'Mark Field is one of the few front
but practically about the long-term i*
Between the Crashes *brings together l*
ing the evolution of the crisis, and repres* *contribution to*
understanding how things look from the centre of the Westminster village.'
– Jonathan Herbst, Partner (UK and EU Financial Services Law),
Norton Rose

'Those who despair of the political class and its lack of insight should
familiarise themselves with the refreshing writing of Mark Field. The
Prime Minister should send a copy of this excellent book to George
Osborne and order the Chancellor to read it.'
– Iain Martin, *Daily Telegraph*

'Mark Field's book is a compelling portrait of the development of the
crisis based on his unique insights and understanding of the City.
Between the Crashes *provides a truthful, independent and critical
account of the discussions and key turning points as events unfolded.*

*Mark's perspective is that of a genuine insider and policymaker. He
makes use of an almost unparalleled network of contacts in the world
of finance and commerce to give us a lucid and timely guide to understanding what the issues were and still are.*

*Mark's view is both realistic and pragmatic, this collection of thoughts
is testament to the fact that he did not give in to the temptation to single
out the greedy bankers and instead levels equal criticism at his class of
policymakers and politicians.*

*Clearly, his crystal ball was as cloudy as ours, but the book shows that
he addressed the right issues at the right time.*

*Mark's relaxed and conversational style makes this book an enjoyable
and useful guide to understanding the complexities of the crisis as well
how we might resolve it.'*
– Dr Stefan Georg, Chairman, Delta Economics

BETWEEN THE CRASHES

BETWEEN THE CRASHES

Reflections and Insights on UK Politics and Global Economics in the Aftermath of the Financial Crisis

MARK FIELD MP

\B^b\

Biteback Publishing

conservativehome

First published in Great Britain in 2013 by
Biteback Publishing Ltd
Westminster Tower
3 Albert Embankment
London SE1 7SP
Copyright © Mark Field 2013

ISBN 978-1-84954-553-2

10 9 8 7 6 5 4 3 2 1

A CIP catalogue record for this book is available from the British Library.

Set in Garamond

Printed and bound in Great Britain by
CPI Group (UK) Ltd, Croydon CR0 4YY

CONTENTS

FOREWORD

The global financial crisis over the past four years cruelly exposed the relentless UK economic upturn of the previous decade and a half as illusory. Rising asset prices; cheap credit and easy finance; apparently limitless exports from China and an unsustainable public sector boom. All this turned out to be a transitory boost to the wealth of those lucky enough to be in the workplace or hold assets at the time rather than a paradigm shift in economic welfare. That much-vaunted longest era of global growth and prosperity was based in truth on the West borrowing apparently limitless amounts of money from the East to finance an ultimately unaffordable consumption binge.

The benign economic weather of the past decade also helped cloak some of the fundamental flaws of the eurozone, a currency union that had barely reached its tenth birthday before it hit the rocks. Now caught up in an apparently endless cycle of mini-crises, the continent's politicians lurch from one emergency summit to another, doing just enough at each to buy themselves a little more time to fix the union's deep-seated failings. Which is why this book is entitled *Between the Crashes*. Whilst we may not be approaching another meltdown the magnitude of 2008's, there is still a sense that another major crisis, a further great jolt in the financial markets, lies ahead.

Even from my ringside seat as the MP for the Cities of London & Westminster I cannot remotely claim to have seen the scale of 2008's financial crisis coming. For sure I warned as long ago as 2004 that public sector debt was worryingly – even unsustainably – high. Later that year in a parliamentary debate I lamented the fact that collectively the UK was living beyond its means. Indeed this book begins with the text of a parliamentary speech from a debate entitled *Government Debt* in February 2007, where to an otherwise empty Chamber, the then City Minister, Ed Balls, and I crossed swords.

Nevertheless, like the vast majority I was complacent too. Yes, there was debt in the system, but surely the deflationary effect of economic development in China and India would keep the whole economic machine rolling? Or so we thought.

It would be difficult to overstate how fascinating has been this period for observers of both global economics and UK politics.

I should like to take this opportunity to thank Tim Montgomerie from ConservativeHome who first suggested that we put this collection of essays, articles and parliamentary speeches into book form. Almost all appeared first on that political blog or in the pages of the *Daily Telegraph* and *City A.M.*. They provide a contemporary, and I trust authentic, snapshot of my views of the climactic year or so of the Labour government and, since the inconclusive May 2010 general election, of the coalition government.

As a remorseless critic of government debt and Treasury complacency and its ruinous impact on the public sector deficit during the second half of the noughties, I supported wholeheartedly the Conservative policy shift towards deficit reduction. Indeed if there are any prescient themes which permeate throughout this book, they are all inextricably bound to the debt that clings like fat round the arteries of the British economy – a divide between the generations as the young are saddled with the overconsumption of those that went before; the fundamental shift of political and economic power eastwards as a result of the West's addiction to credit; an apathy and resentment directed towards the political class and capitalism itself, neither of which have appeared to offer the answers they once did; and the absence of the explicit mandate required to pare back the state and get us back on the path to growth, borne of a failure by politicians to level with the public about the pain that lies ahead.

At the likely halfway point of the Cameron–Clegg coalition administration, the political mood music is dominated by the increasingly

desperate attempts to pin the political blame for economic stagnation and a return to technical recession on the actions of the
previous administration and the travails of the eurozone.

Yet despite all the confected partisan political posturing between
the Treasury frontbenches since 2005, it is remarkable just how
much consensus over economic policy there has been amongst the
UK's elite political class during this period.

Indeed nowhere is that unhealthy consensus more evident than
in the conventional wisdom that has taken hold since the formation of the coalition that we are living in a time of 'unprecedented
public sector cuts'. Conveniently this narrative plays to both the
Labour Party's core support but also to the coalition determined in
its plan to continue convincing the financial markets that it is serious about deficit reduction. The truth is that whilst the leadership
of the Conservative, Labour and Liberal Democrat parties fervently
wish the public to believe that they adhere to radically different
economic outlooks, none has been able to offer a credible pathway
to stemming the flow of public expenditure and borrowing. The
electorate has not been offered any stark difference in vision.

Arguably more, much more, should be done to explain to voters
the state of the public finances. Confusion still reigns amongst most
electors between deficit and debt. Until the public grasps that for all
the talk of 'cuts', national debt is still increasing, they will not understand the need to rein back public spending. Few would believe that
this austerity coalition administration will add more to the public
debt than any previous government in the history of the UK.

Even as we approach the end of a third year of so-called austerity, the UK government continues to borrow £1 in every £5 that
it spends (by contrast in 2009 this figure was £1 in £4 of public
spending). Here lies Gordon Brown's great legacy. With the cause
of the crisis in most minds being seen as aggressive deregulation
and the manipulation of markets by greedy financiers rather than
their antics merely being a symptom of over-leveraged governments
and households, his fundamental narrative lives on. The solution
is alleged to lie in government circulating enough money around

through repeated monetary and fiscal stimulus. It remains politically toxic to talk about reining in the UK state that was so fervently expanded in the Blair/Brown years. Cuts are presented as necessary rather than desirable, the opposition to them based on a sense of unfairness that it is the ordinary man bearing the brunt when it should be bankers that receive the greatest bashing. The unavoidable truth is that there is no easy way out of this unholy mess, no matter how much we quantitatively ease or seek to stimulate the economy.

Finally, I should like to take this opportunity to thank my senior researcher, Julia Dockerill, with whom I have written many of these essays, for her advice and support in putting together this book. We are both in turn grateful to Biteback Publishing, and Olivia Beattie in particular, for all their help and advice in getting our work off the ground and into print.

It only remains for me to hope that you find *Between the Crashes* thought provoking and to ask that you do not remind me too loudly of opinions taken which posterity has already shown to be wide of the mark!

Mark Field
January 2013

2007–2008

Government Debt, 20 February 2007

'The economic fundamentals of this country do not look so smart going forward.'

Backbench MPs are able to table adjournment debates in Westminster Hall, an additional parliamentary debating chamber, to which government ministers are obliged to respond. I took the opportunity at the beginning of 2007 to table one such debate about the use by the Labour government of the Private Finance Initiative to keep a proportion of their much-vaunted investment in public services off the public balance sheet. Incorporated into my speech were some of the running themes of this book – mounting government debt and the risk of inter-generational tensions as we saddled the young with paying it off. Replying on behalf of the government was City Minister, Ed Balls MP.

Politicians in this country are neither being open nor transparent about the state of the public finances. Too much government borrowing is being made to fund current consumption. We are in this way mortgaging the future and expecting subsequent working generations, some of whom have not yet been born, to foot the bill for the excessive costs of today's health care, education and pensions. This approach is neither prudent nor sustainable.

Unfortunately this cavalier outlook to public expenditure has a fairly long political tradition. In the aftermath of the Second World War, Britain frittered away its Marshall Aid on welfare consumption in stark contrast, of course, with the Germans under Konrad

Adenauer and Ludwig Erhard who invested the US-backed aid in rebuilding a world-beating, income-generating German industry.

I have to say that my own Party has also failed to address this fundamental problem. During several periods in recent decades, particularly in the early 1970s and early 1990s, the national debt rose as a result of an unwillingness to take difficult and unpopular political decisions to curb current public sector consumption.

The current Chancellor of the Exchequer's own diversionary tactic over the past decade has been to use the mechanism of the Private Finance Initiative (PFI) to remove from the public balance sheet a proportion of the capital costs associated with the government's much-vaunted investment in the public sector. The Treasury's response to criticism over PFI has always been robust.

The Chancellor argues that the Private Finance Initiative was set up by the previous Conservative administration and the current government is simply adopting the same rules but under tighter accounting standards.

Unfortunately, however, this defence does not hold water. The concept of 'unitary payments', the amalgamation of the capital and service costs of PFI projects, has been adopted as a supposedly simple method of allowing easy comparison between contractors during the PFI bidding process.

However, so far as the public accounts are concerned, this means that a huge amount of current capital expenditure is transferred to future revenue. In short, PFI acts as a form of disguised borrowing, with repayment being postponed for as long as twenty or thirty years.

In reality there is no economic difference between PFI projects and the raising of cash from issues of government debt: the principal and the interest need to be paid in both cases. The shrewd device of the unitary payment, therefore, simply gives rise to a misleading picture of future government financial commitments. In truth the obligation to repay principal sums under PFI projects should be accounted for as a government debt obligation, and unitary payments which contain a capital equivalent component should be accounted in the same way as ordinary government debt.

It is a little difficult to describe the workings of PFI projects without being beset with arcane or complex terminology. However, in straightforward terms, my contention is this the lack of transparency and use of off-balance-sheet funding would not be regarded as acceptable in the private sector.

Any company, never mind its auditors, adopting such tactics would rightly be subject to critical scrutiny. The supporters of PFI frequently claim that one of its greatest benefits is the ability to transfer the risk of project or service failure to the private sector. Indeed this assertion is often used to justify the superficially generous deals that operators of PFI contracts appear to have won in the course of negotiation. However, the significant profit potential these contracts endow on operators – evidenced by the inflated share price of many companies who have won lucrative PFI contracts for school, transport system and hospital building here in London – comes at a real cost to future generations of taxpayers, who will be footing the bill for today's consumption.

In reality, all too often very little risk is transferred. I suspect that some of this is down to poor negotiation, with most operators – take, for example, the bus companies in London – running rings round their public sector counterparts in drawing up the repayment terms.

The Treasury admitted to the absence of risk transfer as long ago as July 2003 when it said in the document, 'PFI: Meeting the Investment Challenge':

> It is impossible to predict with accuracy the percentage of PFI projects which may fail, but it is important to understand that in the extreme circumstances of failure, the government will be prepared to terminate such contracts in accordance with its legal rights, even if at a loss to financial participants in the scheme.
>
> Where this happens it will also act within its legal right to ensure that public services will be maintained.

On the one hand the government commits itself as the ultimate guarantor – and in truth many PFI projects cannot be allowed to fail if only for purely political reasons, as evidenced by the vast and unsustainable deficits accrued by many NHS Trusts.

Yet on the other hand, there is often no sum representing that cost on the government's balance sheet.

Whilst admittedly some £20 billion of the capital value of PFI projects has actually been included on the current government balance sheet, estimated payments on the PFI contracts for the twenty-five years until 2030 total £138 billion, leaving £118 billion of debt payments unaccounted for. This of course takes no account of those PFI contracts which are set to last beyond 2030.

Most independent calculations suggest that at the very least an additional £25 billion should be added to the balance sheet by including a risk-rated percentage of total liabilities arising from PFI. However, even this aggregate of £45 billion wildly understates the truth of the situation.

The fact is that the great majority of PFI projects are undertaken by local authorities, as my own constituents will soon discover to their horror when the financial implications of many contracts agreed to by the current Mayor of London become apparent. Worse still, there has never been any pretence about the balance of risk assessment being made for any of these projects and once again, given the vital social and political importance of the schemes, central government as the ultimate guarantor will have to cough up. We have already seen early skirmishes in a battle between the Treasury and the Mayor of London in relation to the budget of the 2012 Olympics which has, as some of us have always predicted, spiralled totally out of control. Clearly a guarantee from the Treasury would have immediately placed this entire project on the government balance sheet and would amount to public borrowing.

There is also a further category of debt which is classified as 'contingent liabilities' by the Office of National Statistics. The general rule here is quite plain – financial reporting should follow the substance of the commercial effect of a transaction, not the form in which it is dressed up. As a result, some £1.25 billion of bonds issued by London and Continental Railway – the body responsible for the Channel Tunnel rail link – were reclassified as government debt in August 2005, because the debt was ultimately guaranteed by the government and the bond holders were not deemed at risk from default. It had been hoped that the Statistics and Registration Services Bill, which has received its second reading in this House in January, would provide the opportunity to end the uncertainty surrounding the government's accounting.

Inevitably, as some of our brightest investment banking brains create ever more complex financial instruments, the line between substance and form becomes ever more blurred. Transparency in these matters may not always be easy to achieve. However, the case of Network Rail gives rise to the strong suspicion that this government has deliberately manipulated the calculation of government debt.

Following the collapse of Railtrack five years ago, Network Rail was set up in such a way as to be legally independent of government. The management restructuring and the fiction that Network Rail was under the control of 'members' has helped mask the fact that some £18.2 billion of debt has been run up by the company up until July 2006.

Just over two years ago the Office of National Statistics received advice from the Department of Transport that the government's support for Network Rail's borrowing was 'contingent liability of government' and was classified as such in the national accounts. Nevertheless, the government has guaranteed the debt, and the fact that Network Rail, a company limited by guarantee with almost £20 billion of debt, is still regarded as having a credit rating of AAA gives rise to the presumption that the market at least recognises these debts are effectively owed by the government. It should therefore be on the public balance sheet.

One of the reasons that criticism of PFI has been so muted is that private sector operators, contractors, consultants, lawyers and accountants have all made hay over the past decade playing their part as advisers in a process which has proved to be extremely lucrative. It is incontrovertible that the explosion in PFI projects will vary from bad to appallingly bad value for the taxpayer, although as a means of avoiding upfront government debt, this device has also allowed for an almost unprecedented level of school and hospital building.

We need to stand back and face some harsh political facts. In the same way as privatisation under the Conservative government in the 1980s and early 1990s proved irreversible (even Labour's pledge to reverse rail privatisation in the final year of the Conservative administration had to be quietly dropped), so too will PFI. In many ways, from the Labour Party's point of view, that is the great genius of the vast expansion of such projects that has taken place since it came to office. The cost the taxpayer will have to pay for PFI projects now agreed will amount to an ongoing additional burden on public expenditure over the next twenty-five years or so. Yet the political fallout of trying to unravel PFI schemes in essential services means that the room for manoeuvre open to any future Conservative government in the areas of public expenditure and taxation will be considerably limited.

The economic fundamentals of this country do not look so smart going forward. We are simply kidding ourselves about the true costs of accounting the future. Ironically the Chancellor of the Exchequer recognised this expressly in his early justification for his 'golden rule' (that over the economic cycle, the government will borrow only to invest and not to fund current spending) when he stated that 'the government does not pass on the costs of services consumed today to the taxpayers of the future – each generation is expected to meet the current cost of the public services from which they benefit'.

I have spoken in this House before in relation to the principle of generational conflict. Nowhere is it more pronounced than in the area of pensions reform. Unfunded public pension liabilities mean that tomorrow's taxpayers will be obliged to fund today's ever larger deficits.

Alternatively, those who have made their pensions contributions in good faith will see their entitlement collapse. Pensions payments are another example of deferred expenditure – or to put it another way, of government borrowing.

The government has claimed that its unfunded public pension

liabilities were £460 billion as of 31 March 2004. However, this figure was calculated on the basis of a discount rate of 3.5 per cent which the government actuary's department has now revised downwards to 2.8 per cent. In answer to parliamentary questions on this matter, the Treasury accept that the liability of unfunded public pensions amounts to £650 billion and the unfunded element of local government pensions scheme around £70 billion.

Once more there is no easy way out. In essence, today's pensioners and those retiring in the near future will be able to rely upon considerably more generous benefits than those just entering the workplace who are paying for these liabilities. Given the fact that there are twice as many voters over the age of fifty-five as under the age of thirty-five, and that they are twice as likely to vote, it is unrealistic to expect anyone in the political arena to state some bald facts about this matter. Nevertheless, in spite of the orchestrated campaigns, today's pensioners have never had it so good. The reason why many pensioners in their seventies and eighties believe they have so little is because they have failed to pay anything like enough into the system to warrant what they now expect to receive.

These unrealistic expectations have been created and are periodically raised by politicians across the spectrum. That somewhat unpalatable message plays no part in the policy prospectus of any major political party, perhaps for rather obvious reasons. The unspoken message of the political class to anyone under the age of thirty is that their generation will not only have to foot the unfunded cost of pensions for those who are older, but they will also need to lower significantly their financial expectations when it is time for them to retire. I believe that we run the risk of quite serious social unrest in the decades ahead as the evidence of this appalling generational pyramid sales scam becomes evident. For there is little doubt that future government spending will have to be much higher, not least because there will be ever fewer people in the workforce having to subsidise an ever larger number of dependants, whilst the costs of the National Health Service, for example, continue to rise exponentially as the population ages.

This off-balance-sheet financing is delaying some very tough decisions that need to be made about the future of public spending. It also delays our debate on the way we need to manage public services in future to deliver equity and social cohesion as well as providing for the vulnerable and voiceless in our society. One of the more depressing prospects is that in the years ahead my generation will be seen as having had it easy.

This era will be seen as the best of times.

‡

In Defence of Capitalism, 8 October 2008

With the nationalisation of British bank, Northern Rock, in February, the rescuing of US investment bank, Bear Stearns in March, and the placing of US mortgage lenders, Fannie Mae and Freddie Mac, under government conservatorship at the beginning of September, the clues in 2008 of major financial upheaval were all there. Yet few could have guessed the scale of what was to come.

On 15 September 2008, Lehman Brothers, the 158-year-old American investment bank (the fourth largest in the US at that time), filed for the biggest bankruptcy in US history. Heavily invested in securities linked to the US sub-prime mortgage market, the bank was forced to make write-downs of $7.8 billion, causing Lehman's share price to plummet by over 95 per cent. The US government chose not to bail the bank out and panic spread across global financial markets about the robustness of other financial institutions, leading to a severe contraction of liquidity.

I began sketching this article out at Conservative Party Conference, held that year in Birmingham. Prime Minister, Gordon Brown, had just delivered his warning to the nation and his Party that 'this is no time for a novice' in a bid to stave off internal threats (in the form of David Miliband) and external ones (in David Cameron) to his leadership. At my Party's own conference, so rapidly were economic events moving that David Cameron was forced to rewrite his keynote speech.

He reassured the nation that he was 'a man with a plan' whilst Shadow Chancellor, George Osborne, cautioned that the era of excessive personal and state borrowing was over and as a fiscal conservative, he would prioritise the reduction of borrowing over upfront tax cuts.

These are dangerous times for capitalism and free markets. In the past few weeks we witnessed an unravelling of the global financial system at a speed so breath-taking that even seasoned financial experts have little certainty as to its eventual implications.

The political class is reeling. How best to balance the need for swift and decisive action to restore stability with concerns at the law of unintended consequences? How to protect depositors and maintain confidence in the markets without protecting and rewarding bankers for reckless risk-taking? And how to convey security and certainty to a dismayed public whilst struggling to grasp how this financial turmoil will affect the real economy?

For sure, supporters of free markets and globalisation have been dealt a sore blow. There is certainly a degree of truth to the notion that we are where we are as a result of untamed greed and we shall have to take stock.

But what we must not do is allow a narrative to develop which heralds the current crisis as the start of a new era of corporatism and ever more restrictive regulation. Capitalism, whilst wounded, has not been discredited. Indeed, without the dynamism of free trade and markets, billions across the globe would not be enjoying (in many cases only starting to enjoy) the fruits of innovation, creativity and enterprise.

My constituency houses the City of London; hedge funds and alternative assets in Mayfair and St James; a residential population of wealthy global business folk and a service and entertainment sector in the West End which has blossomed from the disposable incomes of a busy London workforce. Capitalism has thrived here. But Conservatives have never shied from exposing some of the problems caused by this wealth explosion.

Last year, to the dismay of some of my wealthier international constituents, we articulated the importance of an equitable tax system for the non-domiciled in response to a growing sense of despair and resentment from hard-working Londoners. The debate on non-doms followed hot on the heels from that over the preferential tax rates enjoyed by those working in private equity. This was essentially a middle-class revolt over the unequal rewards to labour. To their surprise, many highly educated professionals working outside the gilded corridors of the financial services sphere saw themselves losing out as the world became more integrated and interdependent.

It has come as no shock to me, therefore, that many people feel little sympathy for the current plight of the investment banker. For a large proportion of British workers, the growth of the City's power has simply increased the cost of living and reduced to a wistful dream any prospect of getting on the housing ladder. Now with a culture of two decades of financial services dominating the central London landscape since the 1986 Big Bang, the banking industry (previously keen to keep government interference or regulation to a minimum) asking for a public bailout has quite understandably been met with distaste. In such a climate, I am deeply worried that the centre of gravity of public sentiment on economic and financial matters has in recent weeks moved firmly to the left. The clamour for heavy regulation and government control in the financial services sphere will increase.

So I was very encouraged to see at last week's Conservative Party Conference David Cameron and George Osborne take a brave stand on this issue. They made clear that whilst irresponsibility in banking must be curbed, populist and rushed measures designed to rein in City excess should be avoided.

In the current climate, it would have been all too easy to play to the gallery, a reckless temptation I fear the Prime Minister has failed to resist. As the Shadow Chancellor rightly pointed out, however, Gordon Brown has no place lecturing the City when he has played such a significant role in shaping the failed regulatory system and racking up colossal government debt whilst hubristically claiming to have 'ended boom and bust'.

Similarly, whilst it is easy for us all to target bankers as the most obvious recipients of the decade's boom, we must not forget that the racking up of over £1 trillion of personal debt was the responsibility of the public at large. Nor were the banking fraternity the sole beneficiaries of a house price explosion, which has seen many people accrue more profit from property inflation than they could ever have dreamed of earning over a similar period of time.

It must now be the role of politicians soberly to reflect that this crisis will affect not only the financial services world. The public needs to know that the economy as a whole now stands to be sorely tested in the years ahead as the combination of much diminished liquidity, historically high commodity prices and a weak currency begins to bite.

There is no easy short-term fix and I detect that the public are increasingly receptive to politicians who tell it as it is. We must accept that to a great extent, the housing bubble should be left to deflate. We should reconcile ourselves with the potential loss of some large banking and corporate institutions. At the same time, confidence needs to be restored to our markets through restructuring and recapitalising the financial system and the core of that system sustained – something which will require the determination of a strong government.

Demands for quick-fire solutions and superficially attractive regulation should not be indulged. The Sarbanes–Oxley legislation introduced in the United States after the Enron and Worldcom scandal has taught us two things. First, that recent additional regulation to protect consumers in that country did nothing to stave off the current crisis and second, that in a global economy, business will have no hesitation in relocating if regulation becomes too cumbersome. One option now being discussed in the City is the possibility of mopping up in the years ahead should other countries, notably the US, be tempted to over-regulate again and further push business our way.

It is worth reflecting at this point that when financial institutions are described as 'too big to fail' implicitly we are also recognising they are 'too big to regulate' and are ultimately beyond the pale of prudential sanction. Perversely, the recent set of defensive megamergers in the financial services world will make this worse since regulation is the strongest barrier to entry to the market. This in-built lack of competition will continue to result in a remuneration regime that means the rewards to investment banking employees are roughly seventeen times that of the general economy. The demand for robustly large balance sheets makes for unregulatable institutions, cushioned from competition and able to charge exorbitant fees.

These new business opportunities will not be welcomed by the public unless we attempt to modify our own regulatory framework and make regulators more proactive and credible. This can be achieved without stifling financial innovation and flair or introducing unnecessary legislation.

Since 1997, we have had a three-pronged system which divides responsibility between the Financial Services Authority (FSA), the Bank of England and the Treasury. After a decade of clement economic weather, the first time the system was tested saw the lack of accountability, division and conflict between each institution and the emergence of competition between regulators. Streamlining must now take place – perhaps through the merging of the FSA with the Bank of England – and the disparities between the regulators and the bankers should be evened up. The huge salary differences between the regulators (on civil service grades) and those they pursue mean that the brightest minds are consistently attracted to the banks, outwitting those who seek to check their excesses.

Banks themselves must in the future become more responsible. Huge success-driven bonuses have until now been based largely on short-term results. Instead, reward should be pegged to share price performance (I accept this did not prevent the collapse of Lehman Brothers where employees were given generous shareholdings) and longer-term profit goals. Furthermore, rules should be introduced to preside over banks' capital requirements to prevent what risks unravelling into excessive borrowing.

We should also look at the operation of credit agencies, the bodies which rate an organisation's ability to keep to their agreements, resulting in the advance of many billions of dollars a day. Currently, agencies are paid by the same companies having their credit rated, providing a clear incentive for an agency to produce a favourable result. A better system would see agencies either being paid by those lending the money or a general market levy to ensure neutrality.

It should be kept in mind that whilst mergers facilitated by the government can create short-term stability, they are ultimately highly risky. Large banks cannot be allowed to fail and in the event of their faltering, financial meltdown quickly looms. As time passes, we must look to maintain smaller institutions which can keep alive an element of competition in the market place. This will be ever more crucial as consumers and businesses find themselves restricted by the offers available from money lenders.

Finally, the United States looks set to take on the greatest burden in sorting out the current mess. Rather than strive to deal with global financial problems, our focus should remain on sorting out our own house. Painfully, this may mean deepening a huge fiscal deficit but if this is to be done, it has to be vigorously and relentlessly driven down the moment the economy recovers.

A daunting task lies ahead and getting it right means resisting the emotional pressure of a public resentful of the money makers and fearful of what is in store. A large part of that pressure can be mollified if the public is made aware of the danger the wider economy is in, the pitfalls of poor regulation and the collective pain which we may all have to grit our teeth and get through.

Indulging in the bashing of bankers and global capitalism will prove tempting for many – even amongst Conservative Party supporters. As a defender of free markets, free trade and global capitalism, I am willing to bet that whilst government needs to play a crucial role in stabilising and revitalising our confidence-battered economy, it will eventually be hard work, enterprise and freedom in the market place which will ensure our economy thrives once again.

‡

Power Moves Eastwards, 9 October 2008

We can all be forgiven for being bewildered by the implications of the turmoil in the global financial markets. Over the past seven months most of the UK's biggest mortgage lenders – and all of the US investment banks – have ceased to exist as independent entities. We are witnessing the first signs of a seismic shift of power from the United States/Europe to China, Russia and the Gulf States.

I believe that the near collapse of the global banking industry will serve to accelerate trends which are already in play. Indeed the US economy may never recover its dominant position in global markets. With hindsight the current financial crisis may be as crucial to the undermining of US economic dominance as the outbreak of the First World War was to Britain's.

The erstwhile expectation that by the middle of this century China and India will have attained the standard of living and inter-national power on a par with the US now needs revising. We may be there considerably sooner.

I write these words at a time when US and European govern-ments are desperately trying to underpin the global banking system. Amidst a doubling of US national debt as a percentage of GDP there has been a massive destruction of shareholder value. The much vaunted US $800 billion bailout is not only unaffordable but may fail to restore confidence to the financial sector let alone corpo-rate Main Street America. For our part, government borrowing will spiral well beyond the predicted £43 billion this year and £38 billion next. The suggestion that next year's out-turn will see a public sector over-run of £90 billion plus no longer seems so fanciful.

In the midst of all the damage and destruction to the value of the West's financial resources, we also face a major loss of economic power and international prestige. The seriousness of the current situation is only just beginning to dawn on the public at large. In the year since queues snaked outside branches of Northern Rock, there has been a strange calm as if the travails of the financial services sector might somehow be ring-fenced from the 'real' economy. Everyone – whether they yet see it or not – is going to be affected by the seizing up of inter-bank lending. Most worrying is the possibility that the recapitalisation of the UK banking sector may not lead to a restoration of normal credit flows. This is already having a serious impact on future domestic economic growth and is unlikely to be ameliorated even by an aggressive strategy of interest rate cuts.

Whilst European governments try frantically to fix the system, there is a real danger that their co-ordinated long-term commitment of taxpayers' funds will be regarded as unfair both by domestic electorates and by key policymakers in trading partners outside the West. Unfortunately, economic theory and public sentiment may pull in opposite directions – to be seen to reward greed and incompetence in the banking sector could prove fatal to any rescue programme.

To put it simply, money is power. Financial power and global political leadership go hand in hand. The bailout of US and European banks will essentially be underwritten by the flooding in the global capital markets of US and European government bonds which will be mopped up by cash-rich sovereign wealth funds in China, the Gulf and Russia. Their money will buy them power. This power will be used to exert more influence – in the case of China and Russia, backed by military force around its borders. Our entire model of democracy and free markets will be put to the test.

As we have seen in recent months, one of the few impediments to Russia exercising military power around its borders is the influence of an educated, wealthy and fast-growing domestic middle class. To date, India and China (beyond Kashmir and Burma/Tibet) have shown relatively little interest in exercising their military muscle. As their global financial clout becomes more apparent, so too will their appetite for interference in world affairs.

The Islamic world will also see the West's ongoing economic crisis as an opportunity to exacerbate conflicts in its region. One has to ask who in the West will have the financial clout – or political will – to spend on policing any new flashpoints?

Having visited China three times over the past five years, I have seen with my own eyes the rapid pace of development there. If the US and Europe lose moral leadership in the management of global financial markets then there is little doubt that within a decade the West will be forced to accept China as an equal.

I have spoken several times over recent years in parliament about the impact of debt. We have been living well beyond our means as individuals and collectively. The use by this government of PFI to fund capital projects is little more than a pyramid sales scam against future generations of taxpayers. The reckoning is upon us.

In short we have been mortgaging our future, expecting subsequent working generations to foot the bill for the cost of today's health care, education and pensions. Back in February 2007 I warned:

> As some of our brightest investment banking brains create ever more complex financial instruments, the line between substance and form becomes ever more blurred … This country's economic fundamentals do not look so smart going forward, and we are simply kidding ourselves about the true costs of accounting in the future.

Today's much vaunted recapitalisation of the banking sector is in essence more of the same – a further debt for future generations to repay.

For some years it has been clear to me that any incoming Conservative government's room for economic manoeuvre would be desperately limited. Now, on top of already historically high levels of government debt and off-balance-sheet financing, we face having to grapple with the costs of sorting out the turbulence in the financial industry.

There will be no winners – at least on these shores. These momentous few weeks underpin an accelerated shift of global power eastward.

‡

A Brave New World for Bankers, 24 October 2008

There was no let-up in the drama being played out across the global economy in the five weeks between the collapse of Lehman Brothers and the release of this article. In the UK, Lloyds announced a £12.2 billion takeover of HBOS; the ailing Bradford & Bingley was rescued by Spanish bank, Santander, which bought its branches and savings book, leaving the taxpayer with its toxic mortgage book; the government increased bank deposit guarantees to £50,000; Icelandic banks collapsed, placing the funds of British savers, including many local authorities, in jeopardy; the Treasury announced what amounted to a £500 billion bank rescue package; and it was announced that the Royal Bank of Scotland would be given a £20 billion cash injection from the taxpayer whilst its Chief Executive, Sir Fred Goodwin, would step down.

Meanwhile, in the United States, the administration of George W. Bush announced its intention to buy stock and warrants from the nine largest US banks under the Troubled Asset Relief Scheme (TARP), a $250 billion pot (in its first tranche) to which financial institutions could apply for a preferred stock investment by the US Treasury.

Lord (Adair) Turner, chairman of the UK's Financial Services Authority, warned that the days of soft-touch regulation were over.

Amidst the bewilderingly swift developments of recent weeks in the financial services sector, many in the City can be forgiven for failing to appreciate the extent of change in the landscape that lies before them. Some complacently regard the recent turmoil as a short-lived upheaval and that business will 'return to normal' before long. I fear this will prove wishful thinking.

The decision to launch a full-scale rescue of the domestic banking industry need not have required nationalisation. The enforced recapitalisation of a relatively healthy bank, Lloyds TSB, has – to date – met with only muted opposition from ordinary shareholders whose investment has been largely destroyed. Once the dust settles, pension funds, reliant upon dividends, are unlikely to be overjoyed by the government diktat that deprives them of this crucial source of income for up to five years.

One key area the government has failed properly to address is that of competition law. The extreme circumstances that prevailed in early October meant the Lloyds TSB buyout of HBOS was given the go-ahead even though in less turbulent economic conditions it would have fallen foul of anti-trust legislation. In such extreme circumstances it appeared supportable. However, by the time the government's bailout package was unveiled – seeing £37 billion of taxpayers' cash being pumped into RBS and the new Lloyds TSB/HBOS entity – it was no longer clear why it should be exempt from these considerations. Competition law is designed to protect the public – not as an extra layer of bureaucracy, but as a crucial guarantor of choice and diversity in the free market.

Which begs the next question – whither the level playing field? The US government in its decision to hose down the financial services market with vast sums of taxpayer cash has used the expedient of insisting that financial institutions such as Goldman Sachs and J. P. Morgan take government money even though, at this stage at least, it was neither needed nor requested.

In the UK, however, we face a potentially serious structural problem in the banking industry looking ahead. The government (courtesy of Lloyds TSB/HBOS, Northern Rock and Bradford & Bingley) now controls 45 per cent of the UK mortgage market and it is difficult to see how innovation, flair and consumer choice can be enhanced by such an arrangement. Moreover, the two of the big four banks which have not taken public money, HSBC and Barclays, will almost certainly have good cause before long to complain that their products (without the foundation of a government guarantee) risk being less attractive to the consumer.

As a condition of giving banks public funds, the government have insisted that lending activity is kept on a par with that which existed when there was more clement economic weather. This is also dangerous territory – first, will this result in the creation of another credit bubble albeit with lower interest rates than we have experienced over the past decade? Second, with the government as a guarantor of last resort, might part-nationalised banks, in order to satisfy the government's demand for volume business, skew the market by selling their mortgage products at unsustainably attractive rates?

There is public distaste and anger for the banking fraternity which I fear has a long way to run. Indeed, when the recession begins to bite hard in the 'real' economy there will doubtless be a vociferous demand (led by the tabloid press) that corporate UK should have a similar right to be bailed out as the banking industry. Indeed, the Conservative announcements on small businesses in the last few days implicitly pre-empt this. I fear that there is a lot of complacency in the financial services world over the level of public anger still to come to the fore. Simply put – things cannot be the same. The adoption in the UK of a rules rather than, as hitherto, a principles-based regulation system will now be the norm. Worse still, so much of the banking industry is now in public hands there has to be a real concern about the place of the City of London within the ranking of globally competitive financial centres.

Furthermore, unravelling these recapitalisation arrangements will not be a short-term affair. I suspect that it will take many years – possibly as long as a decade. In truth the deal was done without full political scrutiny. The power of the executive in the UK and shorter-term political considerations meant that effectively the government was presented with a blank cheque which it has brandished with relish. It is slowly dawning on the public that there has been a far more extensive nationalisation of banking assets than was envisaged when bipartisan support was offered.

An integral element of our ongoing scrutiny of the bailout must be a forensic analysis of the failings of the Bank of England and the Financial Services Authority. Our ambitious plans to encourage a process of Bank of England-led reconstruction in preference to financial services nationalisation requires respected and credible personnel at the highest ranks of the institution.

In short the bailout is far from being a 'done deal' and our role as an Opposition should be to side with the hapless taxpayer in holding the government to account. Looking forward we need to provide a compelling vision of global capitalism, free markets and a small, more effective state for the recovery stage of this economic cycle.

‡

Time to Tell it as it is to the Electorate, 10 November 2008

As the crisis marched on, the Bank of England lowered the base rate by 1.5 percentage points from 4.5 per cent to 3 per cent and revealed that the world's financial institutions were nursing losses of $2.8 trillion. Meanwhile, US automotive sales fell off a cliff leading to calls for emergency funding and the Chinese authorities announced a $586 billion domestic stimulus package. Gloomy British retailers looked ahead at a tough Christmas.

Politically, after eight years of President George W. Bush, the United States elected its first black President in Barack Obama, who ran on an optimistic platform of hope and change.

The state of the public finances is a national disgrace. Over eleven years of Labour administration too much government borrowing has funded current consumption. Instead of building a secure future we are borrowing from it and condemning future generations of Britons, some still to be born, to pick up the bill for the cost of current welfare, health care and pensions expenditure.

It is an approach which is neither prudent nor sustainable. It falls to Conservatives to condemn this cavalier approach to public expenditure and show the nation that there is a better way forward.

The recent banking bailout following the credit crisis has provided the government with an alibi for exorbitant levels of public debt which were already spiralling dangerously out of control. Public sector borrowing was due to reach £43 billion in the current financial year – we shall now be lucky to avoid doubling that sorry figure. Next year the total may well exceed £100 billion; that is around

£300 million spending in excess of tax receipts each and every day of the year.

Just as it has been difficult for a bewildered public to grasp the true meaning of the wild fluctuations in the stock market in recent weeks, I fear that it will now be unaware of the seismic implications of the unprecedented level of government debt now locked into the system.

We must ring-fence the billions accrued for the banking bailout from the enormous sums that were already on – and indeed off – the balance sheet. The new spirit of the age should be for value for money out of the public purse – instead the idea of big government as an ever-benevolent cash cow seems to be entrenching even further.

Remarkably, a narrative on the need for greater austerity has really not yet emerged. Whilst Conservatives no longer feel any pressure to match Labour's spending plans nor to 'share the proceeds of growth', the urgent questions we now face are whether we are to match government on massive, costly infrastructure projects – or better still to make the political weather perhaps by promoting a fiscal stimulus by means of a targeted tax cut to the less well-off which will readily be recycled into consumer consumption.

In truth there remains an eerie sense of calm in the 'real' economy. But not for much longer. For now, the tumultuous collapse of the finance sector appears to many an isolated incident which has been contained. Whilst the newspapers might be littered with credit crunch tales – falling house prices, squeezed company profits – I just do not believe that this crisis has really bitten the public yet, as demonstrated by the crush of shoppers at London's new super shopping mall, Westfield, last weekend.

More worryingly this is coupled with a notion that however bad things get financially for the individual, the state will move to soften the blow, a perception that the government's intervention to protect depositors in Northern Rock, Icesave and others has only served to increase. Labour is returning to its comfort zone with an economic narrative of interference in the name of protecting the public through continued high spending. We saw the Prime Minister developing this idea last week in the House of Commons as he sought to exploit the outcome of the US election as evidence of an international mandate for big government. If there is a lesson to be learned from Barack Obama's success this should not be it.

For sure, the world has changed but that is no reason for Conservatives to be bystanders – we must not be mesmerised by the tumultuous events into lacking the confidence to present a distinctive pathway forward. The era of cheap and easy money is now behind us yet too much government borrowing is targeted at short-term consumption rather than building for a better future. This was the case before the credit crisis and remains the case now. An increase in state intervention may soften the financial blow in the immediate term, but the looming level of interest payments alone on rising debt risks the lowering of living standards for decades to come.

It will soon dawn on younger voters that the unspoken message of the political class to anyone under thirty is that their generation will need to not only fund the cost of pensions for those who are older, but they will have to lower significantly their own financial expectations when the time comes for them to retire. The availability of cheap goods – clothes, technology, alcohol – has created a false sense of material wealth in the young. Unfortunately, the longer-term prospect of being able to pay off student debt, enjoy a standard of living as good as their parents, live on a decent pension for a retirement likely to last decades and expect a generous range of state benefits that those currently in retirement take for granted looks less rosy.

Any failure by government rapidly to grasp this nettle risks serious social unrest in the decades ahead. Our society will otherwise be economically divided as never before between old and young; those working in the comparatively secure and well-pensioned public sector and those in private wealth creation; those with globally transferable opportunities and others in an increasing tail of low-skilled, chaotic lifestyles.

Conservatives need to connect these realities and provide a

convincing financial and moral narrative as to the importance of balancing the collective books. Outside of wartime it is almost unique for any generation to conclude (as is the case today) that its children and grandchildren will most likely be worse off than it has been. Unless radical action is taken to halt and reverse these unsustainable levels of public sector borrowing and to re-educate people as to the economic realities of maintaining a cradle-to-grave welfare state, that will be the sorry fate to befall the future generations of Britons.

At the next election we can offer the electorate change and a distinctive agenda which shows we are ahead of the game. If the best of times are to lie ahead the Conservatives must make the case for a smaller, more efficient State and understand there is an untapped appetite amongst our fellow Britons for discipline and prudence. We should relish the real opportunity that comes with giving the bewildered general public a convincing narrative for the future based upon our enduring principles.

‡

Procurement: A Route to Reducing Expenditure and Funding Tax Cuts? 20 November 2008

As the state of the public finances deteriorated further, I made a series of Freedom of Information requests to government departments to ascertain just how much was being spent on procurement. My aim was to identify areas of expenditure that an incoming Conservative administration might be able significantly to reduce through efficiencies and by exploiting the government's muscle as a major purchaser.

Public sector purchasing policy is not exactly a subject designed to make the pulse race. But perhaps it should. At a time when scrutiny of the public finances has never been greater, a prudent procurement policy offers a heaven-sent opportunity to rein in public expenditure.

The lack of visibility of so much of this spend means that the cost to the public purse risks spiralling out of control. There are straightforward disciplines which the public sector could adopt which can be taken from the private sector. Reduce the number of suppliers, manage those suppliers better, don't let them change the terms mid-contract, negotiate well, bring transparency and disclosure to those with whom money is spent.

In essence, purchasing impacts the public sector more profoundly than you might imagine. Everything which is neither salary nor distributed as a grant or as welfare is regarded as public sector purchase. For this an estimated annual budget of £150 billion is up for grabs. Even a relatively modest 10 per cent saving in this category would bring with it substantial dividends.

Goods and services that the public sector purchases vary from IT systems (not noticeably good value in recent years), buildings, highly sophisticated defence equipment and stationery. Meanwhile, services include the acquisition of childcare, consultants and call centres.

The science of sales is well known. It is certainly the somewhat sexier counterpart to purchasing. Top sales professionals are stars in the corporate world – their dark arts are the subject of an extensive body of learning and training. By contrast, the procurement industry is very much in its infancy – regarded as less easily understood or easy to define and its practitioners undervalued compared to sales staff. Moreover, purchasing managers are rarely motivated to beat their suppliers down on price – this culture is especially common in the public sector.

Indeed, it is estimated that there are some fifty times more professional sales people than trained procurement people and procurement performance is rarely tracked in the way that sales are. The scale of public sector expenditure across a range of sectors is mind boggling. Grouped by department, Local Government (£39.8 billion), Health (£30.1 billion), Defence (£16.9 billion) and the devolved administrations (£15.4 billion) are the largest public sector purchasers. The goods and services purchased across departments include construction (£22.3 billion), pharmaceuticals (£8.9 billion) and the slightly more mundane transport (cars and business travel – £5.4 billion), telecommunications (radio and TV – £3.6 billion), IT services (£4.2 billion), down to food (£3.2 billion) and furniture (£1.2 billion).

The desire to 'cut waste' is one shared by opposition politicians across the world. The important thing surely is to drill down to determine the precise nature of the procurement and purchasing budget as well as examining why people are so bad at the science of buying.

In essence there are three variables – price, quantity and specification. When you buy a single good such as utilities, like electricity or water, there is a fixed price which hinges upon the quantity consumed. A poor purchasing deal is often done because of ignorance, lethargy, personal preference for a particular supplier or a misperception of the risk or product concerned. Whilst sales people are highly focused, all too often the purchaser of a single good fails to recognise the market is moving all the time and cannot keep up with these crucial changes.

By contrast, purchasing decisions over a multitude of items (such as stationery) involves pricing a basket of goods based on the volume of each item sold. In this model, high-value volume items should be less expensive. The total paid depends on the purchaser predicting the volume of each item and negotiating the price accordingly – get the prediction wrong and the high-volume items will end up being rather more expensive.

Buying professional services can be trickier still. For example – something once close to my own heart – buying the services of a lawyer usually depends upon fixed day rates, quantity of consumption that can vary massively and a specification which is not visible at the time of purchase. The odds are typically firmly stacked against the purchaser when compared to the party making the sales. Mistakes include poor upfront thinking which can lead to an inadequate analysis of the specification and inefficient use of a supplier: using an overqualified and therefore more expensive professional for more mundane work or else agreeing to pay for the A Team but getting the less qualified and less efficient B Team for most of the assignment.

Buying services also involves a leap of faith – as a sales person it is easy to promise but hard to deliver. Defining and measuring of outputs and their quality can be so difficult that the entire process can be overly focused on inputs (such as time sheets for hours inefficiently spent undertaking the task at hand). Naturally the fee model can impact on behaviour by any supplier – day rates understandably encourage both prolonged and more complex work.

Even buying services over the longer term when many of the pitfalls should be foreseen can lead to problems. For example, the supplier may start cheaply and then charge overrun fees in the knowledge that the costs of changing supplier are prohibitive or would cause more delay to the process. Once locked in, the effective rate shoots up. Almost inevitably, if a decision is made to pay the service on inputs then the project time (and expense) will extend. Similarly, a supplier of long-term service who may identify a problem may not also be that person delivering the answer. All of these factors make for a bad deal for a purchaser of services.

Then of course there is the problem that striking a deal is attractive but managing the subsequent process is far less so. All too many organisations – especially in the public sector – are notoriously bad at managing suppliers both commercially and operationally. Sales people, the suppliers in this context, are trained to be better at exploiting this.

It is also the case that the biggest savings often mean internal change. The easy part is to renegotiate the price of an existing supplier but changing to a new supplier (which may in the short term be more costly as well as inconvenient) is potentially the efficient way forward. If the buyer whose job it is to determine the volume of services of goods being bought as well as the specification is poor at managing the process of buying then costs will begin to spiral.

Unfortunately, the public sector seems unusually susceptible to changing specifications as it goes along. As anyone who has employed a builder knows, this is not a good idea. The maxim here is straightforward – the better you plan, the better you buy. Much of this may sound like common sense but it requires a meticulous approach. At the outset it is crucial that the individual charged with purchasing goods and services fully understands the objectives and payment around pre-determined delivery in the public sector.

This is an area of opportunity for the Conservatives to say something new by addressing ways of capturing value across a third of the public sector expenditure budget. At a time when the economic clouds are gathering and there are increasing pressures on the public purse, adopting a more systematic approach towards procurement should not detrimentally affect the services to the public.

2009

Tales from the Front Line, 5 January 2009

By the end of November, the UK government had taken a 58 per cent share in RBS with Stephen Hester taking the reins from failed Chief Executive, Sir Fred Goodwin. Chancellor Alistair Darling revealed in his Pre-Budget Report that the government planned to borrow Britain out of recession, leaving the country with a deficit of 8 per cent of GDP, the highest level in post-war history. He also cut VAT temporarily to 15 per cent in order to boost consumption in the economy.

By the end of the year, the value of the pound had decreased dramatically, taking it to near parity with the euro. In the States, the FBI had arrested financier Bernard Madoff for his part in a Ponzi scheme which totalled $50 billion, considered the largest financial fraud in US history.

With the passing of 2008, those in government, business and banking looked ahead to 2009 with trepidation. The bailing out of Britain's banks complete, the big question was now whether this would work both in stemming the panic and getting money flowing to the nation's businesses once more.

Few in the financial services industry will mourn the end of 2008, which will rank as its most tumultuous year, certainly since 1974, or perhaps even 1931. Few wise men (or women) would dare predict how the year ahead will shape up.

One thing seems for sure, however. The gloss on the Prime Minister's much-vaunted global recapitalisation of the banks is already wearing off.

As much as Gordon Brown has relished his portrayal as a grand Keynesian economic genius whose lead the United States and Europe follow, the political weather may be about to turn stormy for our Prime Minister. In his international showboating, he has sought to take the credit for the government's display of apparently bold and swift action to save the nation's economy. Household-name banks have been provided with an injection of cash so colossal that the UK's already spiralling levels of debt seem like small change, allowing the Prime Minister to continue the conceit that he has been a steady hand on the economic tiller for the past debt-laden decade. No doubt he will try to articulate a similar fantasy when the wheels come off the recapitalisation plan. The banks will offer a ready scapegoat.

For now as fear stalks the land, people are understandably desperate to believe the government has the answers. Indeed, back in November I wrote that the broader economic crisis had not yet bitten and people viewed the implosion of the financial sector as a problem that had been contained. But sentiment is changing swiftly and in painting himself as an all-powerful global saviour, Gordon Brown will surely find it ever harder to escape blame when the fear turns to pain and then to anger. Now that the season of goodwill is behind us, harsh reality will assert itself. It will not be a pretty sight.

With a residential population of just under 70,000 but with a daily workforce close on 1 million, my constituency mailbag is filled every week with ever more letters from increasingly alarmed business folk. Most seem to boil down to the same question: given that the government has poured billions into propping up the banks, why will no one lend to my otherwise viable small business which is unable to access credit?

The first indication that the credit crunch would extend beyond inter-bank lending came a couple of months ago when a former lawyer at a leading international firm wrote to me outlining the problems he was having setting up a new solicitors' practice in the constituency. Despite fulfilling the criteria, he found it impossible to get a quotation for professional indemnity insurance. He could only suppose it was due to a lack of available capital in the insurance market and wrote:

> The Prime Minister has, to date, focused on the transparent costs of the credit crunch that fall on small businesses ... it seems, however, little has been done to address the less transparent costs of the credit crunch on SMEs [small and medium enterprises]. I am told by my broker that the insurer has 'lost its appetite' for property-related risk. Very quickly, then, what was once a viable business could become unviable.

Another company in the constituency informed me that under the DTI Small Firm Loan Guarantee Scheme they were given a loan of £50,000 of which they had spent £10,000. They requested that Lloyds TSB defer the capital repayments on the loan to maintain enough working capital for the business. The bank had refused, saying they were bound by the terms of the DTI guarantee. The letter concluded, 'The rhetoric the government is feeding us is not backed by any support in reality despite the billions of taxpayers' pounds served up to rescue the banks without our electoral consent.'

Another long-standing small business said:

> Despite the massive efforts by the government to refinance the banks and to encourage a return to normal commercial practice, the facts on the ground remain dire, putting the life of our company at risk. In the past months we have seen our overdraft facilities cancelled, all merchant services provided by our bank subjected to huge cost increases and a strict refusal to envisage new terms for short-term loans or overdraft facilities. Ours is a seasonal business – without some financial flexibility, our cash-flow fluctuations can quickly lead to difficulties.

I could provide further examples. In the meantime, rather curiously, a resident wrote to tell me that on going to his now partly nationalised bank, he was offered a loan out of the blue and unsolicited of

£27,000. He pondered whether the banks were seeking good risk customers to lend to in an attempt to appear to meet the government's aims without involving themselves in intrinsically riskier loans to small business.

I suspect he is right, and small wonder when one looks at the perverse incentives contained in the recapitalisation package. The banks are absolutely desperate to run down the capital they have been encouraged to take from the government as quickly as possible. Whereas the US Treasury has lent money to its banks at an interest rate of 5 per cent and in Germany at between 5.5 per cent and 8.5 per cent, the British government demands a 12 per cent coupon on its preference shares. As Eric Daniels, Chief Executive of Lloyds TSB said, 'In the case of the UK, the recapitalisation was done on pretty punitive terms, and that can cause the wrong behaviours.'

As the banks see it, the quickest and simplest way of reducing the size of their balance sheets and repaying the government is to stop lending new money. In the meantime, the government demands that lending continues to SMEs at rates far more favourable than those it has imposed upon the banks. Simultaneously it orders them to shore up their own balance sheets and buy government bonds to equip themselves better for future crises (and, conveniently, to fund the swelling national debt). To accuse the government of sending out mixed messages is an understatement.

Unfortunately the banks, all too aware of their grim public profile, are wary of publicly saying anything of their reservations. Speaking to a representative of RBS recently, I was told that the banks are prepared to act as fall guys in the short term, but they are not fools: they realise that this narrative enables the government to deflect criticism for its own policy failures. For UK plc this can only end in tears. It is not simply that confidence in our financial institutions has been shaken to its core – in truth, trust has been shattered and this will take a long time to restore.

In the year ahead we may well discover that our bashful, activist government has conjured up a fantastical rescue plan that has not only come at colossal cost to future generations of taxpayers

but may not work on the ground. For the time being, the public
has placed a conditional trust in the Prime Minister as someone
who can best make sense of a fast-moving and bewildering financial
catastrophe. But be in no doubt. Before this year gets much older
the public's fright and apprehension will turn to real pain and anger.
The real question then will be whether trust will be corroded more
in government or the workings of a free market economy. Neither
outcome makes for a cheery prospect for the year ahead.

‡

Time for Parliament to Lead, (*Daily Mail*), 23 January 2009

*'Collectively the House of Commons has failed to show itself in a good
light over allowances but we now have a real opportunity to display
some leadership in these difficult times.'*

*Alongside the financial crisis ran a political one concerning revela-
tions about the use and misuse of MPs' expenses and allowances which
was eventually to corrode utterly the nation's trust in its politicians. At
the time of writing this article, however, the* Daily Telegraph *had not
yet published the leaked, explosive details of MPs' claims. Since I had
been warning that the rules governing MPs' expenses were a scandal in
the making for some time, I strongly advocated a transparent, proactive
approach to Freedom of Information requests that were being made for
the disclosure of claims. Similarly, with the depth of pain being inflicted
on the nation as a result of economic turmoil, I thought it right for MPs
to take a lead in confronting the thorny issue of public sector pensions
whose cost the financial crisis helped expose as unsustainable.*

Out in the real world beyond the Houses of Parliament there is
growing alarm at the next tsunami threatening to engulf our beleaguered economy – the inequitable state of affairs between public
and private pensions.

Businesses faced with the prospect of lean times or liquidation
are being forced to look upon their pensions obligations with

a more discerning gaze. In December, the Pensions Protection Fund revealed that Britain's final salary schemes' pensions deficit has increased to £195 billion as companies struggle to raise funds. Meanwhile this week it was reported that more than half of those defined benefit pension schemes still open to new members will be closed due to the current economic situation. This came hot on the heels of a warning from the National Association of Pension Funds that we are likely to see final salary schemes being closed even to existing members.

The scrapping of pensions benefits, falling equity and bond yields, lower interest rates, increasing life expectancy and even the risk of employers' default on pensions provisions all now combine to create a sobering economic outlook for those reliant upon occupational or private pensions. The government should take heed.

For amidst all this private pension gloom, the taxpayers' bill for public sector pension provision seems to grow exponentially. People retiring from the wealth-creating sector with inadequate, money purchase pensions – or in fact none at all from their failed employers – are not going to watch happily as folk from the public sector, whose wages they have paid over many years, retire on guaranteed index-linked final salary pensions. The greatest vitriol will no doubt be reserved for MPs whose gold-plated pension scheme (admittedly underwritten by generous contributions from parliamentarians) will be even harder for people to stomach amidst private sector woe and further controversy over parliamentary expenses.

Collectively the House of Commons has failed to show itself in a good light over allowances but we now have a real opportunity to display some leadership in these difficult times. As a matter of urgency we need to change the structure of our pensions and lead the way for the entire public sector. Failure to grasp this nettle risks serious social unrest – with society being economically divided as never before between those in the public and wealth-creating sectors.

Pensions are vital to everyone's aspirations. But our expectations – especially in the public sector – must be made more realistic in the light of this country's financial plight. Now that public sector workers are paid on a par and often above private sector equivalent levels, the time when final salary schemes were seen as compensation for low levels of public sector pay are well and truly over.

MPs, whose pension arrangements are invariably regarded as the most generous of all, are the right people to show they are not immune from the turbulence of the British economy. For new entrants to the contributory parliamentary pensions scheme, there must be a defined contribution (not final salary) outcome. Existing MPs should set an example by voluntarily agreeing to pay more into the scheme or accepting that future contributions should be on a 1/60th rather than a 1/40th basis (which means that MPs would have to make full contributions for forty, rather than only twenty-seven, years to qualify for a full pension).

Only by agreeing to such a one-third reduction in the benefits of our generous pension scheme, can MPs look the rest of the public sector in the eye when asking for similar sacrifice and restraint.

‡

Where Now for British Banking? 3 February 2009

On 19 January, in a bid to contain the banking crisis, the British government announced a second bank rescue plan to kick-start lending and bolster the stability of the nation's financial system. Under the proposals, the Treasury would establish a widescale insurance programme, the Asset Protection Scheme, to protect banks against further losses and guarantee bank assets. It was a move criticised by both the Conservatives and Liberal Democrats as evidence that the first bank bailout had failed.

Alongside this announcement, it was revealed that the government would be converting its preference shares in RBS into ordinary shares, increasing its holding in the bank from 58 per cent to 68 per cent. At the same time, RBS released a trading statement announcing that it could face losses of up to £28 billion from 2008, representing the UK's largest ever corporate loss. On the back of the statement, shares in the bank slumped.

The dismal plight facing the UK economy naturally brings to mind rousing and inspirational Churchillian rhetoric.

I am sad to report, however, that we are not even at the end of the beginning of this financial and economic crisis. Its impact on the fortunes of us all will be felt for many years to come. It is important not to heed some of the more outlandish predictions of our economic future (such as the so-called City expert opinion that the UK is now heading for bankruptcy) but a turbulent journey lies ahead. For in spite of the astonishing pace and extent of decline over the past twelve months there is no end in sight for the travails facing the banking sector.

The seven largest global investment banks have all lost their independence. One, Lehman Brothers, has gone bust. On these shores the government has spent or guaranteed unimaginably huge sums of public money trying to bring stability to the entire financial system on a scale that is barely able to be comprehended. Such is the price for the UK economy's unbalanced position as a truly global player only in the financial services sphere. Watching the second attempt by the Chancellor of the Exchequer at a definitive bailout my gloomy, but overriding, thought was this: how soon before the government returns for a third bite of the cherry?

The nagging doubt remains that the government lacks any real plan of what UK banking should look like once the worst is behind us. I believe we must soon see a robust vision for restoring free-market disciplines into this stricken sector. For whilst the spirit of the age may point an accusing finger at 'market failure', history teaches us that governments fail far more often. As I have written before, politicians of all parties must explain to the general public some unpalatable home truths – Britons have spent and borrowed far too much over recent times; moreover, too many of us lack the necessary skills to compete effectively as a high-wage player in the global economy. Unless these long-standing failures of government are addressed urgently the UK risks social unrest on an unprecedented scale.

As the financial crisis took hold last October there was a failure of government to send a clear message to the financial system about its priorities at such a difficult juncture. Those UK banks taking government money (RBS and Lloyds/HBOS) were ordered to resume lending at 2007 levels yet simultaneously constrained by an FSA decree to shore-up their balance sheets by increasing their capital reserves. The imposition of a 12 per cent interest rate on government-owned preference shares (roughly double what US or European banks were being charged in what was supposedly a co-ordinated international bailout) led to sheer confusion. Belatedly the UK government has recognised that part-nationalised banks' rational reaction to prioritise the repayment of government loans ran directly counter to its broader economic aims. As a result the government has transferred its preference shares into equity. But this policy confusion since October has cost the UK taxpayer dear.

By 19 January, the day of the second bailout, RBS's total market value had plunged to only £4.5 billion despite the bank having received over £20 billion at what we assumed was the lowest values last autumn. In these short months ownership of RBS shares has cost the UK taxpayer over £17 billion – greater than the UK's entire annual defence budget.

Speaking to City professionals in recent weeks my clear understanding is that the problem facing the financial system is not simply one of lack of confidence: the biggest danger now is that trust in our entire financial system has been so eroded that there is a limit to what government action can achieve. In the eye of this storm the City's demise should not be exaggerated. Better times will return and our critical mass in this sector will stand the UK in good stead for the future. However, the reputational danger to both the City of London and New York means that both centres should expect a markedly smaller slice of the global financial services cake when the recovery comes.

How will this all play out? Whilst historically confidence can often be regained quite suddenly and seemingly without a trigger event, the restoration of trust in a failing system is much more difficult.

By the time the government has a third stab at a widescale banking industry rescue, RBS may well be fully nationalised. The Lloyds
Banking Group and Barclays (notwithstanding the terms of its deal
last autumn with Abu Dhabi investors) may well by then also have
the government as a majority stakeholder. At which point, given
the imperative to protect the taxpayers' financial interests (an issue
which seems to have been forgotten in all the turmoil to date), the
competition implications may force even the final 'big bank' HSBC,
to sacrifice its independence in the interests of a 'level playing field'.
It would then be a short step from nationalising the banks to bringing large parts of UK industry and commerce under government
influence, control or ownership. We already see the first signs of this
in high-level discussions over what remains of the UK car industry.
Indeed, the fast-deteriorating state of their corporate client portfolios represents the most serious short-term threat to the balance
sheets of the UK banking sector.

This scenario would also open the door to the creation of a 'toxic
bank', a step which the government has so far resisted. Whilst the
creation of a vehicle to take on all the toxic assets of the major
banks should in theory free up inter-bank lending and with it the
credit markets, it comes at a tremendous risk. In these turbulent
times it is almost impossible to set an accurate value to such toxic
assets. Valued too low and the beleaguered banks stand to be crip-
pled by their debts for years to come and unable to contemplate
a return to private ownership. Value the toxic assets too highly (a
more likely problem) and the taxpayer will foot an unfathomably
large bill, further delaying the restoration of confidence and trust in
the broader financial system.

This nation needs to go back to the enduring values of personal
responsibility, thrift and enterprise. We must recognise that the
debt-fuelled credit bubble of the past decade – and the current
government's strategy for repairing the damage – is little more than a
pyramid sales scam against the young. Future generations of British
taxpayers will foot the ever-increasing bill for the 'rescue', which
fails to halt, yet alone reverse, the unsustainable levels of public

sector borrowing. To pay for the years to come for present-day consumption also makes it difficult to promote the much-needed savings culture for the future.

The world of finance will look different. However, we have paid the price for short-termism, financial products being improperly understood and over-exuberant speculation in the past. This downturn is new only in its extent and the elusive ingredient, trust, will take a long time to restore.

Above all, at this of all times, politicians need to defend capitalism and free markets as the only bulwark against an all-powerful State. For whilst government's role in stabilising our beleaguered economy cannot be denied, it will only be the hard work, enterprise and flair of our wealth-creators building businesses which will ensure that our economy rises again.

‡

A Few Home Truths on Banking Bonuses, 9 February 2009

Only weeks after the announcement that the government was increasing the taxpayer's share in RBS, news emerged that the bank was planning to pay out £1 billion in bonuses, insisting that it had contractual obligations to many of its executives. It was a story that provoked a public outcry.

Our nation needs a thriving financial services sector. The spiritual home of the UK's banking industry is in the City, but its importance as an employer and engine for economic growth extends throughout the land.

As the City's MP I regard with dismay the attempts by some in public life to make banks and bankers scapegoats for the recession. We should recognise that many thousands working in this sector have already lost their jobs; others, relatively modestly paid, are fearful for their futures in finance. The great majority of bank employees are caught up in events outside their control or influence and are as bewildered as the rest of us at the collapse in their sector.

This only adds to my disbelief at reports that the directors of RBS and Lloyds Banking Group, entities which survive courtesy of huge taxpayer loans and guarantees, now propose to pay billions of pounds in bonuses to reflect performance over the last year. The public outrage at this news is entirely justifiable. No bank which is in receipt of government bailout funding should be paying bonuses to staff this year. After all, 2008 was for RBS, Lloyds and Northern Rock a year of catastrophic, monumental failure. This state of affairs (resulting in eye-watering sums of government assistance and guarantees) cannot be compatible with a 'business as usual' approach on remuneration. I have sympathy for those hard-working RBS, Lloyds/HBOS and Northern Rock employees operating in profitable divisions, but the notion that they should be ring-fenced from the disaster that has befallen their employers is absurd. Ditto those bankers on 'guaranteed' bonuses. For them, I am afraid, events since last October mean we are living in a very different world. My view is that any such salary guarantees are inapplicable to those banks reliant on government hand-outs.

It is high time that senior management in our leading financial institutions woke up to reality. What better case can they possibly provide to opponents of capitalism and free markets than obliviously to take unwarranted financial rewards when as a result of the credit crunch the UK economy finds itself in such dire straits?

‡

Calling Time on Unsustainable Government Debt, 25 February 2009

As the Conservative Party taunted Gordon Brown over his claim to have ended the days of 'boom and bust', the Prime Minister hit back by contrasting his economic activism with the 'Do-Nothing Party' of David Cameron, a tag he continued to use liberally during this period.

Towards the end of February, it was revealed that the Bank of England's monetary policy committee had voted unanimously to start the process of quantitative easing by buying gilts and other securities in the hope of getting credit flowing through the system again. At the same time, the MPC voted 8–1 for a half point cut in interest rates, taking them to a record low of 1 per cent.

In such turbulent and volatile times it is tempting to suggest that Conservatives should concern themselves more with political positioning than making a cool assessment from economic first principles.

There is little doubt that for a few months around the turn of the year the 'Do-Nothing Party' tag resonated with the public at large. No longer – it is fast dawning on a bewildered British public that frenetic government-by-daily-initiative is no substitute for sound judgement and longer-term thinking.

Whilst superficially the spirit of the age leans towards ever more government intervention and expenditure, so David Cameron's vision of a smaller state and promoting thrift (which all Conservatives should wholeheartedly support) carries short-term risks. In the medium and long term it will be vindicated. Moreover, it is a clear sign that we are serious about the challenges ahead of government.

The next big question on the domestic economic agenda is quantitative easing – the printing of money by the Bank of England, necessary (or so we are told) to reflate the economy. An attractively easy option, but the wrong solution to our economic woes.

Because every other government initiative over the past five months has failed to get the economy moving does not mean we should resort to printing money without a crystal-clear analysis of its dangers.

At the heart of the credit crunch afflicting the global economy is not the quantity of money, but the velocity with which it circulates through the financial system. Printing new money runs the risk of undermining further trust and confidence in the UK government in the bond markets with future inflationary consequences. The current level of government debt already baffles most of the general public. Amidst the mind-blowing announcements that total public debt now stands at over £2 trillion, we need to educate Britons to understand the plain truth.

In the past five short years we have added more to the national debt than we had previously borrowed in the 300 years since the UK was created. And this borrowing has not been investment at all, but for current consumption. For every £5 the government will spend in 2009, it will have raised only £4 in taxes. This is the lamentable legacy we pass on to future generations of taxpayers footing the bill for today's consumption.

Printing money now would simply represent more of the same. I fear it will lead this nation to fiscal and monetary ruin. Conservatives should not now shy away from making the case that enough is enough. After all, sticking closely to the financial orthodoxy of so-called banking industry experts over recent years has got us to this place. For the sake of future generations of taxpayers, Conservatives must now stand up and be counted. We must call time on unsustainable government debt.

‡

The Unacceptable Face of Capitalism? 27 February 2009

Just over a month after the government's second rescue of RBS, it was announced that the bank had agreed to take part in the government's asset protection scheme, allowing it to pass most of the potential losses on its riskier assets to the taxpayer. At the same time, the bank raised up to £25.5 billion in new funding from the taxpayer meaning that the government would come to own over 80 per cent of the ailing bank.

Hot on the heels of this news came revelations that RBS's failed Chief Executive, Sir Fred Goodwin, had his pension topped up to £16 million after being sacked. This represented an annual pension for life of £650,000 from the age of fifty. That this story broke on the same day that RBS's new management announced a pre-tax loss for 2008 of £40.6 billion – a net loss of £24.1 billion – sparked widespread horror.

Chancellor Alistair Darling called upon Goodwin, now nicknamed 'Fred the Shred' by the tabloids, to give up his pension or face it being clawed back legally.

On the day the Royal Bank of Scotland announced the largest annual loss in UK corporate history, paving the way for another huge cash injection by the government (bringing the taxpayers' investment in RBS to £45.5 billion since October), the story eclipsing all others is the size of the pension pot of RBS's Chief Executive, Sir Fred Goodwin. Let's face facts – this is a smokescreen to divert attention from the appallingly bad deal that government intervention in RBS represents to each and every one of us.

It is a sign of the times that the idea of a £24.1 billion annual loss fails to raise many eyebrows. Yet at a time when billion-pound losses are being posted almost routinely, it is understandable that public anger rests on something easier to comprehend. On learning of the potential £16 million pension pot, we can all make a direct connection between the money we pay in tax and its destination – Sir Fred's bank account – and ponder the disparity between success and reward, the treatment of top bankers and ordinary workers, our own financial circumstances to the rewards for failure in the boardroom.

This is why this story is so dangerous to capitalism.

I have some sympathy with Sir Fred's argument that he should keep his money if it is established that the government agreed to leave his pension arrangements intact in return for his sacrificing severance pay and options. I even have a sliver of admiration for his refusal to give in to a government whose self-righteous, politically calculating public face contrasts with its private desire to cut a deal without properly appraising itself of the implications. Indeed, if there is one area of consistency from government over the past months, it has been in the blaming of bankers for all of our emerging economic woes.

But let us not forget that Sir Fred's stewardship of RBS has been a monumental failure – catastrophically the worst failure in this country's corporate history. Had the government not intervened to save this failed institution, Sir Fred would have had to rely on some sort of pension protection fund which no doubt would have capped his pension at around £20,000 per year.

I support capitalism. I believe in honouring contracts and recognise the importance of these concepts in our global economic relations. Incentives should rightly be offered for good performance. But the end result of this particular episode can only be utter distaste for politicians, bankers and – most damaging of all – capitalism. Far from upholding the free market values and the honour of the law of contract, those who support Sir Fred's entitlement as it was back in October will only help to undermine capitalism and all it does to create wealth.

For the truth is that we now know that the profits, bonuses and other emoluments for many banks and bankers over recent years have been massively overstated. If it is impractical to restate those earnings to reflect reality that has become apparent since last autumn, it is equally absurd to invoke the sanctity of contract law to prevent some move towards an equitable claw back for those unwarranted rewards.

‡

Levelling with the Public About the Action Needed to Restore Britain to Economic Health, 17 March 2009

'Anyone in management not planning to spend considerably less in the next year is living in cloud cuckoo land.' This was the bleak, yet candid, commercial assessment of a high-profile businessman in my constituency.

Most people in the political world accept that the same strictures must apply to government. At some point, some unpalatable and politically difficult decisions will have to be made on public spending. But in the final year of this parliament, how open and honest should the political class be with the electorate about the scale of the troubles that lie ahead? Should we Conservatives be the first to tell some home truths about our nation's economic future?

I have long argued that we should tell it as it is to the electorate and believe we must continue to do so for one compelling reason: in the event that we are elected, it is crucial that we have a strong and clear mandate to do what is necessary to put the public finances back on track. After the next election it will not be enough simply to freeze or trim public expenditure. Instead much more radical solutions will be necessary. Policymakers will need to re-evaluate where the State's empire should properly start and end.

I accept that this message is not an easy one to deliver. Indeed there are some sound political reasons to avoid even starting down such a path.

For a start, the extreme economic volatility of recent months is likely to continue well beyond the forthcoming election year. There can be few certainties about the state of the economy to be inherited by any incoming administration. Specific policy commitments are arguably unwise.

It is also worth reflecting that for many, this recession is still 'happening to someone else', with the real pain and anger being felt by only a minority. For those in (relatively) secure employment – including most in the public sector – the cost of living has fallen dramatically over the past year. Many with tracker mortgages are paying less than half the cost servicing housing debt than they were a year ago. Similarly a visit to the supermarket or filling station has become noticeably cheaper in recent months.

In these tumultuous times, the overwhelming emotion for many is utter bewilderment. Understandably most electors fail to grasp the magnitude of the current economic difficulties, when unfathomable levels of spending and debt running to hundreds of billions of pounds are routinely banded around in news coverage. Reducing departmental government expenditure by a few billion seems small beer when compared to the colossal sums expended in the banking bailout. So why try? In the run-up period to the general election, do we really need to rock the boat on public spending? It will be unpalatable to many that taxpayers' money can happily be spent bailing out banks and bankers whilst public services are cut back. Similarly to the 750,000 more working in the public sector than twelve years ago, the prospect of public spending cuts is unlikely to appeal.

It is also conceivable that this state of denial will continue, especially as government continues to lead the public to believe that it will always be there to cushion the blow.

The Conservative leadership is mindful of the experience of the last two general election campaigns, when our proposals for what in the current situation seem like pathetically modest savings in government expenditure were misrepresented as 'severe public spending cuts' by our political opponents. Moreover, a bleak and uncompromising economic message runs counter to the positive, optimistic outlook that the Party has sought to project under David Cameron's leadership.

As a counter to the more general state of disillusionment with the political process, we must offer a positive programme that does not focus solely on the blame game. This requires avoiding an economic message that looks dangerously unappealingly in the face of unrealistic spending pledges made by a Labour Party with nothing to lose and a Liberal Democrat Party unlikely to be probed deeply.

Putting these concerns to one side, there is no doubt that an incoming Conservative government will have to be incredibly robust about the extent of the public sector's scope. Indeed, matters are far more serious than in 1979. At least then we inherited an economy which, courtesy of the IMF, had been subjected to monetarist policies for two and a half years. Three decades ago the tough decisions on spending had already to a large extent been made.

Even if the government's own, almost certainly optimistic, projections on public spending come to pass, during 2009 it will raise only £4 in taxes for every £5 it spends. Remember too that we are only at the early stages of the recession. Things will probably get much worse before there is any sign of global economic recovery. Today we must start to come to terms with the fact that there are entire areas of current central and local government activity that arguably should no longer qualify for public funding. The overall state of the public finances suggest that even in the areas of education, health and defence – which during more economically clement times the Party pledged to ring-fence – further scrutiny will be necessary. Whilst there has been a marked improvement in school and hospital infrastructure over the past decade, much of this has been financed via the PFI, which will need to be paid off balance sheet for many years to come. Even here there will be no short-term public spending benefit to be derived from putting any future infrastructure commitments on hold.

I cannot accept that everything that government does today is essential. In a brighter economic climate we can be more expansive, but for the foreseeable future there are whole silos of expenditure that will have to be removed from the public purse. In truth, such radical plans can only really be carried out in the first weeks of a new government with a strong mandate. The planning must start now.

Whilst it is prudent to avoid overly detailed commitments along the lines of the James Review before the 2005 election, it may prove unexpectedly popular to the electorate if before the next election we display awareness of the seriousness of our nation's economic plight. In 1979, contrary to the myth that has since grown-up, we were clear with the public in advance of the election about the necessary medicine our economy required. It may be no coincidence that we were swept into office with the then biggest swing at a post-war election.

At a time when people are paring down personal and company budgets, the call for restraint by government will surely become even louder. I detect the public becoming weary of frenetic activity by political leaders, which yields little result other than to rack up yet greater national debt. Furthermore, a rather interesting phenomenon has revealed itself in my postbag in recent weeks. Constituents who are encountering the benefits system and Jobcentres for the very first time after being made redundant are finding that in spite of paying into the system for years, they either do not qualify for assistance or are bitterly disappointed with the help they do receive. Add them to the legions of pensioners dependent upon income from hard-earned savings and there may soon be significant demand for more value from a smaller, cheaper state by a hitherto silent majority.

A message of responsibility and thrift; the appeal of representing reinvigorated values of reward for work; the encouragement of innovation and flair; a choice apart from the activist, intrusive government that we are told is the essential response to this crisis – these are all positive things that can accompany our levelling with the public sooner rather than later.

The momentous change that Conservatives aspire to offer our nation requires an explicit mandate.

‡

Which Way Now for Banking and the Economy? 23 April 2009

On 22 April, Alistair Darling delivered his Budget statement. With the British economy in recession, rising unemployment and record borrowing, it was one of the most hotly anticipated Budgets of recent years. The news was every bit as gloomy as anticipated with projected GDP growth for the year as a whole of -3.5 per cent, the deepest contraction of modern times and markedly worse than the Chancellor had predicted only months before in his Pre-Budget Report. Darling also revealed that public sector borrowing for the year would stand at £175 billion, almost double that of the year before.

But stealing headlines was his announcement that the top rate of tax would rise to 50p for earnings over £150,000, breaking a key election pledge not to raise income tax and signalling a firm break from the New Labour strategy of reassuring the rich. A car scrappage scheme was also announced to shore up the ailing British automotive sector.

If there are any crumbs of comfort to be gained for the Chancellor in this week's Budget – and I suspect there are very few – no one can accuse him of putting an overly bright face on our nation's bleak economic prospects.

It lacked any credible narrative of a pathway for economic recovery. Yet still the seriousness of the situation is only slowly dawning on the political class, let alone the general public.

Last year's Budget predicted £40 billion public borrowing for 2009/10, by autumn the figures were £78 billion for last year, £118 billion this. Now we know that over the next two years' aggregate borrowing will be around £350 billion. In short, over the near term – whoever is in government – for every £4 that government spends, it will raise only £3 in tax. This overspend cannot possibly be described as 'investment' – it is purely spending to consume today what will need to be financed by a future generation. Remember too this is only if the government's figures – persistently over-optimistic – prove accurate.

There has been a precipitous collapse in tax receipts, especially from business. But this also applies to the government's slice of bonuses earned by the wealthiest in more clement economic times. No bonuses means no tax, which means as ever that it is predominately middle-income salary earners who will foot much of the future bill for the government's over-expenditure.

The government have flunked the really tough decisions on public spending that needed to be made. Instead action on this has been delayed until a general election is behind us.

Attention is understandably moving away from financial institutions as the 'real' recession takes hold. But as the City's MP I would highlight some pressing issues that will emerge in the months ahead.

Two of the big four domestic banks are all but fully nationalised. One, Lloyds Banking Group, contains 'assets' from HBOS which engaged in a series of balance sheet boosting debt-for-equity deals during the boom years in the middle of this decade.

As a consequence, LBG has large holdings in a swathe of leading UK companies. Doubtlessly many such household names will require refinancing as the downturn proceeds. Such financial rescue will come from the taxpayers' coffers – in short, before long, considerably large parts of mainstream corporate UK will be effectively nationalised.

49

Whilst the days of financial sector governance by blind form filling may be numbered, it is wistful to imagine a return to the days of regulation by informal eyebrow raising from the Governor of the Bank of England. This will apply even if many of that institution's traditional powers are restored. However, we need to use smarter intelligence to nip regulatory problems in the bud. An enhanced role for the Bank of England must be accompanied by the appointment of high-calibre, respected professionals in its top roles. I believe this should be augmented by the emergence of prosecutors with US-style status in place of the discredited Serious Fraud Office (SFO). Nothing less will restore confidence from market professionals and trust from the public at large.

The banking bailouts have proved an expensive failure. No further nationalisation should be undertaken in this sector. The lesson we must learn is that any institution deemed too big to be allowed to fail will forever be prey to reckless risk-taking. If banks cannot fail, they cannot be effectively regulated, for regulation requires the eradication, not reward, of recklessness.

The operation of capitalism requires corporate failure. This is not 'market failure': it is a sign that capitalism is working properly. Instead the message that banks will not be allowed to fail only serves to make their effective regulation all but impossible. Regulation creates barriers to entry and favours large corporations over smaller start-ups. The wisest policy option should be to create smaller, more competitive financial institutions. Manifestly, nationalisation takes us in precisely the wrong policy direction. The best form of regulation must be open competition; public ownership – other than on a strictly temporary basis – is anathema to this policy goal.

The conventional wisdom is that the heightened phase of the economic downturn since last autumn has come about as a result of the US government's decision to allow Lehman Brothers to collapse. But letting a leading bank like Lehman fail will in time, I suspect, not be regarded as a mistake at all.

For by nationalising banks, governments have protected not only depositors (unarguably essential in preserving trust in a market economy) but also bondholders. The latter's interests have been preserved at the expense of taxpayers, present and future.

Essentially this has been political gambit – much of the banks' borrowing has been funded by insurance companies and other institutional investors and the risk of contagion in the event of their collapse was deemed too great. Yet bondholders, as lenders of capital, are supposed to take risks (and receive ample rewards by way of interest payments). In a 'heads we win, tails you lose' inversion of classic capitalist practice, when all has turned to dust they too have expected – and received – a taxpayer bailout.

The current consensus promoting Quantitative Easing will find less favour as the year wears on. With little evidence that the velocity of money within the economy is any less sluggish as the real recession takes hold, printing money in vast quantities increasingly seems like a desperate last throw of the governmental dice when nothing else has succeeded. Inflation is clearly not an immediate problem, but mark my words, this unprecedented pumping of money into the system is certain to be inflationary. History suggests that an unsustainable mini-boom will be on the cards by the end of next year, but stagflation (a toxic mix of inflation, rising unemployment and low growth/diminished competitiveness) will follow. Indeed the commodities and futures markets are already factoring this in when pricing for the early years of the next decade. I suspect the government has not seen the back of the problems it has recently experienced in trying to sell gilts as our national credit rating is hammered in the global capital markets.

This crisis – now that globalisation has taken hold – is certainly different in magnitude to those we have seen before. One of the grand old names of British banking, Barings, collapsed owing £780 million only fourteen years ago: today RBS survives courtesy of a £26 billion bailout. However, there are clear lessons we can learn from the past. First, we need to restore the distinction between retail and investment banking which – in the US at least – existed for over six decades until the repeal of Glass-Steagall by the Clinton administration in 1999. The purpose of what was regarded as outdated 1930s throwback legislation is the protection of the ordinary depositor from high-risk, if innovative, banking practices. It now seems mighty apposite.

How then to deal with the toxic assets that banks still hold and find so difficult to quantify? Curiously enough, the UK has a template close at hand. The near collapse of Lloyds of London was avoided almost twenty years ago by the creation of a government-backed Equitas fund. This experience should be the starting point for consideration of any further large-scale government-backed rescue expenditure. In fairness the government has begun down such a path, although we should all be fearful of the ultimate overall cost to the taxpayer.

The nagging sense of insecurity amongst the majority of the UK workforce that the spoils of globalisation are being spread inequitably will grow and has the makings of serious social unrest. The hollowing out of large swathes of 'traditional' UK industry as job employment has been exported to low-cost China and India has not even been accompanied by higher middle class professional earnings (at least for those outside the gilded world of financial and associated services until last year). Over the past decade the mirage of higher living standards was maintained only by the credit-fuelled residential property market. The sharp correction here has exposed the reality – international free trade has done little to enrich personally the majority of our fellow countrymen in recent times.

It is dawning on many middle class folk that the losers from free movement of labour and capital are not simply the unskilled forced to compete with ever large numbers of immigrant workers. It is also increasingly apparent that the generation about to join the workforce will probably be less well off than their parents, not least as they foot the bill for the economic unravelling that began last September. Their phenomenon is almost unimaginable outside times of war – a shocking indictment for my generation of politicians.

So how will we know when the financial system has been fixed? In short, when can government stop pumping vast sums of taxpayers' cash into a system which so desperately needs confidence and trust restored. Surely the main purpose of regulation in this sphere for the taxpayer is the establishment of a system that makes long-term investment worthwhile.

High-profile allegations of mis-selling of financial products from the early 1990s and the near collapse of Equitable Life a decade ago had already done great damage to public confidence well before the credit crunch. Ironically this led to property becoming the invest-ment of choice, rather than savings with pensions. We all now know where this credit bubble has led. It is essential that individually and corporately, the UK reverts to a culture of savings and responsibility with less dependence on debt.

Make no mistake, this path will be a long slog. However, if the problem has been too much borrowing and excessive spending it is difficult to see how yet more government borrowing and a wilful, almost aggressive, determination to impose further public sector debt is the right way forward.

‡

Tax and Tactics, 28 April 2009

It comes as little surprise that early opinion polls suggest an over-whelming majority support the government's plans to impose a new higher tax band on those earning over £150,000. Our Party leader-ship has correctly identified that this blatantly political gauntlet has been thrown down purely to embarrass us – after all, it stands to raise negligible additional income. Accordingly we are entirely justi-fied in declining to play to this discredited government's tune. The most urgent priority of any incoming Conservative government will be to stabilise the public finances.

As I have frequently observed there is an increasing sense of insecurity amongst an ever larger proportion of the UK workforce that the spoils of globalisation are being spread inequitably. This will grow especially amongst middle-class professionals outside the once gilded corridors of financial and associated services. However, the predictable truth of this imposition is that the super-rich will pay not a penny more of tax at all. They are either non-domiciled or in the privileged position of being able to characterise much of their income as capital gains (subject to an unchanged 18 per cent tax rate). Additional revenue will come only from modestly success-ful entrepreneurs (who will have even less incentive or collateral to expand their enterprises) and salaried workers unable to avoid this increase and frequently earning sums not wildly in excess of the threshold, whose instincts to do the right thing on savings and pensions will be blunted as their disposable income falls.

Conservatives understand the critical importance to our national economic health of promoting small, start-up business. Competitive tax rates are essential to encourage entrepreneurs, especially as we make our way out of this deepest of recessions. Conservatives appre-ciate that raising tax now even on the wealthiest in our communities risks prolonging the UK's economic downturn.

A decade or so ago the decision of the then Labour opposition to 'stick to Tory tax and spending plans' was an explicit recognition that our economic strategy was right for this nation. This is in stark contrast to the situation today. Even in these turbulent times the public should not be taken for fools. No one out there believes that the Labour government's recklessness with the public finances is worthy of emulation.

‡

The US and China: A Fatal Dependency? 24 June 2009

Whilst there were many failings that could be laid at the door of the Labour government when it came to the state of the British economy, there was no denying that we were also in the midst of a global financial crisis that had been in the making for years, if not decades.

At no time was this plainer than when the leaders of the world descended upon London at the beginning of April for the latest G20 summit. Gordon Brown sought to use the summit as a means of rebooting

his ailing premiership by seeking global agreement for further co-
ordinated stimulus and in the event, $1 trillion of additional resource
was pledged alongside commitments to strengthen oversight of the global
financial system. The summit also brought protestors out onto the streets
of the capital who wished to demonstrate their anger and resentment
about the failings of the world's economic and political elite.

In this article, I explored some of the overarching global trends that
led us to this crunch point.

The collapse of Lehman Brothers last September triggered an unravelling of the global economy so swift that its cause and scope were
beyond the comprehension not only of a bewildered public but of
most politicians and financiers too. Since that time, jobs have been
junked, global trade has slumped spectacularly and governments
across the globe have borrowed unimaginable sums to shore up our
ailing economies. The implications are so colossal that we know not
yet their true cost.

It is the crucial relationship between the world's biggest economy, the United States, and its eastern pretender, China, which we
should examine if we are to understand the broader reasons why
this unravelling has occurred. This relationship has for many years
driven globalisation and has the potential now to wound that same
project fatally. For a decade or more, the United States (along with
the UK) has pursued a model of growth based on debt-fuelled
consumption, the cash and cheap goods provided courtesy of
China. Pursued to its limits, this relationship has become dangerously unbalanced, the myth of its sustainability brutally uncovered
as the complicated financial mechanisms that hitherto propped it
up, dramatically collapsed.

The consequences of this imbalance are not yet fully apparent. Their impact is still difficult to predict. What looks certain,
however, is that the change will be profound and troubling. The
West's position in the world may never be the same again.

...

In the 1970s and 1980s, Wall Street received a number of breaks, beginning with the dollar's link with gold being broken by the Nixon administration's repudiation of Bretton Woods. Later, Ronald Reagan ended capital controls, the global bond market expanded and the US economy was liberalised, opening up America's savings and pensions. With US pension funds ballooning, Wall Street for the first time had access to a huge new source of finance which it sought to invest to maximum value. Corporations were encouraged to invest globally, exploit new markets and demand highest return for their shareholders – often the ordinary American pension holder.

Alongside this came a 'hollowing out' of the US manufacturing industry as companies looked abroad for cheap goods and labour. Similar trends were afoot on these shores. By the middle of the 1980s, the American manufacturing sector was increasingly taking advantage of competitively priced, non-unionised foreign workers by moving production abroad. This process only accelerated once the end of the Cold War introduced millions more workers to the global economy. Whilst the working classes of America were invariably the losers of this deal, politicians made the case that the benefits to the US would outweigh their collective plight. New employment would be found in services, technology and the like, workers would be 're-skilled' and the vulnerable would be caught, short-term at least, by the welfare system.

China was poised and ready to take advantage of these developments. Following decades of economic darkness since the emergence of Chairman Mao, the more pragmatic regime of Deng Xiaoping adopted an 'Open Door' policy in the late 1970s. The country moved away from command socialism and concentrated on developing strategic industries with a global market in mind. The United States happily paved the way for further Chinese integration into the global economy, culminating in China's eventual admission to the World Trade Organisation in 2001. This final step was partially aimed at shrinking the trade deficit between the two countries. In reality, that deficit ballooned. Whilst China did liberalise and open certain sections of its economy, it kept the door to its domestic market firmly closed. By casting aside the established rules of free trade, China became the overwhelming beneficiary of globalisation, exploiting Western markets whilst reinforcing its role at the centre of a powerful Asian market bloc. It simultaneously built up its own internal market and service sector, accrued vast reserves and began to secure stakes in strategically important commodity corporations and those which agreed to transfer technological know-how.

By the late 1990s, the income of the average US citizen had begun to stagnate as the hollowing out of Western economies continued apace. To disguise this unpalatable problem, politicians in the US (and here in the UK, its closely related economic cousin) eagerly took advantage of the low inflationary environment provided by cheap Asian labour. They turned to a high-consumption economic model fuelled by debt (often racked up against Chinese reserves) in the private and public sector. With easy credit and cheap mortgages, US and UK individuals were able to borrow cash as never before, the false perception of wealth embedded by access to cheap Chinese goods. Meanwhile, financial services in the West thrived to manage the seemingly insatiable demand for new investment instruments.

For politicians in both America and China, the relationship between the two countries seemed a classic case of win-win. In the US, citizens could enjoy cheap money and cheap goods. For China, the immature manufacturing sector boomed as hungry Western markets were exploited. For sure, even in the late 1990s there were nagging doubts about the sustainability of this arrangement. But to rectify them would cause short-term economic difficulties and get politicians into hot water with angry voters. Furthermore, the United States was still in the driving seat. It would always be able to dictate the terms of its relationship with China … or so we thought.

...

Make no mistake, China will not emerge unscathed from this global recession. A slump in demand has already led to extensive Chinese unemployment. Social upheaval may follow. Given that China relies heavily on a healthy US consumer, it is conceivable that the unbalanced, but overly dependent relationship may yet develop into a tight economic alliance. Nevertheless, China remains on a growth trajectory that seems set to take its economy past that of the United States by 2050. The US Treasury and its ailing banks have been stabilised by Chinese loans. The US market remains dependent on cheap Chinese imports. It is hard not to conclude that China holds almost all the cards when negotiating the terms of its bargain with America. What is more, its ascendancy – and that of near neighbour, India – may only just be beginning.

Last year, as the financial system collapsed at breath-taking rate, US and European banks and governments quickly borrowed colossal sums to shore up their operations. In large part that borrowing was funded by China's vast surplus. In this way, a trend that was already in motion – a shift of economic power eastwards – has been markedly accelerated.

The legitimacy of Western capitalism has always been bound up in the idea that it can best deliver prosperity to the masses, offering many millions a route to middle-income stability each year. But as jobs and money have been sucked eastwards, that mass prosperity – for the West at least – may no longer be guaranteed. The wealth of the past two decades is increasingly being regarded as an illusion and the competitive edge the US and Europe have over China and India in services, technological development and scientific research may just as easily be taken from us. China is churning out millions of industrious, well-qualified engineering and technology graduates. As it controls stakes in so many Western corporations, it is also able to transfer and copy intellectual wealth with ease. Soon the powerhouses of Asia could be undercutting Western labour not only in manual but also white-collar and the most highly qualified management positions.

So what will China do with the strong hand it has engineered? Many naïvely assume that along the path towards economic superpower status, China will inevitably become more open, democratic and Western. We assume (or perhaps hope) that it will abide by the Western ideals which have shaped the world's international institutions and laws. It will play by our rules. But all these notions betray a fundamental misunderstanding of how China operates.

Westerners have confused the material wealth brought about by access to cheap credit and cheap goods as a physical demonstration of superiority over the world. However, the debt that has been accrued by the West has come at a cost both in terms of future economic health, and more importantly, global influence. China has played – and continues to play – a patient game. Not for that country the quick fixes and instant gratification inevitably pushed for by Western democracies. Instead a more patient strategy has been pursued, best illustrated by Deng Xiaoping's 'Twenty-Four Character Strategy' – observe calmly, secure our position, cope with affairs calmly, hide the extent of our capacities, bide our time, maintain an assiduously low profile, never claim leadership and make some contributions apparently from the sidelines.

It is inconceivable that China will not now seek to exercise its muscle on the international diplomatic and military stage as a result of the strong hand that has been quietly won. In fact that power is already manifesting itself. Take for instance China's refusal to condemn explicitly Iran and North Korea's nuclear ambitions; its military action in Tibet despite international outcries; the continued unease in Taiwan; the influence it exercises across large swathes of commodity-rich Africa. Similarly from the Caribbean to the South Pacific, it is systematically buying up influence at the UN amongst its smallest sovereign nations. Even under Barack Obama's leadership, China is likely increasingly to reject US economic, military and humanitarian pressure. It will have greater success in any future competitions for resources and greater power to ignore the norms and rules of the 'international community'.

...

What does this all mean for the UK? Curiously, now that the price of our national profligacy has been put into sharp focus, policymakers seem determined to return to business as usual. Further borrowing and the maintenance of historically high levels of public expenditure seem the order of the day, as government remains reluctant to prepare voters for some very inconvenient truths. With typical impatience, the media is already beginning to ask when the recession will end as it hunts for green shoots in every dark corner.

In cold reality, we must accept that for too long now we have been living way beyond our means, riding on a wave of abundant credit, low inflation and high house prices which have combined to create a false hope of ever rising living standards. As a medium-sized economy primarily reliant on a hitherto booming financial services industry, we will remain vulnerable for some time to come. For those middle-income folk outside the gilded corridors of finance who were unwilling to accrue wealth via (largely housing) debt, the economic stagnation had become ever clearer well before the recession. Average salaries and wages have been pretty flat for almost a decade, a fact that has been disguised by grossly inflated asset prices. For younger people in particular, merit and hard work were no longer translating into secure, well-paid jobs and affordable homes. Despite this, the past fifteen years will soon be regarded as having been the very best of times.

The long hard slog of a slow recovery will be difficult to swallow for a nation used to assuming that its debts would never be called in. British employees are owed nothing more than the Asian sweat-shop worker and even the graduate-level openings of tomorrow may equally be filled in the decades ahead by qualified and hard-working twenty-somethings from the East. A rapid return to sustainable economic growth cannot be taken for granted. Complacent hopes of British exceptionalism may not see us through. We might not have the money to cushion this blow as we have in the past with a generous welfare system.

In the short term, we will have to take a long hard look at the books and sharply pare down spending commitments. In the long term we must make a strategic decision as to the direction of our economy; whether to gamble our future on the possible resurrection of our financial services industry, going it alone as a beacon of dynamism, or whether to diversify our economy and – implausible as it may sound today – tie our future more firmly to Europe in the hope that the strength in numbers approach will partially shield us from the stiffest of economic competition from the East.

The recent economic demise has never been outside the bounds of possibility. History is full of banking crises, burst bubbles, periods of economic darkness. But the breath-taking speed at which economic power will shift firmly to the East is new. The fundamental imbalance in the economic relationship between the United States and China will now either cause that relationship to implode or it will be prolonged and made more acute by a continued tsunami of debt. Either way, the coming decades will likely be shaped by the emergence of an increasingly confident China keen to flex its muscle economically, politically, culturally and in short order too, I suspect, militarily.

The West's hope that it can assume continued dominance in the 'knowledge economy' may prove optimistic. I suspect that within the next twenty years, it is quite likely that the intellectual property rights that have underpinned the West's competitive advantage (licensing, patents, copyright protection) are overdue a radical, philosophical shake-up. An ever more assertive China will argue that traditional IP structures are no more than the West's attempt to impose its own form of protectionism to suit its particular demographic. We should not assume that the dominance of 'our' values in determining global trade will remain unchecked.

If there is to be a longer-term price for our collective indebtedness, it will be for the UK to watch with increasing impotence as it becomes our turn to suffer as the rules of the global trading game are changed to our detriment.

‡

Farewell to a Wasted Decade, 10 July 2009

Too few of my parliamentary colleagues have woken up to the enormity of the debt crisis that follows hot on the heels from the economic downturn. Yet the seriousness of what will follow cannot be long denied.

For sure, technically the worst of the economic recession may now be behind us – although it would be premature to conclude that a 'double-dip' recession is not on the cards as the effect of the stimulus dies off in the New Year. Amidst some of the glib green-shoots commentary, we should also understand that the banking crisis represented nothing unusual. Indeed, it signalled the end of another in a long line of boom/bust cycles (positively commonplace in the second half of the last century) caused by speculative eupho-ria and an excess of credit.

The crisis is being presented to serve narrow interests as being an entirely unprecedented type of downturn caused by modern financial alchemy gone wrong, failure by regulators or rank unfore-seeable misfortune. This is not so. It is true that the global nature of the economic crisis has made things worse. But there are also clear lessons we can learn from the past. One of the grand old names of British banking, Barings, collapsed owing £780 million only four-teen years ago; today RBS survives courtesy of a £26 billion bailout. But it is only the extent of the economic downturn, not its cause that is so very different.

The UK economic downturn began when household debt and housing bubbles simultaneously burst. Our house prices rose 88.5 per cent in the decade to 2007 – even in the sub-prime enhanced US this index rose by only 64.5 per cent. Our average household debt leapt from 105 per cent in 1997 to 177 per cent of disposable income a decade later – in Europe and the US both the overall levels and increases during this period were significantly lower. The tolera-tion and promotion of these debt bubbles alongside the growth in financial services and property industries was an integral part of the government's narrative of creating an economic miracle. It had long since given up on encouraging old-school manufacturing and needed to find favour amongst middle-income Britons to secure electoral support.

The past decade seemed for so long like the best of times. However, in our complacency we planted the seeds of catastrophe. Consumer consumption in the US and Europe was maintained by unsustain-able levels of public and private debt. The dotcom revolution was heralded as a 'new paradigm', so whilst almost imperceptibly the wages of middle-income earners stagnated, consumption in a low inflation, low interest rate economy remained apparently robust. In truth – as we have seen – the 'new' economy was sustained by an old-fashioned private debt bubble. Cheap mortgages remained eminently affordable by virtue of the deflationary effects of China and India's emergence on the global economic scene. The Clinton administration's deregulatory policies promoted a love affair with home ownership in the US previously seen only in the UK. Millions of families – including latterly many of the sub-prime borrowers – were able to clamber for the first time onto the property ladder. For so long as the housing bubble inflated, this new breed of property owner was able to borrow yet more on the back of rising house prices. Naturally this also happened with a vengeance on these shores, as became startlingly apparent with the demise of Northern Rock.

As the level of private debt reached dizzy heights the financial risk to the general taxpayer of widespread default suddenly got a whole lot more serious. As we now know there was good cause for retaining the distinction between retail and investment banking, which in the US at least existed for over six decades until the repeal of Glass-Steagall in 1999. Little did we know that the inherent risk of investment banking was to be transferred not to retail banking depositors but to global government balance sheets. Instinctively bankers understood this and once their institutions became too big to be allowed to fail, they had precisely zero incentive to minimise danger. On the contrary, investment banking's short-termist, bonus culture positively encouraged reckless risk-taking.

The abiding lesson of the global banking bailouts is that in future no institution should be allowed to become so large that it cannot be allowed to fail. That way lies the madness of ever more public exposure to financial calamity. An effective regulatory regime requires the eradication of, rather than reward for, risk-taking. It must avoid the creation of barriers to entry that favour large established corporations over entrepreneurial start-ups. Hence the Conservatives' support for a future banking industry made up of smaller, more competitive institutions.

However, there is an uneasy feeling that banking is fast returning to 'business as usual'. Public anger at the proposed £10 million bonus package for the new top team at RBS would perhaps be better directed towards ensuring that risk-taking in future is better managed. Indeed, the crisis of the past nine months has seen those banks that have not collapsed, disappeared or been nationalised suddenly become markedly more profitable as competition has fallen away. Yet whilst money flows again into the hands of bankers the essential structure of the industry remains intact – in short, the taxpayer will be the lender of last resort if all goes wrong. Small wonder that even some Conservative commentators support the notion that banking as a sector whose failure threatens the entire economy must have some added costs and regulatory restraints imposed upon it. After all, the debt now facing future generations of taxpayers courtesy of this banking-led credit catastrophe is more than was ever racked up to fight two world wars. Let's not even speculate at the inflationary prospects ahead if Quantitative Easing proves overly effective.

I have written before about the colossal trade imbalances between the West and China which have spawned a fatal interdependency. This has been made worse by the ending over recent decades of the gold standard and capital controls, the mechanisms by which trade imbalances were traditionally kept in check. Consequently, since the late 1970s, the UK and US have borrowed incrementally more and exported ever less whilst China, especially over the past decade and a half, has built up a huge current account surplus.

Arguably it is these imbalances rather than inadequate regulation that have been the cause of the economic calamity that has beset the global monetary system. A new international framework to secure stability in the management of global trade and the flow of money within the world economy is now overdue.

This economic downturn has been unique in its dramatic global effect. But the core causes are not so very different from what we have seen before. As a result the solutions do not require a bewildering racking-up of unimaginable levels of debt for future generations of taxpayers. Indeed, nothing will more certainly hinder our prospects of rapid economic recovery and a sustainable return to improved living standards.

The biggest threat in the years ahead is that the indiscriminate pumping of money by the Bank of England into the economy will bring with it an unsustainable mini-boom. Thereafter a combination of inflation, rising unemployment, weak growth and diminished competitiveness will produce a toxic mix of stagflation – truly a 'back to the 1970s' phenomenon. The worst-case scenario here is that a future government may regard a sustained dose of inflation as the quickest and most politically convenient way of helping bring down the level of public debt.

In truth, any UK government that is regarded as popular in 2011 and 2012 is probably not administering effective economic medicine. To do the right thing on tax and expenditure in the years to come will not be seen as a politically easy option.

This year, if we follow the government's almost certainly optimistic predictions, we shall be borrowing – I repeat, borrowing, not spending – £450 million each and every day. The billions being borrowed now to ease the impact of the downturn for today's electors will be repaid by future generations in the form of higher spending, higher inflation and reduced living standards. Yet the true cost of all this will not become apparent in the months ahead. The government is desperately hoping that the sands of time and the patience and goodwill of an increasingly alarmed gilt and bonds market do not run out before it has to face the voters. Which makes talk of economic recovery now so very dangerous. This is not a simple, binary choice of 'cuts' set against 'investment'. There is a hard slog ahead for any administration.

If political leaders are unwilling to face up to the stark facts of this long march back to fiscal balance and economic recovery it may even be necessary to bring in the IMF. What better way to encapsulate the power of the quangocracy we have built up for a political class unwilling to take responsibility or court unpopularity than to bring in a neutral umpire to make the really tough decisions on public spending?

‡

Alternative Investment Directive – The Impact on Hedge Funds, 28 September 2009

In November 2008, G20 leaders gathered in Washington DC for a summit on financial markets and the world economy. Their aim was to achieve co-operation in the reform of the global financial system in order to prevent future crises and encourage economic growth. This would involve all significant financial market actors being appropriately supervised and on the back of the summit, the European Commission published in April 2009 proposals to regulate the alternative investment fund management industry.

The Commission's resulting directive outlined rules on how such funds and fund managers might be authorised, operated and suitably transparent in their dealings. It represented a significant change to the regulatory framework governing the private equity and hedge fund industry. Since the majority of the European industry was based in London, the directive was perceived as an attempt by rival continental financial centres to clamp down on the UK's competitive advantages in the field of alternative investment.

The rise and power of hedge funds represents one of the biggest changes to the global economy over the past half-century.

Predominantly limited liability partnerships, most hedge funds are exempted from much of the regulation that applies to investment banks and mutual funds, and as pools of highly mobile capital they have fast developed the reputation of being able to move financial market mountains by anticipating future expectations. Hedge funds thrive on volatility so the crux of the controversy surrounding them is the degree to which they either cause or affect fundamental shifts in financial markets.

This unpoliced, unsupervised and, until recent years, low-profile sector of the financial services world is now firmly in the sights of the European Commission. However, its proposed directive to regulate hedge funds and the private equity sphere betrays a lack of understanding of the workings of the business. Critics of these proposals regard the onerous reporting and disclosure regime as predominantly politically motivated.

The origins of continental Europe's targeting of hedge funds pre-date the credit crunch. Fully four years ago, German economic ministers dubbed as 'locusts' those hedge funds which had precipitated upheaval at the Deutsche Boerse. To many in the Parisian financial community, hedge funds represent the paradigm of the 'Anglo-Saxon' capitalist model. To its opponents, the European Commission's attention in this area appears to have been promoted by an unholy alliance of continental bankers and politicians, most concerned to effect a power grab – 80 per cent of hedge fund assets managed in Europe are accounted for out of London; fewer than one-twentieth originate from Paris.

For the plain truth is that the asset management business has not been directly implicated in the global financial crisis – so why does the EU give such priority to their regulation? Typically hedge funds are small set-up businesses – a far cry from the large, international banking institutions that jeopardised the entire global financial system last autumn. Their offshore domicility owes more to the need for simplicity in tax and regulation with places such as the Cayman Islands not being beset by double-tax treaties and reclaim bureaucracy.

The impetus for a European directive derives from panic in response to the economic crisis alongside a partisan vision of hedge funds and private equity as a Wild West show of amoral speculators and asset-strippers. But there has been no crisis of asset management. Unlike banks, hedge funds neither leveraged themselves to the hilt (they lacked the balance sheet clout to do so even if they had wanted to) nor ran down from adequate levels of liquidity. Indeed, those which have failed have not threatened the entire financial system.

In truth, one of the unsung successes of the Financial Services Authority has been its ability to keep the hedge funds sector ticking along nicely in recent years. So it cannot make sense for a European directive to insist upon onerous hedge fund registration requirements by giving Commission officials the right of veto over their investment strategies. This will simply result in the drying-up of investment from outside the EU to hedge funds here, which is against not only UK, but also French and German interests.

All that investors in this global market ask is that they are free to choose their investment managers. Instead this proposed brave new world for hedge funds and private equity will enforce EU-based investors to abide by a system of rules whereby they will have to instruct EU-based managers and place their assets in EU funds.

A more sensible approach would be to examine how and why private equity and hedge funds became so powerful so rapidly. The homogenising of mainstream institutions in the financial sector – as a result of interdependencies and the converging effect of regulatory creep – gave rise to the demand for a new diversity of off-balance-sheet methods to manage assets and credit. In particular, post the Enron scandal, stricter regulations introduced to control off-balance-sheet activity resulted in an explosion in special-purpose vehicles created to bypass a culture where stifling regulation presented a massive competitive advantage to those institutions able to reap the benefits of economies of scale.

Nevertheless, whilst I believe it is wholly wrong to bury hedge funds, we should be wary of giving them too much praise. There is no doubt that the emergence – in reaction to regulatory overkill – of a largely unpoliced, unsupervised hedge fund sector had significant distorting effects on the entire financial system.

Additionally the huge, largely unregulated profits derived by the most successful hedge funds has had perverse effects on the strategies employed by investment banks, whose profits could never emulate those obtained in the tax-free, regulation-lite regimes enjoyed by the funds. As these profit margins became ever more the talk of the City, unrealistic expectations as to compensation were ratcheted up. By 2004 senior banking executives watched enviously as hedge funds' profits soared and their brightest and best junior staff were poached to make their fortunes there. In retaliation many leading investment banks elected to allow the emergence internally of 'virtual fund' teams specialising in the riskiest but potentially highest return sectors. More often than not such 'star' teams negotiated - and were granted - special shadow profit-sharing status internally. This was the worst of all worlds – giving such teams the green light to indulge in unprecedented risk-taking all the time underwritten by the banks' colossal balance sheets. This seemingly safe umbrella encouraged ever greater leverage and the spectacle – even in the good times – of such a small proportion of banks' profits being retained. Naturally this strategy was only questioned after the credit crisis exposed the folly of allowing the inherently riskier culture of hedge funds to pollute the banking system.

I believe it is right that policymakers engage intellectually with the proposition that rewards (and super profits) be justified only in return for exceptional performance rather than as an arbitrage for tax and regulatory breaks. This requires a systematic analysis of the structure of the financial services sector. Scapegoating hedge funds and private equity cannot be a sensible first step down this path.

‡

Effective Enforcement – Changing the City's Culture, 12 October 2009

Despite grandstanding galore from politicians, there is a growing unease at the paucity of substantial change in the aftermath of the financial crisis. Nowhere does this resonate more than in the field of enforcement, where talks of US-style powers to prosecute alleged wrongdoers in financial services appear to have been dashed.

The general public are not fools. Weak and superficial exercises in chastisement are no replacement for considered and mature discussions between Westminster and the City about the best ways to lead the economy out of the dire mess in which it finds itself. In this way, we must start to look at solid proposals that will make a lasting change to the workings and culture of our financial system. Only then will the banking fraternity earn the public trust so crucial to any economic resurgence.

Two areas at which I suggest we look urgently are the remit of the Serious Fraud Office (SFO) and the related idea of deterrence.

Deterrence is a vital ingredient in any effective financial system. It broadly comes in two forms: the deterrence of losing ground to one's rivals in a competitive market and the deterrence of punishment by a credible judicial or regulatory body, when personal greed or the desire to triumph over one's competitors leads to anti-competitive practice, fraudulent activity or exploitation.

As financial services stand, deterrence is dangerously lacking. As I have said before, the single best form of regulation is open competition. However, in the current landscape – here for some time to come – of large, part-nationalised banks, competition has fallen away. It is the main reason for the rapid return to super profitability, and the awarding of huge bonuses, by some in this sector. Banks have become 'too big to fail', many smaller institutions have either collapsed or been swallowed up by larger banks and a large portion of the risk that remains is guaranteed by the taxpayer. In addition to this sweeping away of competition, we have a fraud-busting body in the SFO that for too long lacked either clout or respect from those in financial services.

Operational since 1988, the SFO is responsible for the detection, investigation and prosecution of serious fraud cases in England, Wales and Northern Ireland ('serious' involves sums of £1 million upwards). Whilst operationally independent, the SFO comes within the remit of the Attorney General and is given the power to bring criminal prosecutions directly. The Financial Services Authority, by contrast, is able to impose civil sanctions and launch criminal cases on matters such as market abuse, in tandem with the City of London Police and Crown Prosecution Service.

The SFO has regularly been criticised for its low conviction rate, a reputation worsened by a series of high-profile cases that have placed the organisation in a poor light. Notably, the organisation was humiliated after it dropped the Al Yamamah investigation into BAE Systems' arms deals with Saudi Arabia in 2006 under pressure from the government. Small wonder it has continued to have BAE's overseas activities in its sights. More recently still, it has come under fire for refusing to pursue criminal charges against the Phoenix Four consortium following their purchase of MG Rover.

Its most costly investigation, however, was Operation Holbein that looked at an alleged pharmaceuticals cartel designed to defraud the NHS. The investigation eventually collapsed after running up a bill of £25 million to the taxpayer. It was this case in particular that raised serious questions about the SFO's ability and role in tackling large, complex investigations. A review of the organisation followed that suggested there was a culture of buck-passing and a lack of internal focus and skill.

Lawyers continue to lament the difficulties associated with securing convictions for fraud, especially given the collapse of highly complex jury trials. It is for this reason that many feel that the introduction of a system of plea bargaining similar to that in the USA would not work – nobody will risk blowing the whistle or turning themselves in when the likelihood of a successful prosecution is so slim.

The SFO's problems are not necessarily of personnel. Speaking to experts in this field, I believe that one of the organisation's main problems is in finding cases to investigate. Indeed, it is only when the police or Attorney General have firm cause to believe that a criminal act has occurred that the SFO is permitted to get involved. When a case does get underway, its prosecutors routinely face months battling defence lawyers before they can get to trial. The defence has a strong incentive to engage in a war of attrition in order to derail a prosecution on legal technicalities.

As such, we face the task of reforming the financial services system and inculcating in the minds of its participants a sense of right and wrong, with an umpire (the SFO) that lacks the tools – or market respect – to do its job properly.

This contrasts sharply with the experience of the United States. For some time, the City has been lagging far behind New York in pursuing, charging and convicting white-collar criminals. From 2003 to 2007, the SFO's conviction rate stood at 61 per cent, which is dwarfed by the 92 per cent obtained by the Manhattan District Attorney's Office.

The differences in our systems are fourfold:

- The whistleblower culture (bringing with it immunities) is far stronger in the US. Regulation 10 (A) of the Securities Exchange Act, for example, puts especial duties on accountants and other professional advisers to report any suspicions. Once such rules are in place here and begin to be used, over time a new culture of responsibility will naturally develop.
- Criminal liability at the corporate level is stronger in America and applies to misfeasance by employees in the US. In the UK it applies only to directors.
- The power of 'deferred' prosecution in the US has no UK equivalent. This mechanism allows prosecutors to resolve criminal changes by the imposition of substantial financial penalties so long as the future conduct of the company involved is agreed upon.
- Finally, in the UK only the FSA can impose a financial penalty on a company. The SFO cannot. This separation of powers in tackling white-collar fraud has contributed to a sense that those committing corporate misfeasance are 'getting away with it'.

So how does the UK learn from the experience of the United States and make the SFO an effective player in the policing of a robust financial services industry embracing the fresh culture that the general public rightly demands?

I believe we should give serious thought to reappraising the role of the Serious Fraud Office by adopting key elements of the US system. First and foremost it should target competition policy, which has been largely bypassed as a result of action taken to stop the haemorrhaging of the financial system over the past year.

In my next article I shall outline precisely how we should go about this task. Getting this key issue right must form a crucial pillar in a credible financial system for the future. As the global landscape of financial services changes, so too must the enforcement of its rules; public trust cannot otherwise be restored and we shall all then be the poorer.

‡

Competition – The Ultimate Consumer Protection, 2 November 2009

Open competition is an absolute necessity as the ultimate consumer safeguard. In the previous article I concluded that government should give serious thought to adapting the role of the Serious Fraud Office and implementing a new, radically improved US-style system for the investigation and prosecution of financial crime. This would form one of a series of strong new pillars in a reformed and effective financial system. So how should the new fraud-busting agency operate?

The Opposition's commitment is to disband the Financial Services Authority and return its supervisory function to a more powerful Bank of England. This poses two problems. First, the FSA is funded by the financial institutions it regulates. Wherever the FSA is absorbed, we will need to claim new resources at a time of highly constrained public spending. Second, what will happen to the FSA's Enforcement Division, which is able to impose civil sanctions and launch criminal cases on matters such as market abuse in tandem with the City of London Police and Crown Prosecution Service? Should those important functions be taken on by an empowered, but potentially overstretched, Bank of England?

My proposal is the drawing up of a robust economic crime policy that places the promotion of commercial competition at the heart of a new code of enforcement designed to deter fraudulent, anti-competitive or criminal activity. Such a policy should centre upon a new agency in place of the Serious Fraud Office which would combine the SFO and the FSA's Enforcement Division.

Incongruously the SFO currently lies under the jurisdiction of the Attorney General. I believe we should place the new investigative agency within the remit of the Department for Business, Innovation and Skills, working closely alongside the Office of Fair Trading. By associating consumer protection with fraud and trust-busting, we give competition its correct place as a central priority in the future commercial landscape.

To effect the necessary sea-change in attitude and create a body with the authority of its US equivalent requires adopting new powers.

1. It would need to be able to impose substantial fines on wrongdo-ers (such fines could, in turn, play a role in covering the costs of any new organisation).

2. Legislative changes would be required to make British companies criminally liable for illegal acts of fraud and corruption by their employees in broader circumstances than now.

3. Measures would be put in place to protect whistleblowers and offer immunity to those aware of anti-competitive practice when they come forward.

4. The new agency would be endowed with greater leeway to inves-tigate any potentially fraudulent activity before a formal inquiry is launched.

5. Perhaps most importantly, a revamped Serious Fraud Office would enjoy a power of deferred prosecution.

   A deferred prosecution enables proceedings in a criminal case to be delayed for a given period subject to certain conditions being met by the company in question. At the end of the set period, if all the agreed conditions have been met, charges can be dismissed and judgement of conviction is entered. Prosecution of the case will continue in the event that the defendant company fails to comply.

Over the past year or so, the SFO has pursued a more consumerist agenda and in view of the fallout from the global financial services crisis, there is great public appetite for the taking of an aggressive approach to fraud in an attempt to rebuild the organisation's battered reputation. A process of deferred prosecution can be made to work in the US, with that pragmatic option reliant upon a willingness on the part of investigated companies to cut a deal.

Ideally, such a system would work along the following lines. A company would be able to approach the SFO to alert them to concerns about certain elements of their operation, for instance in merging with a company whose practices do not necessarily seem sound. Soon after the approach from the company, the SFO would try to establish whether its Board of Directors is committed to resolving the issue and changing their organisation's culture. It would also determine whether they are prepared to work with the SFO on the scope and handling of any additional investigation.

Once both sides are satisfied with the self-investigation, there would follow a without prejudice discussion as to whether further investigation was necessary. Wherever possible, this would be carried out at the company's expense in co-operation with its professional advisers, whilst trying to control costs.

The SFO had been attempting to apply such a method to the BAE Systems case by trying to persuade the company to plead guilty, pay a fine and agree to independent monitoring of its behaviour instead of the embarrassing and lengthy process of a trial. So far BAE has resisted and the SFO is now seeking permission from the Attorney General to prosecute.

The SFO has also introduced the system in the recent Sports Direct/JJB case which was referred to the SFO from the OFT after JJB blew the whistle on alleged cartel activity in the sports retail market. In return for immunity, JJB must fully co-operate with their investigation, withdraw from the cartel and pledge not to act in bad faith. The OFT in its own right has had some recent successes in imposing substantial fines. Most recently it imposed a penalty of £39.27 million on six construction companies that had been engaged in anti-competitive behaviour. In that particular case, a deal had been cut as one of the cartel's whistleblowers was granted an exemption for revealing the operation. The two bodies – either working together or as one – could prove an effective duo in the vigorous promotion of competition and fairness.

One of the biggest problems for the SFO in its current set-up is the difficulty of actually finding cases to investigate. In a system of deferred prosecution, more companies would walk through the door. Though it could lead to an added layer of bureaucracy in fulfilling any new requirements to self-report, discussions with business and professional advisers so far suggest that there is a lot of interest in a system of self-reporting. In return for openness and co-operation there would be effective and proportionate sanctions for any wrongdoing, the prospect of a civil rather than criminal outcome and the opportunity to manage issues and any subsequent publicity proactively.

In a system where no form of corruption is tolerated but a fair and proportionate approach is taken to those who try to reform (backed up by the threat of serious penalties if they do not) a new corporate culture would ideally emerge, creating behavioural changes within businesses and a fresh respect for any fraud-busting agency.

With the UK taxpayer propping up banks that are politically too big to fail and, as a consequence, providing cover for many commercial enterprises part-owned by part-nationalised banks, our economy has a worrying dearth of competition. With a Serious Fraud Office that currently has neither commercial nor industry respect, we lack too a serious, tough and effective body to deter companies from engaging in fraudulent or market-distorting activity. I contend that it is critical that we put the restoration and promotion of competition and fairness at the very heart of future economic policy.

The SFO (or any organisation that replaces it) requires teeth under the Party's plan for sound banking alongside an all-powerful Bank of England. The public will loudly demand more rigorous enforce-ment of regulation across business, but particularly in the financial services sphere. Conservatives need to demonstrate seriousness of intent by outlining robust plans for a tough, not-to-be-messed with agency that values strong competition and clean business dealings as essential to the functioning of an effective financial system. Such an agency should be linked to – or indeed merged with – the Office of Fair Trading and its work made a top priority of the Department for Business, Innovation and Skills rather than a minor one in a Treasury with its hands full. As a blueprint for our new regime, we need only turn to the United States whose system is imbued with a whistle-blowing culture where deals can be cut if a business shows willingness to change, backed up with a tough prosecutorial threat.

The deterrents provided by healthy competition and stiff punishment must form the backbone to the brave new world of banking and business that lies ahead. Nothing less will restore confidence from market professionals and trust from the public at large.

‡

The Future Landscape of Global Finance, 18 November 2009

With the green light given to quantitative easing earlier in the year, the Bank of England began in March to buy £75 billion assets under the government's new Asset Purchase Facility. It proved insufficient and the Bank took a second bite of the cherry in May 2009, purchasing another £50 billion of assets. By August, the total figure was increased to £175 billion and by November, it stood at £200 billion.

Such colossal sums of global taxpayers' money have been spent and immense government guarantees continue to underpin the financial system that it is remarkable how little agreement exists to what constitutes the point at which the banking industry can be said to be fixed. Less still is there any emerging consensus as to the ideal future landscape of the financial services world.

This is no mere academic issue. The imperative to start repaying borrowing at the earliest opportunity cannot be overstated. Yet commercial lending is unlikely to return to anything like normal until the second half of 2011 as toxic assets are gradually removed from bank balance streets. The credit crunch will be with small and medium-sized businesses for some time to come.

Meanwhile this year UK taxpayers are consuming over £4 in government spending for every £3 raised in taxation. This unprecedented burden of borrowing will have to be repaid by future generations in the form of reduced living standards; the UK situation being especially acute as our public finances were already in a dire state as we went into the credit crisis.

To extend beyond £200 billion of quantitative easing puts at great risk our medium-term economic prospects: so when can the Bank of England and the Treasury call time on their short-term fixes? Amidst the euphoria of a narrative suggesting recovery is within sight and a FTSE back above 5,000 I fear that we are in truth some way from being out of the woods. I have written before that the root causes of the global imbalances brought about by the West's financial calamity were the credit/debt bubble along with the East's aggressive desire to build market share in global trade. China's policy of suppressing its currency to soak up the West's debt in the bond markets further helped hold down interest rates. Yet the resultant overinvestment, excess capacity and vast structural debt in the West remains in place. The underlying causes of the crisis have not gone away.

Notwithstanding the ruinously expensive bailouts and capital raising, the losses incurred by banks are probably still not even halfway recovered. Indeed the government's insurance of toxic assets has provided a dangerously false dawn. There is no incentive – or currently requirement – for banks to crystallise non-performing loans because they could not then ignore the losses on their balance sheet. Lloyds Banking Group, for example, with a huge property portfolio courtesy of its disastrous HBOS merger, sits on an enormous pile of assets worth a fraction of their book value at their boom-time purchase.

The collapse in public confidence in financial institutions and their more esoteric products has met with a strong-armed, opportunistic political response. Put simply, we need to ensure that management in banks are able to summarise in simple terms the financial products they wish to sell. If a derivatives product cannot be explained on two sides of A4 then frankly it should not be marketed. Naturally an unworkably complicated regulatory framework risks seriously hitting the future viability and profitability of the entire industry.

Instead, the wellbeing of the institutions in this sector – not to mention its customers – depends upon the development of a workable regulatory system based on commercial principles which pass muster over the decades to come. How else can we persuade those in their twenties to commence a lifetime of prudent saving as a prelude to a financially comfortable retirement? It all comes down to trust. This is an ingredient that no amount of regulation of 'consumer protection' will rapidly restore.

Alongside the promotion of open competition (an end to the heresy that a bank might be 'too big or interconnected to fail') the best government can do is to advance a culture of mutuality. In short, inculcate a sense of accountability between individual policyholders and a diverse range of financial institutions. For this reason, Conservatives should welcome the potential of Northern Rock returning to building society status once it has been stabilised financially. Promotion of as diverse as possible a financial services ecosystem ought to be a goal of future Conservative policy in this area. In future we need ethical values to come from individuals rather than resulting from a hostility which, inevitably, will be mounted against an all-powerful regulator. We should not expect too much from regulation. The buck must stop with all of us as consumers.

Regulation creates barriers to entry and promotes the large and bureaucratic over the small and innovative. A competitive free market can only be promoted by the reestablishment of less concentration amongst all institutions in the financial sphere and ultimately means allowing companies – even huge players like Lehman Brothers – to fail. The interests of depositors and retail investors should rightly be protected from such an eventuality.

A healthy, competitive and innovative capitalist system requires risk-taking, which is why shareholders and bondholders should not naturally expect such blanket protection. The trouble is that too much of the current debate on banking regulation has focused on how we should have stopped the last crash. This has not been helped by a government whose recent economic policy pronouncements are governed less by the national interest and more by a 'scorched-earth' approach designed to limit the room for manoeuvre for years to come of any incoming Conservative administration.

We would be better turning our attention to how best to create a future global financial system that will be trusted by today's children investing in the decades ahead in anticipation of a long, secure retirement income.

‡

Battle of the Bonuses, 4 December 2009

By the year end, attention turned once again to bankers' remuneration as reports emerged that the majority-state-owned RBS was intending to increase its bonus pool to £1.5 billion, a 50 per cent increase on the year before. City Minister, Lord Myners, also revealed that over 5,000 bankers would that year be getting paid over £1 million and collectively, senior executives and traders would earn at least £5 billion in salary and bonuses. All this only twelve months on from the near-collapse of the financial system and a month after an announcement by the Chancellor that the Treasury had agreed to purchase up to an additional £39 billion in RBS and Lloyds Banking Group, taking the state's stake in RBS up to 84 per cent.

These stories sparked a debate on how the government might rein in bonuses at banks in which the taxpayer now had a stake and ministers began to formalise plans to do just that, causing the board of RBS to threaten its resignation.

I appreciate the bewilderment of the general public at the rapid return to huge bonuses in those parts of the City (including the 70 per cent state-owned RBS) which seemed so close to collapse only a year ago.

However, amidst the anger and dismay we need to realise that this is a highly mobile, global business. The only way to introduce an effective cap on banking bonuses would be by a binding, international agreement to cover London, New York, Hong Kong, Singapore, Tokyo et al. This is NOT going to happen.

Conservatives rightly support calls for restraint throughout the financial sector, and in order to open up lines of credit to small businesses it was our suggestion last month that this year's bonuses should ideally be paid in shares, which would only vest in future years.

The government is all at sea on this issue. It should now stop grandstanding with its 'for the many, not the few' line and lead public opinion with a frank explanation of a practical way forward on bonuses.

The real question for the future is this: how can the UK taxpayer get best value for its colossal investments in both RBS and the Lloyds Banking Group?

For sure we can impose stringent rules on bonuses being awarded by those banks which are majority state-owned. But the truth is that the brightest and best will simply leave and join other banks where they will not be subject to a restriction on their bonus and earning capacity.

If we are to repay these nationalised banks' debts and sell off the stakes we own as rapidly and for as much value as possible, how can it be in the national interest to constrain these banks from maximising their financial performance?

‡

The Economic Perils of Political Uncertainty, 14 December 2009

On 9 December, Chancellor Alistair Darling, delivered his Pre-Budget Report. In it, he conceded that the downturn had been far worse than anticipated and presented two contrasting visions of how the UK might go forward. *The choice, he claimed, was 'between securing recovery or wrecking it – between investment to build a fair society where all prosper and a divided society that favours the wealthy few'. The words were pure Gordon Brown and set the scene for the general election that would have to be called within months.*

Pointing the finger of blame for the state of the public purse firmly at the 'global financial crisis', the Chancellor revealed the nation's debt mountain was even more enormous than had been expected and that the government would not be able to cut spending any time soon. Nevertheless, his intention was to halve the budget deficit by 2014.

He also announced a 50 per cent super tax on any discretionary banking bonus above £25,000, a surprise National Insurance hike, a pledge to cap VAT at 17.5 per cent, and a cap on the pay rises of public sector workers.

In response, Shadow Chancellor, George Osborne, declared that Labour 'had lost all moral authority to govern'.

The relentlessly breathless press coverage of the financial crisis over the past two years may have persuaded the electorate that we have already been through the worst of the recession. The truth is that such optimism is dangerously unwarranted. The economic reckoning for the general public has yet to begin.

The relative calm and stability in the bond and currency markets owes more to the imminence of a general election and the markets' confidence that an incoming administration will put politics to one side and administer the tough economic medicine the UK so desperately needs. For it is certainly not some miraculous solving of our dire public finances that has soothed the markets over the past few months. Indeed the IMF has calculated that over the course of the next decade, the UK government should ideally impose a fiscal tightening of 12.8 per cent simply to restore the national debt to pre-crisis levels – an option considered by most to be so extreme that it would prove politically impossible to implement.

As we saw in last week's Autumn Statement it is only the Conservatives who have begun to wake up to the enormity and seriousness of the debt crisis that will underpin domestic politics for much of the decade to come. In essence this is why, with our Party riding high in the opinion polls, the markets are calmly assessing the nation's economic prospects.

The prospect of a hung parliament and further delay to the required radical decision-making, pending a second election, risks tipping sterling and the gilts market into a catastrophic state. I repeat – the general public has spent the past two years believing they are living through a financial crisis without having to start paying the price. The effect of the current government's pumping money into the economy (however economically orthodox such a strategy may have been) has been to deceive the electorate into thinking this period has represented the worst of the economic downturn. It is one of the biggest indictments of this government that it has continued to borrow recklessly whilst failing to educate the public as to the medium- and long-term consequences of such policies.

Understandably the public remains reluctant to have the comfort blanket pulled away. I totally support Conservatives unashamedly levelling now with the voters and making the case for an urgent restoration of stability to the public finances. For the colossal scale of this debt crisis brings with it the urgent need for fundamental rethinking as to the extent of the State's empire. Unarguably this comes at some potential cost at the ballot box.

Nothing would be more damaging to our economic prospects than for a layer of political uncertainty to be added to our economic uncertainty. The markets have factored in firm action in the near future. Even as the sands of electoral time move inexorably towards next spring, the sterling and gilt markets risk being tipped over the edge if further delay results from an inconclusive election result. Just imagine the unseemly horse-trading that would result from a hung parliament simply to form a government.

In the absence of firm political decision-making about public spending and tax, market activity would certainly fill the void. The currency and bond markets would probably turn sour; there is a substantial risk of a sterling crisis; long-term interest rates would soar and the nation's essential triple-A gilts credit rating might even face a downgrading. If political leaders – concerned only in gaining tactical advantage – showed themselves unwilling to face up to the stark facts of this long march back to fiscal balance and economic recovery it could even prove necessary to bring in the IMF. A political class unwilling or unable to take responsibility or court unpopularity may in this way be forced to bring in such a neutral umpire to administer the really tough decisions on public spending.

Nor should anyone rule out the prospect of inflation being allowed to run riot as the most politically palatable way to assist in running down the debt burden. Moreover, a dose of inflation provides the expedient route to enhancing the tax take as fiscal drag is allowed to run its course. The inflationary pressures brought about by the fiscal stimulus and quantitative easing may in any event make this path difficult to avoid in the years to come.

So how to bring about the decisive leadership on the economy that the country so desperately needs?

We have spent the past few months systematically discrediting the government's record for economic management. This has been an unqualified success. We have also been upfront about the collective task that lies ahead and we have made some difficult statements about the need to pare back public spending. But there remains a fundamental disconnect with the public – as well as a lingering sense of fear – that could well prove the difference between a working majority and a hung parliament. Rather than to continue to define ourselves in terms of negatives, I believe we now require a sweeping, positive, uplifting vision to counteract the dismal deficit of aspiration in today's Britain.

From now on Conservatives need to promote a consistent and well-articulated case for sustained economic growth. The truth is that rapid action to correct the deficit will be the quickest route to the promotion of growth and recovery. A rigorously thought-out timetable to sort out the public finances boosts confidence and – as all the international evidence shows – promotes more rapid recovery. Note too that nothing risks choking future growth more conclusively than tax rises. Cuts in public expenditure, rather than additional taxes, especially those on income, are more likely to result in economic expansion.

Above all let us not forget that the opportunity this financial crisis lends us is incredibly exciting. Far more enthralling than the prospect of holding office during the placid past decade. Victory in the battle of 2010 has the potential to provide Conservatives with explicit consent to reshape the entire country, redefining the government's role in the domestic economy and Britain's role in the world. Let us now articulate that sense of excitement as to the challenges ahead. For sure, the public needs to know the scale of our problems and have a taste for the solutions. Once again it falls to us as Conservatives to give our fellow Britons something to believe in.

2010

Uneasy Calm Settles Over Financial Markets, 4 February 2010

As 2010 dawned, President Obama gave his first State of the Union address which took a much harder tone following a year in which his personal ratings had dropped. Telling his nation that he hated the bank bailout, he suggested new measures to clamp down on the financial sector that were presented as the strictest restrictions on banks' activities for seven years.

Meanwhile in the UK, it was revealed on 27 January that the economy had come out of recession through growth in the final quarter of 2009 of 0.1 per cent – a rate weaker than expected. UK unemployment was also seen to have fallen for the first time in eighteen months. Nevertheless, the economy was still operating at far below its pre-crisis level with only an extremely lacklustre recovery.

Over recent months, global financial markets have been enveloped by an eerie stillness. The fear remains that this calm is unlikely to last – our fundamental economic imbalances have not been solved, merely parked. The recent indication from the Chinese government that it is to put a firm break on bank lending to ameliorate the effect of speculation is just one sign that points towards the likely return of market turbulence. The most negative effects of the crisis may well be most painfully felt in the stagnant aftermath of statistical recession.

As things stand, the global economic patient lies in an induced coma. Over the past eighteen months we have had near-zero interest rates and governments worldwide have gone on an unprecedented spending spree – whether through quantitative easing, car scrappage schemes or bank bailouts – that has filled the gap left by the ailing private sector. The absence of an immediate market reaction to this, and the lag from credit ratings agencies in adjusting their assessments, has given rise (with the exception of Iceland, Greece and Ireland) to unwarranted complacency. But past economic experience reminds us that the State is not infallible to debt crises of its own. Sovereign default may not be the outlandish prospect we believe and the notion that huge deficits can be racked up without any medium-term implications as to the cost and availability of credit may prove desperately naïve.

Remove the measures taken by governments to stem the downward spiral and our economic fundamentals do not look too smart going forward. There remain deep structural problems that may see our economic woes become harder to deal with once induced low interest rates, quantitative easing and enthusiastic investment in government bonds are removed from the equation.

For one, Britain's labour market is looking sickly. This recession has been characterised by graduate and youth unemployment and experience suggests that prolonged unemployment early in one's career risks longer-term productivity. Not only that, but I have long feared that our nations' much-vaunted 'skills training' is failing to deliver a flexible and competitive workforce to face up to the challenge of competition from the millions of young Chinese and Indians graduating into the global marketplace.

In this post-crisis period, the temptation towards protectionism is likely to rear its head in the guise of demands for employment creation and retention schemes – the uproar over the Cadbury takeover will be just the beginning. Politicians need to make the case that any short-term gains from this activity would inevitably involve longer-term loss. Let us not forget that Britain has benefited significantly from the inflows of foreign capital over the past two decades.

We also face an increasingly powerful anti-capitalist sentiment. In every recession, a society inevitably wishes to punish those who have apparently precipitated the economic downfall. In our case, it is the banker. I understand the appetite for revenge but we must separate sensible measures to curb excess and risk to the taxpayer with punitive measures designed only to twist the knife. Amidst this feverish pre-election political atmosphere, let us not ignore the case for the UK's imperative, competitive advantage in financial services. To be frank, we may wish in future for a 'more balanced economy' but no other sector will be a world beater any time soon on the scale of banking for UK plc. Nor should we forget the complementary industries of law, insurance, retail and entertainment – to name but a few – which all benefit massively from this sector when it thrives.

In this respect, I believe there is an urgent need for reliable, qualitative and quantitative evidence about the exodus from the City of London and the impact on London's financial markets following the imposition of a 50 per cent higher rate income tax band from April this year. The Mayor of London has understandably taken it upon himself to defend the capital's key role as a global financial centre. He, like me, has received plenty of anecdotal evidence in recent months of individuals and institutions already leaving these shores at the mere prospect of higher marginal rates of income tax.

Nevertheless, it is equally important that politicians refrain from bandying around figures in a way that can all too easily be regarded as hysterical. Indeed it can all too often be seen as special pleading from an industry that wishes to exempt itself from any form of restraint yet, in spite of the colossal sums of taxpayers' money spent to underpin, gives little indication of how the landscape of financial services should look in the future. Whilst recognising the potential for catastrophe if we delay the review of these matters until tax cuts are politically palatable, similarly little would be more undermining for the place of financial services in London as to be seen to be crying wolf about the numbers leaving. A robust case needs to be made and only reliable empirical evidence proving the effects of changes in tax rates can support it. For my part, as the MP for the City, I shall be working with the City of London Corporation to amass such evidence in advance of this autumn's Pre-Budget Statement.

President Obama's attack on Wall Street excess comes at an especially dangerous time. The astonishingly rapid bounce-back in profitability this year for those banks still operating is a function of a diminution in competition in much of the sector and the effect of low-to-zero interest rates as easy government money has lubricated the system. These factors will be unsustainable even in the short term, so it is unwise to construct the terms of trade in global banking on the basis of this unusual period of super profits.

Nevertheless, the Conservatives here are right to press for a global accord to ensure that banks are no longer too big or interconnected to fail. Historically the City of London has benefited from arbitrage with Wall Street from withholding tax under President Kennedy (which precipitated the creation of the Eurodollar and Eurobond markets) to Big Bang in the mid-1980s and the effects of Sarbanes-Oxley (2002) in the aftermath of the Enron and Worldcom scandals. This time we must have an international agreement on the future landscape of the financial services world.

The rise of hedge funds owed much to stricter regulations post-Enron to control off-balance-sheet activity. Hedge funds were often the special purpose vehicle of choice created to bypass the culture of stifling regulation which always favours existing institutional players. Whilst asset management (whether hedge funds or private equity) has not been directly implicated in this global financial crisis, I believe that Obama's proposals may as an unintended consequence help promote a further explosion in less regulated investment, which may prove the cause of the next financial crisis. As ever, too much political and regulatory energy tends to be expended in solving the last crisis rather than looking far enough ahead into the future.

For this reason, Conservatives must continue to impress upon the nation that the end of the recession will not inevitably herald the beginning of recovery. This is not the Opposition talking Britain down. We are merely facing up to the reality that the avoidance of bitter economic medicine for some years to come is not an option. To coin a phrase, when it comes to the recovery, and repaying the nation's vast collective debt burden, the Conservatives at least will not stand by as the Do-Nothing Party.

‡

Still the Biggest Game in Town, 21 February 2010

With the financial crisis exposing just how much the British economy relied upon its financial services sector, calls for a rebalancing of the economy began to increase. I wrote this article in response to these calls, many of which I feared were motivated out of a desire to shrink the City rather than to expand other areas of the economy.

Since time immemorial, the City of London has enjoyed an international reputation as a bastion of commercial certainty and reliability. It has promoted financial innovation, provided an international market to global merchants and in commercial affairs has rightly been seen as a watchword for justice, neutrality and fairness. As a result London has emerged as the global financial centre.

But this priceless asset to the UK economy is now being scrutinised as never before. The financial crisis has painfully highlighted our economic dependence on the City and our collective exposure to the risks taken by the banking sector. As we contemplate our future in the new, post-crisis economic landscape, many now suggest that it is time to wean ourselves off the City's false riches by diversifying our economy. But is this a realistic or desirable goal?

That failure in any single sector of the economy overexposes the domestic taxpayer seems unwise. The City's dominance over the past decade has also had wide-ranging social consequences. For a large proportion of British people working outside the financial services industry, the growth of the City's power simply increased the cost of living and reduced to a wistful dream any prospect of getting on the housing ladder (except via colossal personal debt). It could also be argued that the City precipitated a brain drain from other professions and industries, with our brightest and best graduates tempted away by the unrivalled starting salaries in banking jobs.

Framed in these terms, the desirability of a movement away from over-reliance on the financial sector seems sound. But when we talk of reducing our economic dependence on the City, are we sure that the UK offers similarly strong sectors to take its place? My fear is that many desire a smaller City, not out of pragmatism but rather an ideological distaste for financial services. In this feverish political atmosphere, let us not forget why – on the whole – a thriving City makes for a successful Britain.

It is not just banks that benefit from our financial sector but complementary industries such as law, insurance, retail and entertainment. So too do top-flight universities and the arts and social charitable sector gain, the latter two from cultural funds or corporate responsibility grants often provided by the City's top banks and bankers. The presence of our large financial sector gives London the critical mass to attract the best professionals from across the globe.

The banking bailouts notwithstanding, the City contributes massively to the Treasury's coffers in terms of tax revenues and employment. It also plays a critical role in supporting business, whether that be in drawing huge inward flows of foreign capital to help build our infrastructure and prop up our companies or in providing British companies access to diversified sources of capital to enable them to invest and expand.

Even if opposition to City dominance is practical not ideological, I suspect that not only is it unlikely that any other sector will be a world beater anytime soon but that London's population is insufficiently equipped to deal with significant growth in new industries. Few people realise that at 9 per cent, London has one of the highest levels of regional unemployment in the UK. With Britain wedded to a model of high housing and employment benefits, those living in the capital need to earn considerably more than the minimum wage to make it worth their while to work. As a corollary, it has been far easier in recent years to encourage hard-working migrants to fill the jobs that Londoners have been unwilling or unable to take up themselves. We now have a large proportion of the indigenous working-age population without the skills or inclination to fill jobs of any description.

A nation of only 60 million people should be grateful to have one world-beating industry that is, in normal times, incredibly lucrative and feeds a panoply of other sectors. By all means, we should build up other sectors if we can and reduce the exposure of the taxpayer to risk. But economic diversification will be no easy option and should not lead to the neglect or diminution of the City – indeed if it does, the task of diversification will be far harder. Global businesses and their highly skilled work forces do not necessarily have an innate loyalty to the UK. They will go where the legal, fiscal, regulatory, physical and social environment works best for them.

In this respect, more pressing than diversification must be the need to make the UK a place of possibilities, enterprise and entrepreneurship. It should be the priority of politicians of all colours to get that most important of messages out: that the UK welcomes business, whether in the financial services sector or indeed any other industry.

‡

Our Broken Infrastructure, 22 February 2010

On the morrow of her 1987 election triumph, Margaret Thatcher pledged that the Conservatives would devote themselves to transforming Britain's inner cities. The urgent regeneration task for an incoming Conservative administration this year will involve transforming our increasingly shabby suburbs at a time of dire constraints on the public finances.

The regeneration of the centres of cities like Glasgow, Manchester, Liverpool and Manchester – to name but a few – has been one of the triumphs of the past twenty-five years. These areas have become attractive places to work and live. Even in my own central London seat I never cease to be amazed at the number of people in their fifties and sixties who choose to downsize from the Home Counties and move into a city centre apartment where they can benefit from an excellent retail, health, transport and entertainment offering. Alongside a more diverse and mobile younger population, they help provide a social glue that ensures many inner city areas now thrive.

Unfortunately the same cannot be said of our suburbs. One of my not-quite-so-secret pastimes is exploring the streets of suburban London on foot in an almost Betjeman-like way. Beyond the seven square miles of my constituency, I travel by tube or overground about once a month to a far-flung suburb and wend my back home through areas of the capital that very few outsiders ever see. It is rare that anyone takes a leisure trip to the Barkings, Crayfords or Dollis Hills of this world, but the furthest tentacles of our tireless capital can tell the visitor so much about modern British life.

For one, the pace of demographic change since the turn of the century in London's suburbs has been staggering. As life in the centre has become ever more expensive, it has been the outskirts of London that have absorbed those pushed further out and borne the brunt of the large waves of immigration over the past decade. Whilst authorities such as Westminster City Council have a long history in dealing with some of the challenges of a hyperdiverse, hypermobile population – providing health care, schooling, language services and housing quickly to new arrivals in the area – local councils unaccustomed to an unstable and diverse mix of residents are finding their area's fast-changing population difficult to cope with. On top of logistical challenges come huge financial pressures. With government grants to local authorities calculated according to inaccurate population estimates, councils often find themselves servicing large 'hidden' populations alongside registered residents.

My walks also reveal neglected, rather shabby suburban districts that appear to have been passed over by the glitzy visions of urban planners keen to revive more central areas of the capital. Potholed roads and pavements and tatty looking street furniture make way for scruffy high streets, where the credit crunch leaves many shop units empty.

This bleak picture will be exacerbated by the grim economic outlook revealed in December's Pre-Budget Report. Following the general election, any government will have to slam on the spending breaks. Nowhere will this be more profound than in infrastructure projects – yet this is precisely where a track record of patchy investment has left the public realm in some areas falling apart at the seams.

Limited investment in infrastructure in the 1980s and 1990s was understandably identified as a political opportunity by Labour in the run up to the 1997 election. However, their grand building projects since, notably of schools and hospitals, have proved desperately poor value to the taxpayer, present and future.

Gordon Brown's diversionary tactic over the past thirteen years has been to use the mechanism of the Private Finance Initiative (PFI) to remove from the public balance sheet a proportion of the capital costs associated with the government's much-vaunted public sector investment. As I have pointed out, the cost the taxpayer will have to meet for PFI projects agreed over the past few years will amount to a huge ongoing additional burden on public expenditure typically over the next twenty-five years. Indeed the taxpayer is now firmly locked into making annual repayments for some 650 or so schools; hospital and other public sector programmes at a total liability so far stands at £262 billion, some of which will not be paid off until 2047.

Remember too that the capital value of these PFI contracts was only £55 billion – the vastly higher sum reflects the huge mark-up costs of lengthy long-term contracts. Needless to say this comes at a time when public spending will already be under extreme constraint.

Yet the future political fallout of financially unravelling PFI schemes means that the room for manoeuvre open to any future Conservative government in the areas of public expenditure and taxation will be considerably limited – a fact acknowledged by Alistair Darling when in opposition he said of PFI, 'apparent savings now could be countered by the formidable commitment on revenue expenditure in years to come'.

The Treasury's response to concerns over PFI has always been robust and disingenuous – this means of long-term funding was set up by the previous Conservative administration and the current government simply adopted the same rules but allegedly to tighter accounting standards. However, the principle underpinning PFI of private firms building schools, hospitals, prisons, bridges or roads has enabled the public sector to be charged often for decades ahead, leaving a generation-long legacy of debt. Broader public criticism has been muted because of the sheer number of private sector operators, contractors, consultants, lawyers and accountants who have all made hay over the past decade as advisers in a process that has proved extremely lucrative.

The true cost of accounting the future presents the sternest of challenges for Conservatives at a national level. But it will also fall to a group of relatively inexperienced senior Conservative council leaders to fight desperately to keep control of their districts at a time when infrastructure investment will by necessity have to be slashed.

Explaining to the public that this is a result of the extravagant costs and poor value of infrastructure projects already in the frame will be tough. Employ the acronyms PFI or PPP and the public switches off. It is the size of Sir Fred Goodwin's pension and the moats and bell towers of MPs that capture the public's imagination, not the couple of hundred billion pounds indiscriminately, incompetently splurged on PFI.

Conservatives face the challenge of reviving our suburbs and transport infrastructure amidst this depressing indifference to the true costs of Labour's decade-long spending spree. The risk is further decline of these outer districts continuing alongside ballooning youth unemployment and increasingly fractious community relations. A serious situation risks being worsened by the systematic understating of population figures unless urgent attention is paid to the methodology of next year's nationwide census.

So much of local government in England is now Conservative run that we confront the sternest challenge in the face of a populist Labour campaign in the years ahead. Our task will be to reverse the waste of the past decade and reassert values of both economy and community in our suburbs.

‡

Warnings for the Road Ahead, 1 April 2010

On 24 March, Alistair Darling delivered his final Budget and set the scene for the general election, a date for which an announcement was expected imminently, by warning voters not to put the tentative recovery at risk by switching to the Conservatives. David Cameron retorted that the 'biggest risk to the recovery is five more years of this Prime Minister'.

The Chancellor cut the forecast for the year's borrowing by £11 billion to a 'mere' £167 billion; announced a cut in stamp duty for first-time buyers; staggered the planned rise in fuel duty; hiked tax on strong cider; pledged 20,000 university places; and announced a growth package to boost job numbers. It was also announced that his one-off bank bonus tax had raised £2 billion, double the amount forecast, and that RBS and Lloyds Banking Group would provide £94 billion in small business loans.

Now that the dust has settled on a highly political Budget, it has become ever clearer that our nation desperately requires strong Conservative governance to put our national finances back in order. Whatever the remedies within our reach should we secure office at the imminent election, we will also have to keep a close watch on events in the global economy which will surely have a significant bearing on the British economy in the years to come. There are already some worrying signals about the pitfalls ahead:

1. If their governments are to be believed, the only way out of these economic troubles for all Western nations will be 'export-led' growth. I am afraid this begs the obvious question of just who will be doing the importing?

When the financial crisis hit, China acted earlier and more aggressively to forestall a serious downturn than any other large economy by engaging in massive fiscal and monetary stimulus. However, as most countries now agonise over how to keep their barely reviving economies growing, China is already looking to slam on the brakes. With policymakers becoming more concerned about containing inflationary expectations and managing the risk of asset price bubbles as a result of last year's aggressive expansion of credit, China's central bank has now moved to reduce lending to companies and individuals by, amongst other measures, requiring large commercial banks to increase the amount of cash they put in the central bank.

This is just one sign that points towards the likely return of market turbulence. If China brakes too hard, it risks slowing global growth overall and throwing other countries, including the United States, back into recession. Indeed, when China announced its policy, share prices were sent sliding across Europe and America now that China's commercial banks have become ever more important lenders to the rest of the world following the contraction of lending by US banks. It is perhaps for this reason that despite the significant devaluation of sterling, widely expected to revive exports, a majority of British companies have reported that their export order books remain below normal.

2. We should also beware the looming threat of protectionism. Lessons from the crash of the 1930s over trade protectionism appear, to date, to have been learned. However, 'beggar thy neighbour' sentiments may manifest themselves in monetary policy (especially exchange rate). In the UK we have already seen the benefits of devaluation by some 25 per cent over the past two years which may help alleviate the worst economic ravages in the months to come but we should not assume that this competitive advantage will persist. Indeed we may be losers as other currencies devalue in the years ahead; China, to name but one economic rival, also seems determined to use monetary policy to avoid what many would regard as a realistic revaluation of its own currency. The impending US legal judgment over alleged unfair competition might also result in tariffs being levied against Chinese imports. Clearly this would represent a dangerous escalation in economic tensions.

3. Finally, the global imbalances that were the underlying cause of the financial downturn have not been solved, only parked. Unless there is a smooth transition away from the racking up of huge trade deficits and currency surpluses, the risk is that we simply repeat the

policy mistakes culminating in a further crisis by the end of this decade with even greater imbalances.

We can no doubt take a positive hold of a large part of our economic destiny but it will inevitably involve a great deal of pain, a reappraisal of our expectations and a cold dose of reality over the degree to which we are at the mercy of global events (which will likely be primarily influenced by the way in which China handles its economic policy in the years ahead).

Our goal upon emerging from the economic gloom must be a fundamental rebalancing of the economy in favour of the wealth-creating sector, not a further public spending splurge. It is for this reason we should take little heart from the recent fall in unemployment, caused primarily by a growth only in public sector jobs. What we truly require is a proper strategy for growth, low taxes and a smaller state as a choice apart from this activist, intrusive government.

Sadly, in addressing precious few of our national challenges, the Budget perfectly illustrated the legacy of an administration that any objective observer must sincerely trust is now in its dying days.

It offered woefully little hope and inspiration to our young people, who are now beset by the ravages of an unprecedented growth in graduate and youth unemployment. If our nation continues to believe that 'Big Government' is the answer to all our travails and marginalises enterprise and entrepreneurship small wonder that many of our most promising youngsters will conclude that their future lies elsewhere.

A little over two decades ago I left university convinced that the UK was a place of infinite possibilities. I set up my first business as an undergraduate, got myself professionally qualified, sold my business, set up a second enterprise – all by the age of twenty-nine and all here in the UK. Today's most talented young Britons will graduate with average debts in excess of £20,000 and the twin prospects of uncompetitive, high tax when they find work and collectively needing to repay the debts that my generation and my parents' generation have racked up over the past decade.

Essentially we are telling them that the price of British citizenship is to clear up the financially catastrophic economic complacency of this Labour government and foot the bill for over-consumption by our generation.

Unless we can contrive to present our brightest and best youngsters with a more attractive financial proposition we should not be surprised if they leave these shores. Some have highly globally mobile skills and we urgently need to convince them that this nation offers the exciting opportunities and limitless potential. If we do not, it is they who will vote with their feet.

‡

Winning the Battle of Ideas, 12 April 2010

On 6 April, Gordon Brown announced that the general election would be held exactly one month later. In this article, I raised some of my concerns about the absence of debate on the tough decisions over public spending that would have to be made by any new government, and my fear that these decisions would be eminently tougher if an incoming Conservative administration lacked an explicit mandate to make them.

In the weeks ahead we can be sure that commentators will be ever eager to draw comparisons between today's domestic political scene and that of 1979 when the Conservatives were last swept to office.

Contrary to the myth that has since grown up, at that momentous general election Margaret Thatcher presented a distinctive and radical offering to the electorate. I was a fourteen-year-old schoolboy at the time and recall the keen consensus that this was a crossroads election which had the potential to change not just political personnel of the day but our entire national direction.

We all fervently hope for a similar, sweeping victory after polling day. Indeed I passionately believe that a convincing result is not only what our Party needs but is essential for our nation's future well-being. However, I fear that this time the political backdrop is markedly different.

For one, the economic situation in 2010 is considerably more serious. Three decades ago we inherited a rocky economy, for sure. But we should remember that by the time we took control of the public purse, the country had been subject to monetarist policies for two and a half years, courtesy of the IMF. In essence, the toughest decisions on public spending had already been made.

Second, the public was ready to embrace change in 1979. Today it seems the electorate has still to grasp the seriousness of our national economic situation. The hyperbolic media coverage of the past two years, charting dramatic stock market swings, house price crashes and global turbulence, has probably convinced many that the worst is behind us without the headlines having ever truly translated to the situation on the ground. This makes it all the more difficult to persuade a complacent public that an era of financial reckoning lies ahead.

Finally, the spirit of this age is uncompromisingly ugly for those of us who instinctively support capitalism, free markets and global trade. There is open hostility to banks, bankers, big business, the wealthy, private education, private health and the profit motive. This is in stark contrast to 1979 when the case for empowering people, the smaller state and individual responsibility had already been made.

Today, we are poised for electoral success without having needed to convince the public of the superiority of our case. Indeed domestic politics continues largely to be defined by New Labour's rhetoric, with our commitment to cutting public spending sold on the grounds of necessity rather than our natural instincts for a smaller, more efficient state. Conservatives have yet to challenge conclusively the contention that a government which devotes huge swathes of taxpayer cash to tackling 'social inequality' through a lumbering welfare system is more caring than one which believes in empowering the individual. Nor have we sufficiently defended ourselves against our opponents' class war politics. We acquiesce in higher taxes on the wealthy without making clear the very practical reasons why, in an age of global mobility, the brightest and best of our young people will simply leave these shores if their plans to create wealth and promote enterprise are stifled. As the election approaches, we must now make the political weather, dictate the terms of debate and set out a distinct, positive pathway to a prosperous future. The tough times that lie ahead are sure to be infinitely more hazardous without such an underpinning.

To be tempted into a tussle for the centre ground is to rob the electorate of choice – which in part explains the sense of so-called apathy that continues to beset political debate in spite of our living in such tumultuous times. The floating vote slips with the tide and our task as Conservatives is to seek to influence the flow of that tide. If, as we widely believe, the electorate is repulsed by the politics of spin and illusion, then surely I am right in suggesting that authenticity and candour are the most effective weapons in the Conservative armoury?

Going along with the consensus that public spending and current living standards were sustainable even before the financial crisis took hold also robs the young of hope. Let us be clear: the political class has managed to avoid conflict over the past decade with older voters, homeowners and those using unreformed welfare services only by consuming today and borrowing against future generations of taxpayers. A failure to grasp this nettle and secure an explicit mandate for the rapid administering of strong economic medicine, risks generational conflict and public disorder of a sort not seen on Britain's streets for a generation.

This is more than a mere academic debate. The global economic and political outlook is shifting so fast that any incoming Conservative government will need also to strike out urgently with a distinctive and convincing vision of the UK's place in the world in the decades ahead.

Let us be under no illusion, by the end of this turbulent decade it is quite conceivable that our status internationally will have diminished considerably. First, our reduced military capability means we may soon no longer enjoy the prestige of a permanent seat on the UN Security Council. Moreover, as the geopolitical shift to the East gathers pace, the UK may find itself excluded from the top table of economic nations. The Centre for Economic and Business Research recently suggested that Britain may no longer be one of the world's top ten economies by 2015 and even if we do maintain our relative position amongst European nations, by 2050 we shall account for just 2.5 per cent of global output (roughly where Benelux stands today in world rankings). Who is to say that in the coming years a G5 or so of the largest economies will not be instituted, with the UK's role confined to appearing as a bit-part player at occasional G20 summits? This readjustment will have a deep psychological effect on us all. No doubt it will reshape the way in which we look at the UK's multilateral obligations and should certainly inform a Conservative view on the forthcoming Strategic Defence Review.

I do not say these things to be unremittingly gloomy, merely to underline the importance of Conservatives having a consistent, resolute plan for the forthcoming election. The consequences of the political decisions taken in the next few years for the future prospects of our country cannot be overstated. We must make the UK a place of possibilities, enterprise and entrepreneurship; a place that inspires young, bright people, not drives them away.

Let us not lull the electorate into thinking that their choice in this election is not an important one, just a matter of swapping one lot for the other. No, this is a defining moment for our nation.

The forthcoming election must not be framed simply as a clash of personalities. It is far too important for that – it must be a battle of ideas.

‡

Capital Gains Tax, 17 June 2010

Unfortunately the open debate I called for during the election campaign on the state of the public finances never happened and discussions were confined to whether any new government should cut £6 billion from public expenditure immediately or slightly later.

By 7 May 2010, the day after polling day, the only thing that was clear was that the result was inconclusive. In the words at the time of former Liberal Democrat leader, Paddy Ashdown, 'the people have spoken, but we don't know what they have said'.

In the end, a coalition was formed between the Conservatives and the Liberal Democrats and new Chancellor, George Osborne, signalled on 17 May that he would be delivering an Emergency Budget at the end of June. One of the proposals mooted in advance was a doubling of capital gains tax.

We now know for sure that the nation faces a huge hole in its public finances. So amidst an economic crisis that has opened wider the social divide between the haves and have nots, a rise in capital gains tax (CGT) to 40 per cent seems to be an especially easy sell. After all this levy on second homeowners and rampant speculators is designed to fund a laudable income tax cut for the lowest earners. However, taxing capital gains and income differently is not an anomaly.

Like many MPs, I have received an avalanche of letters and emails from angry and perplexed constituents since the rise in CGT was floated. These do not come from the ranks of the super wealthy or short-term City speculators. Instead my anxious correspondents are predominantly people who have 'done the right thing' – those who have worked to build up a business, employees who invested in their company; workers close to retirement who have painstakingly acquired small share portfolios or those who, having lost trust in the pensions system, turned to property as a safe haven for their retirement fund. In short, rather than representing a neat redistributive tax from rich to poor, the proposed rise in CGT risks squeezing those caught in the middle and stifling aspiration and self-reliance to boot.

Capital gains tax is a levy on the gain or profit you make when you sell or otherwise dispose of an asset, such as shares or property. In addition to an annual CGT allowance (currently £10,000) and Entrepreneur's Relief, in the past taper relief (which modifies the levy according to the length an asset has been held) and indexation (the taking into account of inflation) have offset some of the burden placed upon individuals.

Capital gains have hitherto been taxed at a different rate from income for good reason. They come from investment and those investments inevitably involve risk – risk that does not necessarily deliver a return. Indeed, given the current state of the economy, there is no guarantee that investing in shares or property will prove as beneficial in the future as it has been. Reduce further the incentives to make those investments in the first place, therefore, and you will find there are some unwelcome knock-on effects.

First, strong and growing economies depend upon high levels of investment. These have to be financed out of savings and the existing pool of capital. The UK has a serious problem already in this respect because our savings ratio has slumped to around 5 per cent, compared to 35 per cent in fast-growing economies such as China and India. Accordingly in the UK we will have to depend on our current pool of savings and inward investments (which will result in ever more dividends and interest being sent overseas to the detriment of our own living standards). Higher levels of capital gains tax will only serve to reduce further the pool of savings available for future capital investment. Indeed, yet more of the UK's capital risks being used to fund current expenditure – a state of affairs that will continue for so long as we continue to run a deficit.

Second, capital is highly mobile. For that reason economic competitors of the UK's such as Australia, New Zealand, Switzerland and the Netherlands, have abolished capital gains tax. All these countries recognise that high capital gains tax rates discourage investment.

Capital gains tax also clogs up the capital markets. Nobody is compelled to sell an asset so uncompetitive rates of CGT will simply encourage those who do not need to realise their gains to switch into other assets or securities. As such, there is a real risk that any sharp rise in the rates of CGT will produce a precipitate drop in the government's tax take from this source. Aligning capital gains tax rates with those of income tax will most likely worsen the deficit as it will cost revenue to the Exchequer.

Moreover, high rates of CGT reduce turnover and liquidity levels in the stock market. In turn the most successful growing companies will find it more difficult and expensive to raise capital to the detriment of the UK economy as a whole. Naturally this also applies to foreign companies who have traditionally looked to the City of London to raise money for expansion.

Having been overwhelmed by individual respondents, I convened a meeting in parliament last week with representatives from the Institute of Directors, National Landlords' Association and the UK Shareholders' Association to test the breadth of concern over capital tax rises. Nearly every representative accepted the inevitability in the current economic plight of an uplift to CGT, but raised wide-ranging worries – the general competitiveness of the UK economy and the problems of uncertainty in the financial environment; the constraining effect on the private rented sector that stands to affect young renters and social housing tenants; the penalising of the small investor; the impact on company share schemes and mobile talent; the perverse message being sent out to pensioners and those saving for retirement.

If the headline rate is to remain, all representatives pushed for softeners, namely the reintroduction of taper relief or a return to indexation. This may be the only way yet seems contrary to the laudable aim of simplification in our tax system. In his famous 1988 Budget the then Chancellor, Nigel Lawson, brought into line the level of CGT with basic and higher rates of income tax. This was achieved at a time of aggressive reductions in the latter. Similarly two years ago Alistair Darling introduced a flat rate of 18 per cent by removing indexation and taper relief.

Restoring a complicated regime of allowances and reliefs to take account of the effects of inflation and length of time over which chargeable assets has been owned sadly might prove an unavoidable compromise to part-protect the interests of the prudent and the elderly, long-term investor.

Whilst the new Business Secretary, Vince Cable, assures us that the proposed higher rates of CGT are not aimed at entrepreneurs, but are designed at 'essentially private capital gains, financial capital gains and second homes', he perhaps fails to appreciate fully that many second-homeowners have sought to save in such an asset as a consequence of the widespread lack of trust in pensions and other financial products over the past couple of decades.

Similarly, he seems not to have taken into account the disproportionate impact higher rates on property will have on Londoners and those in the Home Counties. Many people who buy a second home outside the capital as an addition to a small London base do so not because they are enormously wealthy but precisely because they are not. It is virtually impossible even for many of those earning multiples of the average national wage to trade up the property ladder in the capital. For those with growing families, the only option is often to buy a house with garden outside London.

Above all, an increase in the rate of capital gains may in the event generate neither fairness nor additional revenue. Our nation more than ever needs to be able to repay its debts by wealth creation and selling our skills, products and expertise in a highly competitive global market. This cannot be done by disincentivising small businesses and entrepreneurs with higher tax for risk and investment now or by punishing those who have done the right thing by saving for their future.

‡

Budget Speech, 24 June 2010

On 22 June, new Chancellor, George Osborne, delivered the coalition's Emergency Budget with the aim of balancing the books by 2015/16. He announced a hike in VAT to 20 per cent; a freeze in council tax and child benefit; an increase in capital gains tax from 18 per cent to 28 per cent for higher-rate taxpayers; maximum limits that could be claimed for housing benefit; a two-year pay freeze in the public sector for those earning over £21,000; an annual cut in corporation tax until it reached 24 per cent; and a new bank levy. This was my speech at the ensuing Budget debate.

The first Budget of any new administration is always a momentous event. It inevitably sets the seal for much of what will follow economically. This is a ground-breaking and very brave Budget, which has expressly changed the terms of trade. In his speech, the Chancellor made a robust case for the nation to have a future that would be underwritten by the success of business and enterprise.

It is only the third time in more than three decades that such a Budget has been delivered. In the infinitely more clement economic weather of 1997, the then Chancellor, Gordon Brown, whilst ostensibly sticking to his predecessor's spending plans, announced fatefully his intention to restrict private pension tax breaks. At a stroke, the culture of personal savings was undermined, and a distinct shift from individual responsibility to collective state provision was flagged up. It has, perhaps, taken a full thirteen years for us to appreciate the true implications of what many then regarded as a technical manoeuvre born largely from a need to secure an easily available pool of cash to spend on pet projects, a state of affairs that was necessitated by the making of an orthodox manifesto pledge.

In the Emergency Budget of 1979, the incoming Conservative government signalled a desire to unleash the power of the free market from the state's grip, and to promote free trade after a characteristic spell of Labour mismanagement. Indeed, in the run-up to the general election this year, it became the pastime of many political commentators to draw comparisons between that momentous 1979 election and the political and economic landscape that faces us today. Yet, of course, that simplistic analysis ignored the significant differences between the two episodes. When the Conservative government took control of the public purse in the final year of the 1970s, our nation had been subject to monetarist policies for two and half years courtesy of the IMF. In essence the very toughest decisions on public spending had already been made at that time.

In contrast, this year, whilst there was a superficial acceptance that the best of economic times was over, the sheer gravity of our economic problems has been too lightly skated over during the campaign skirmishes. Indeed, it served the expedient interests of all three main political parties to confine any economic discussion to a somewhat fatuous battle over public spending cuts of £6 billion; a sum of money that we borrow, not spend, every fortnight.

I am delighted that this Budget starts to make the case for empowering people, the smaller state and individual responsibility.

The election is now of course behind us. I remain concerned that our coalition government does in all fairness lack the critical and explicit mandate to make some of the very tough economic decisions that are required as a matter of urgency to get the public finances back on track, for this Parliament – indeed probably for the entire decade – stands to be dominated domestically by the need to take a firm grip of the public finances.

This year's public budget deficit of some £155 billion represents 11 per cent of GDP and means that we continue to borrow fully £1 in every £4 that we spend. This colossal living beyond our means is made up of consumption rather than investment in any meaningful sense of the word. Correcting that imbalance will necessitate diminished living standards for the generation of taxpayers yet to enter the workplace. In a large measure, that means that we have to take an axe to public spending, and that has of course been a remarkably rare event.

I am delighted by the generally positive media response to the Budget, but I should point out that the pain of the tax rises accounts for only 23 per cent of the overall measures. Details of the adjustments to public expenditure will be hammered home in the months to come and will become fully apparent only in 2011/12. That is when the real logistic and political tests will come.

There is much to learn from history about those very few previous episodes when we have needed to make a substantial cut in public spending. The single most significant period of efficiencies and reductions in public spending came in the aftermath of the First World War and, perhaps significantly, was also in a time of peacetime coalition between the Liberals and Conservatives under Lloyd George. The wartime economy at that juncture was characterised by huge unprecedented state control, so much so that when the conflict came to an end, there was a massive upswing in the economy as pent-up demand, wartime savings and the removal of wartime controls caused a boom. However, the first peacetime Budget in 1919 actually led to a budget deficit of 6 per cent of GDP after the then Chancellor concentrated on building homes fit for heroes and embarking on an ambitious social programme rather than balancing books.

Hot on the heels of that boom, however, was a grim slump. Having been one of the world's largest overseas investors before the First World War, Britain became one of the biggest debtors with interest payments taking up some 40 per cent of all government expenditure. The value of the pound was depressed, yet the antici-pated export boom failed to materialise. Even preceding the slump there had been a public outcry at the government's extravagance. As the economic gloom descended and tax increased, the outcry against government waste became a thundering clamour.

It was against that background of public pressure and economic misery that the then Prime Minister Lloyd George appointed Sir Eric Geddes to chair an independent review of government spending in the bitter year of 1921, the aim being drastically to cut spending by eliminating the waste that had been identified. The Geddes committee was to become the most thorough and rigor-ous outside investigation of public expenditure ever conducted in Britain. It was also, of course, highly controversial. Its membership consisted of only a single elected MP and five unelected business leaders, and whilst it was lauded by the world of commerce and Conservatives and taxpayers, it was attacked by the fledgling Labour Party and the trade unions.

In the end, Geddes was able to slice some £54 million off govern-ment expenditure. That seems an almost risibly small sum today, but in those days it amounted to a 10 per cent reduction. We should soberly remember that, once ring-fencing is accounted for, depart-mental cuts of about 25 per cent are likely to be required next year.

Back in the 1920s, a clear message was sent to Ministers,

Whitehall and the general public that spending in any form would be very closely scrutinised like never before. The committee's work marked a crucial turning point in rebalancing the public finances from a distorted war basis to a peacetime basis. It is a lesson we need to learn in the months ahead as we go about the work of ensuring that these departmental changes happen.

The committee's success in rapidly achieving its goal was due to a number of factors: it had professional and respected committee members; it enjoyed unstinting political support; it worked to a very swift timetable, which I think we will have to do again this time; there was widespread public support for its aims; and it was willing to compromise on proposals that proved to be politically unfeasible – I believe we will find ourselves in that situation again in the months to come. The experience of nine decades ago has demonstrated that whilst securing public expenditure cuts is very politically difficult, it is far from an impossible task, as is often claimed. We undoubtedly need to try to achieve great public support. The experience of the 1920s showed that whilst voters might agree in general with cuts, they almost never agree with specific cuts that directly affect them. To put it simply, we need to ensure that the cuts are fair, focused and effective.

History also provides important perspectives and pointers to the future. Wisely, the coalition government has an even more recent precedent in mind. It has been rightly pointed out that the Canadian model of deficit reduction in the first half of the 1990s took place in an era of great global growth and plenty. We should not underestimate how much easier that made its very painful readjustments, under which a quarter of public sector employees in the country lost their jobs. By contrast, today's reductions in the head count will, to an extent, be tomorrow's unemployment rise.

In Canada in the 1990s, the government had already levelled with the voters over a period of time. They then proceeded to provide very clear evidence, on a year-by-year basis, of the gains as expenditure was reduced. They also made the moral case that the living standards of future generations of taxpayers should not be diminished to pick up the tab for the consumption and debts of current taxpayers. That is absolutely crucial.

This has been an extremely brave Budget from the Chancellor. The fact is that despite the – at times contrived – anger from Opposition Members, those who are most likely to suffer are Middle England voters, who are the very people the Conservative Party has relied upon for electoral support. The Budget's promise to be tough but fair is largely borne out, especially in its protection for the poorest and most vulnerable in our society. Indeed, I have been calling for some years now for the removal of the very lowest earners from income tax altogether, and I am very pleased about the steps that have been taken in that regard.

I sound only two notes of caution. First, I believe that the Office for Budget Responsibility projections have been over-optimistic. Indeed, such has been the unreliability of economic forecasting over recent years, that I suspect that unemployment will not peak this year, but that it will be higher in both 2011 and 2012. Secondly, I fear that there is a real risk of serious sovereign default in the eurozone, as has been discussed.

I do, in part, accept the Opposition's view that there is a significant element of risk in this Budget, with many of the toughest measures coming in next year when the coldest winds may well be sweeping across the continent. However, for the sake of this nation's economic welfare, I believe this calculated judgement is well worth taking. Given that denial, debt and delay are part of the problem, I cannot see that they will be the solution to this crisis.

‡

The Next Financial Crisis May Already Be Upon Us, 5 July 2010

Alongside the global financial crisis were growing tensions on the continent as problems began to afflict the economies of members of the euro, a currency barely ten years old. Greece in particular threatened the stability of the currency union after racking up colossal debts which the markets began to fear its government would not be able to pay off. By April 2010, the nation's debt was downgraded to junk status and the world waited with baited breath to see whether and how the eurozone members and International Monetary Fund would bail the ailing Greek economy out. Since any bailout would be conditional on tough austerity measures, on 1 May the Greek Prime Minister, George Papandreou, announced a deeply unpalatable policy prescription that included public sector pay cuts, a raft of tax rises and an increase in VAT, sparking widespread protests.

I fear that the acute financial woes in Greece are but a side-show to a much more serious sovereign debt crisis that threatens to engulf the eurozone in the months ahead.

The lesson of this week's global stock market jitters is that the UK, whilst proudly standing outside the eurozone, will not be immune to its political and economic impact.

The coalition government's Budget set out a determined programme of decisive action to deal with the domestic deficit. Inconveniently this long-overdue transfer from stimulus to austerity is being faithfully emulated by many other EU nations, led by a German government constrained by a constitutional requirement to move to a balanced budget. This battening down of the hatches in key EU nations augurs ill for prolonged evidence of consistent renewed economic growth in mainland Europe. The twin worries of an unrequited policy of 'export-led' growth and monetary protectionism which I wrote about after Labour's last gasp Budget in late March, now look very real indeed.

The main concern for the near-term is of contagion – to Portugal, Spain (an economy four times the size of Greece) and even to Italy (two times the size again). Leading City figures working in European banks tell me that they are increasingly alarmed at the prospect of sovereign default by the turn of the year, especially as much of the debt of many of the struggling eurozone countries – unlike the UK – will need to be refinanced over the next two or three years.

The more optimistic view is that some of the weakest economies can be persuaded 'voluntarily' to leave the euro. These nations would take with them huge write-offs and guarantees on existing debt obligations, although it is difficult to see how such countries would ever again be able to finance their debt by selling bonds in the global capital markets. The lack of a mechanism to expel recalcitrant nations from the euro may persuade the worst offenders simply to soak up support from the emergency fund for the European currency. Alternatively a two-tier euro may enable Germany, France and others to draw away from the worst excesses of the currency crisis.

But make no mistake, the UK will be caught up as this drama unfolds even though we smugly sit outside the eurozone. Some 55 per cent of our external trade is with the countries that make up the eurozone and our exports are already becoming considerably less competitive as the euro depreciates against sterling.

Moreover, the fiscal and economic squeeze now underway in Europe designed to correct the sovereign debt crisis runs the real risk of promoting a renewed banking crisis. The truth is that in this low-to-zero interest rate environment (a deceptively benign state which provides a strong disincentive to foreclosure) many banks, both domestically and in mainland Europe, still have huge unquantifiable toxic 'assets' on their balance sheets. The interconnectedness of the global finance industry means that whilst British banks are not directly exposed to Greek debt, their German and French counterparts are. If Spain, Portugal or Italy falter then the exposure of our banks is more immediate still.

If this were to precipitate a renewed credit crunch, it is difficult to see how the British SME (small and medium enterprise) sector can play its crucial part in the export-led, private sector recovery on which all our hopes for economic growth are pinned.

Business expansion requires the smooth operation of a banking sector, willing and able to loan money freely.

It also requires confidence.

Sovereign default in the eurozone in the next twelve months – if it happens – will have as profound an effect psychologically as it does economically. In truth the outcome many now regard as inevitable may prove every bit as seminal an event on global affairs as the collapse of Lehman Brothers in September 2008.

‡

Offshore Financial Centres, 21 July 2010

As international organisations and major governments seek to understand the cause of the global financial crisis, small international financial centres (IFCs) have repeatedly endured political attacks and misguided criticism. From pejorative sniping about their being tax havens for avaricious bankers to allegations that they provide secrecy jurisdictions for shady figures in the international business community and are in part to blame for shortcomings in the financial markets, the debate over the role of small IFCs has been, to date, remarkably one-sided. This is unfortunate as it demonstrates a fundamental lack of understanding of their function and the benefits they provide to the wider global economy.

Before the UK and our international partners look to develop further international standards on financial regulation, it is critical that politicians and policymakers formulate and implement policy in an informed, consistent and balanced manner. As such, it is vital that we now take a dispassionate view of IFCs that looks sensibly at the benefits they can offer our nation as well as the broader global financial system.

The UK has a unique position in this debate. We have a constitutional relationship – through our Crown Dependences and Overseas Territories – with half of the top thirty offshore financial centres. With the Chinese government successfully lobbying the G20 to have both Macao and Hong Kong excluded from any OECD grey list on matters of tax transparency, it looks increasingly likely that the standards and regulations currently being formulated may well be imposed in some jurisdictions yet overlooked in others. Not only is this incompatible with the need to find a global response to the formation of new financial regulation but it risks undermining the UK's financial sector and the wider British economy which is a major recipient of investment capital raised through small IFCs.

...

Small international financial centres, such as Jersey and Guernsey, are used by the global financial community for a variety of reasons. They include political stability and a favourable economic outlook; familiar legal systems often based on English common law; a very high quality of service providers; the ability to meet important investor requirements such as the legal infrastructure to sell shares; a lack of foreign exchange controls that remove restrictions on the payment of interest of dividends; tax neutrality (not to be confused with tax evasion) that enables investors from multiple jurisdictions to ensure they do not meet multiple layers of taxation as funds pass through the global financial system; and legal neutrality that ensures no one nationality is given special treatment.

It is for this reason that there has been a mutually beneficial relationship between the City of London and many Crown Dependencies and Overseas Territories, demonstrated not only by the massive capital flows between the two which aid market liquidity and investment in the UK, but also legal and constitutional similarities and the transfer of skilled professionals. To give some idea of the scale of those capital flows, UK banks had net financing from Guernsey alone of $74.1 billion at the end of June 2009.

Unfortunately, because the public debate is largely myopic when it comes to IFCs, these benefits are often overlooked or conveniently ignored. This is in part as a result of small IFCs' relatively low profile, from, for instance, a lack of seats at the intergovernmental bodies which design global financial regulation.

There now needs to be a much greater understanding of the role and proven benefits provided by small international financial centres as part of the City of London's transaction chain. I therefore seek to dispel some of the popular myths surrounding such centres.

Firstly, that IFCs have a negative impact on growth in the global economy. In reality, many small IFCs are able to offer a stable, well-regulated and neutral jurisdiction through which to facilitate international and cross-border business. Investment channelled into small IFCs will in turn provide much needed liquidity, further investment opportunities, competitiveness and access to capital markets for businesses and investors in both the major developed economies and emerging market countries.

Indeed the recent Treasury Review of this area undertaken by Michael Foot concluded that: 'The Crown Dependencies make a significant contribution to the liquidity of the UK market. Together they provided net financing to UK banks of $332.5 billion in the second quarter of 2009.' These funds are largely accounted for by the 'up-streaming' to the UK head office of deposits collected by UK banks including Lloyds Banking Group and Royal Bank of Scotland as well as Barclays, HSBC, Santander and a number of building societies.

In addition to aiding capital flows, a report by University of Michigan economics professor, James Hines, on the relation between IFCs and the world economy reveals that expanding investment opportunities through offshore centres leads to increased domestic investment and employment, creating jobs both at the financial centre and in the domestic economy.

Small IFCs play an important role in helping to allocate capital efficiently. To this end they act as important financial intermediaries which match the capital provided by savers in one country with the investment needs of borrowers in another. Whilst this has led to concerns over 'round tripping' in which capital is recycled through an offshore centre in order to give it the appearance of foreign investment and attracting a more favourable tax treatment, the experience of China and India throws this into doubt – both countries have removed tax breaks for foreign investment during the past decade and both have seen inward investment continue to soar.

As a major net recipient of capital flows from small IFCs, it is possible that our firms may suffer if they were to find it more difficult to access capital via the international markets.

A second myth is that small IFCs played a part in causing the global financial crisis. Whilst it is convenient to blame far-off countries for causing the crisis, even those who work in the financial markets do not accept that small IFCs were a major cause. Last year, for instance, the Treasury Select Committee found that Guernsey did not contribute at all to global financial contagion. Indeed it could be argued that the liquidity provided by the small IFCs was a significant positive to the UK during the crisis.

Thirdly, that IFCs engage in harmful tax practices. The Foot Review suggested that the potential for tax leakage from so-called full tax jurisdictions such as the UK towards low-tax or zero-tax regimes is relatively limited. Whilst the TUC has argued that the tax gap created in UK government tax receipts as a result of offshore centres is £25 billion, the Deloitte Report, commissioned by the Treasury at the time of the Foot Report, showed that only £2 billion is potentially lost in tax leakage per annum, with Foot concluding that the real figure could be even less than that.

Concerns about the UK's tax base being stripped by unfair competition have been overstated. It is clear that the debate around tax competition needs to be redefined and any further policy initiatives need to protect the important principle of tax sovereignty as well as adequately recognise the impact of tax regimes on the productive sector. The OECD has clearly warned on the detrimental effects of high corporate tax on productivity.

The recent attacks on the zero-ten tax regimes reveal a worrying trend which not only undermines the sovereignty of independent states to set their own tax rates, but which also sees high tax countries seeking to export their high tax rates around the world.

Economic models vary country by country, and the adoption of a tax regime premised on the principles of lower tax burdens, efficient government and dynamic private sector activity is legitimate and some degree of tax competition should therefore be recognised as positive. Regardless of this, small IFCs have shown willingness to engage with the concerns raised over their tax regime and Guernsey, for example, is currently voluntarily undertaking a Corporate Tax Review to act within the spirit of the EU Tax Code of Conduct Group.

A fourth myth suggests that small IFCs have a negative impact on transparency, regulation and information exchange. With the G20 placing tax transparency at the top of its agenda, small IFCs are actively participating in the expansion of the Global Forum on Transparency and Exchange of Information. Indeed an IMF review of Jersey's regulatory standards in September last year concluded that Jersey was in the 'top division' of financial centres and gave it the highest ranking ever achieved by a financial centre in terms of its compliance with FATF (Financial Action Taskforce) recommendations.

Fifthly, it is often thought that small IFCs do not benefit developing countries. Small IFCs have been accused of supporting capital flight out of developing countries. Yet the Commonwealth Secretariat is publishing a new report this month illustrating how small IFCs often play an important role in aiding developing countries by enabling such nations effectively to 'rent' financial expertise from other countries whilst they develop financial centres of their own. Crucially, they also offer investors greater protection of their property rights against domestic political uncertainty. It is no exaggeration to say that without smaller offshore financial centres many developing countries would not secure key funding for project finance which makes a substantial contribution to the improved lives of the most vulnerable global citizens.

Furthermore, the Financial Action Taskforce gives many small IFCs a positive assessment in meeting its forty-nine recommendations on anti-money laundering and terrorism finance. In fact, centres like the Channel Islands perform better in fighting financial crime when compared with major countries such as France, Italy, the US or even the UK.

Finally, that the UK's Crown Dependencies are fiscally unsustainable. The debate within the UK government has naturally been framed by events surrounding the collapse of Iceland's banking system. When the Icelandic banks imploded in September 2008, it quickly became apparent that the contagion would spread to British savers and ultimately to the British taxpayer. Furthermore, the role of the Isle of Man as a core financial intermediary between British savers and Icelandic borrowers illustrated the UK's exposure to offshore centres.

However, the subsequent Treasury Review undertaken by Michael Foot went some way to allaying the two main concerns. In particular, the worries over the fiscal sustainability of UK Crown Dependencies proved to be overstated. Throughout the past years IFCs like Gibraltar, the Isle of Man, Guernsey and Jersey have amassed large budget surpluses whilst diversifying their tax base as Foot recommended. Indeed the Foot Report commented on the fact that none of the Crown Dependencies have taken on significant levels of borrowing.

...

To conclude, too few people who now seek to impose regulation on offshore jurisdictions truly understand how those jurisdictions actually operate, their positive rankings of compliance with major international regulatory standards (IL1), or their beneficial role in promoting investment and growth in the wider global economy. Whilst it is inevitable that governments attempt to prevent further financial crises occurring, and that this will result in the development of global standards which should have an impact on all jurisdictions, it is critical that politicians and policymakers do not depart from the need to formulate and implement policy in an informed, consistent and balanced manner. When it comes to our naked self-interest, it would be foolish of the UK to ignore the proven benefits provided by small international financial centres as part of the City of London's world class operation.

‡

The Looming Threat of Protectionism, 28 July 2010

In 2009, US food giant, Kraft, launched a hostile takeover bid for Cadbury, the beloved British chocolate maker founded in 1824. The chocolatier initially actively resisted the Kraft takeover but eventually the deal was sealed on 19 January 2010 and Cadbury was purchased for £11.5 billion to the dismay of the British public and Cadbury's workers in the UK. It was one of a number of stories around at that time which emphasised a business's nationality, another being the devastating oil spill in the Gulf of Mexico where blame was heaped on British company, BP, by the American press and US politicians. I used these stories to highlight my fear that increasing economic national-ism stoked by the financial crisis might spark a wave of protectionist measures that risked stifling world trade.

'A Double Raid on UK plc as Overseas Buyers Swoop' was how the *Evening Standard* fearfully described both a recent bid by a US-Canadian consortium to buy British manufacturing firm, Tomkins, and the revival of merger talks between France's GDF-Suez and the UK's International Power.

That news of either deal would have raised eyebrows in alarm a few years ago seems unlikely. And yet how the coalition government reacts to the selling of these British assets to foreign buyers is being watched with close interest.

With the furore over the hostile takeover of Cadbury by American giant, Kraft, the attacks by the Obama administration on British Petroleum, and worry over the number of companies being sold to buyers from the Middle East, China, Russia and India, the ownership of business has become increasingly politicised. Against a backdrop of rising unemployment and deep-seated economic unease at home, any perceived failure by a government to stand up for the 'national interest' against ruthless foreign invaders risks domestic uproar.

Unfortunately, however, I fear these awkward collisions between the worlds of business and politics are merely the outward manifestations of an underlying trend towards protectionism that is beginning to infect the global economy. But why the urge to batten down the hatches and what does it augur for the future?

I would contend that growing protectionism is in reality only a symptom of a far deeper, more fundamental anxiety – that of the colossal trade imbalances that the financial crisis has so painfully exposed (and which were in truth one of its main causes). How these might be overcome and what the world will look like once they have been unravelled may eventually tell the story of the global economy in this century.

...

Since the rapid unfurling of the global financial system in 2008, politicians have been anxious to avoid the policy mistakes that followed the banking crisis of the 1930s. Uncomfortably aware of the speed at which the Wall Street Crash of 1929 led to the Great Depression, focus has rested primarily on public spending. It is for this reason that we have been subject to the continual invocation of Keynesian economics when it comes to the bailing out of banks, quantitative easing and the maintenance of historically high levels of public spending.

Of rather less interest, however, seem to be the equally important lessons that the 1929–33 era taught us about protectionism. As the global economy entered recession, the Smoot–Hawley Tariff Act of 1930 raised tariffs drastically on over 20,000 goods imported into the United States in a bid to protect American jobs from foreign competition. Initially the Act appeared a great success with domestic industrial production increasing sharply. However, whilst imports into the US dropped by 66 per cent within only a few years, US exports also decreased markedly by 61 per cent over the same period.

In essence this Act had sparked a domino effect amongst America's trading partners who were provoked into imposing similar measures to protect their own domestic economies. The result was a slump in world trade that decimated economic growth and caused unemployment to soar. We need not be reminded of the political upheaval and military conflict that followed hot on the heels of those deep economic troubles.

It is with an eye to this dark historical period that world leaders have continued to reassert their commitment to free trade at each meeting of the G20 since 2008's economic crisis. At the most recent summit in Toronto, further pledges to resist protectionism and avoid new barriers to investment and trade once again tripped easily off tongues. Yet these laudable promises disguised a rather less palatable reality that goes some way to explaining why the final declaration at the Canadian meeting reportedly dropped a promise to lift any protectionist measures that have been enacted since the economic crisis.

The truth is that since the global economy hit the skids, ailing nations have failed to resist domestic pressure to shield their own companies and workers from the coldest recessionary winds. Independent monitor, Global Trade Alert, has estimated that discriminatory measures applied worldwide since the beginning of the financial crisis now cover $1.6 trillion – a staggering 10 per cent – of global trade. To reinforce this, a 2009 study by economists David Jacks, Christopher Meissner and Dennis Novy suggests that the costs and obstacles that exporters faced in 2008 and 2009 increased by almost the same scale as in the early 1930s.

Such costs and obstacles may not be the blatant protectionism of Smoot–Hawley, but they could still prove potent. Let us look at some specific examples.

First, the terms of the banking bailouts. When RBS was bailed out by the UK government, explicit clauses were inserted into the agreement that ensured that lending to domestic customers would be prioritised over businesses or individuals overseas. Similarly, in the United States foreign companies were restricted from accessing government bailout money and some important government contracts, and specific 'Buy American' clauses were inserted into the stimulus package. Granted, some of these measures were put in place to prevent leakage (in other words to guard against the drastic dilution of the stimulus effect in the event that government money was used to pay for cheap foreign imports or investment abroad). However, the provisions were palpably protectionism by the back door.

Turning to trade, the European Union has been putting ever more burdensome requirements on products and production processes that have been having an especially negative effect on developing countries' ability to export to EU nations. The new Renewable Energy Directive, for example, has been branded green protectionism for its use of environmentalism as a fig leaf in favouring French and Spanish rapeseed producers over cheaper foreign competitors in the production of biofuels.

Meanwhile a war of words has erupted between European business leaders and the Chinese government over access to China's domestic market. The President of the European Chamber of Commerce recently warned China that not enough is being done to create a level playing field for foreign businesses, a sentiment shared by the US Chamber of Commerce. New rules promoting 'indigenous innovation', for example, explicitly favour Chinese companies in government procurement and encourage the forced transfer of technological know-how or intellectual property as the price of foreign companies doing business in that country.

Recent disputes between the Chinese and high-profile global companies, Google and Rio Tinto, have served only to heighten tensions. The arrest of senior Rio Tinto executives for bribe-taking happened to coincide with tough negotiations with the Chinese over the price of iron ore as well as Rio's decision to pull out of a deal with a Chinese state-controlled firm. Whilst the Rio Tinto employees have found themselves subject to a corruption trial, the Chinese felons have not been brought to book.

Eclipsing all these examples, however, is the increasingly fraught relationship between the United States and China. US politicians are under pressure domestically either to press vigorously for the revaluation of the yuan or else impose anti-dumping duties and countervailing tariffs on the cheap Chinese goods perceived to be undermining US exports and jobs. China, on the other hand, treats requests for currency revaluation and a reduction in protectionist measures as deeply distasteful. To their minds a nation so indebted is in no position to negotiate; nor should a nation that bails out its carmakers, enacts Buy American legislation or restricts Chinese companies from government contracts be regarded as being in any position to lecture others.

Perhaps alone none of these examples is critical. But in the event that nations across the world become convinced that others are retreating from free trade, the rush towards protectionism could prove highly contagious. We need only remind ourselves of the 1930s to grasp the economic and political implications.

...

Such a rush would only be the symptom of a much more fundamental problem – the overarching struggle between nations with trade surpluses, on the one hand, and nations with trade deficits on the other.

Countries such as China and Germany have enjoyed for some time export-led growth that has allowed them to accrue vast reserves. This has, of course, been achieved in large part by the industry and enterprise of their people. Yet both have undeniably benefited from currency manipulation too. For some time the undervalued Chinese yuan has viciously undercut foreign competition. Meanwhile the adoption of fixed exchange rates within the euro by Germany has kept that nation's relative labour costs competitively low. Both countries have also relied upon the willingness of neighbouring countries to buy their goods, lending vast sums to its trading partners if necessary to fund their imports.

Over the past decade or so these deficit countries – the United States and Britain, above all – have undoubtedly enjoyed the cheap goods and easy money. But when the financial crisis hit, the resulting indebtedness was sharply exposed. They have therefore spent the past two years uncomfortably realigning expectations and slowly coming to terms with a new reality of constrained spending. But they are also gradually beginning to ask why they should continue to provide a dumping ground for cheap exports and burden future generations with vast debt simply to provide Chinese and German jobs. It is these questions that are beginning to manifest themselves in the rhetoric of economic nationalism and the increasing allure of protectionism.

Having convinced themselves of occupying the moral high ground, however, surplus nations are asking questions too. Why should they relinquish economic power by unleashing some of their surplus and why should they look again at currency revaluation at the risk of undermining export-led employment? As these issues are grappled with, so we see greater economic bullishness from the likes of China and an assertion of the right to protect jobs and favour companies domestically.

In truth, however, both predicaments reveal the mutual symbiosis of today's global trading relationships. By definition, not every country can have a trade surplus and those that do have now been made aware that any deep imbalance in their relationships with trading partners can leave the lender as vulnerable as the debtor.

The path ahead for the global economy therefore presents a choice – the massive trade imbalances can continue or somehow a healthier equilibrium has to be found. The first scenario is vulnerable to shocks, as we have seen. But the second inevitably entails the tense unravelling of trade imbalances.

In the face of such adjustment from both deficit and surplus nations, protectionism is deeply tempting. The combination of fear, anger, xenophobia, nationalism and anxiety over each country's role in an ever competitive world, could suck the global economy into a dark spiral that, in the worst-case scenario, could prove the precursor to more physical conflict. Unfortunately the less immediately perceptible benefits of global trade are far harder for politicians to articulate to anxious countrymen than the emotional pulls of national pride and the easy political capital to be gained from standing up against foreign competition in the face of rising unemployment.

It is for these reasons that it becomes ever more vital that the World Trade Organisation and national, political and business leaders make the case in the years ahead for the massive benefits of free trade. Efforts to roll back the protectionism of the past two years and break down the remaining barriers of all kinds to trade in goods and services must be redoubled. Only then will the path to prosperity become clearer for all.

‡

Welfare Reform Never Comes Cheap, 14 October 2010

In advance of the government's Spending Review, delivered by the Chancellor on 21 October, ministers were asked to put forward proposals for cutting spending within their own departments. It was revealed at the beginning of October that Work and Pensions Secretary, Iain Duncan Smith, proposed replacing the existing, complex benefits system with a single Universal Credit. This represented a significant victory for the Secretary of State who had been locked in a battle with the Treasury over the cost of the proposals, which he was convinced were essential to his long-term reforms aimed at making those in work better off than those on benefit.

No one can accuse the government of paucity of ambition as it seeks to overhaul the paralysingly complicated array of welfare benefits. Wisely it also recognises that such wholesale reform cannot be rushed. It will – electorate willing – prove a two-term task.

The holy grail of ending the welfare trap for those in the workplace, who otherwise stand to be better off claiming benefits, has been tantalisingly elusive to generations of politicians. Yet one of the key stumbling blocks in the immediate future is that there may well not be jobs available for many who find themselves transferred from Incapacity Benefit to Jobseeker's Allowance. These changes all promise to take time.

They will also cost money. Probably far more money than we might think.

I believe the government is spot on in identifying the overriding need to enhance skills as an integral part of this entire agenda.

However, the fact is that many millions of Britons lack the basic skills, aptitude or consistent record of employment to justify the level of workplace earnings they have come to expect as a matter of course in this highly competitive global economy. My concern is that the unskilled – assuming employment of any description can be found for them – will find employers who will regard the statutory minimum wage as a maximum to be paid. Once employers are confident that any shortfall between an individual's statutory minimum entitlement and the wages he or she requires 'to be better off in work' will be covered by the State, they will have precious little incentive to pay more. As with tax credits, the unintended consequence of assisting the less well-paid at work may be a starkly deflationary impact on wages. To repeat, why will many employers pay more when the government has agreed upfront to pick up the tab to cover the gap between the national minimum wage and an employee's total benefits entitlement?

These reforms to our welfare state are essential. But they are also likely to cost the taxpayer considerably more than is currently envisaged.

‡

MP Hits Out at Attacks on the City (*City A.M.*), 3 November 2010

I tabled a Westminster Hall debate in parliament to highlight the importance of the City of London to the health of the UK economy in light of persistent attacks on the financial services sector following the credit crunch. The debate was previewed on the front page of City A.M. *and the paper's editor, Allister Heath, commented, 'Mark Field's excellent speech is unusually brave and lucid. Others must now stand up for London's most important industry, taxpayer and employer.'*

Amidst feverish analysis of the size, scope and impact of the government's chosen spending cuts, a fresh debate is emerging about the desirable blueprint for Britain's economic future. Such is the near universal distaste reserved for financial services that a determination no longer to rely on its economic contribution seems one of the only certainties in these discussions.

As a result, 'rebalancing' is the new economic watchword. For sure, the financial crisis painfully highlighted the UK's dependence on the City and our collective exposure to the risks taken by the global banking fraternity. My worry, however, is that it is being used as code – even by Conservative coalition ministers – for a playing to the gallery as part of the general banker bashing sentiment.

It is superficially convincing to promote trying to stimulate growth more evenly throughout the regions and stepping up our game in the innovation and incubation of companies in the high-value-added areas of high-tech manufacturing, engineering, pharmaceuticals and biotechnology. But we *must* be wary of how the aim of rebalancing is pursued. Unwisely, most of the focus so far has been on how we might *shrink* the City to reduce its relative importance rather than how to provide the positive economic climate in which other sectors flourish. Before we pursue such a dangerous strategy any further, I wish to make the case for why financial services must remain a central plank in Britain's bid for continuing relevance in the global economy.

A strong financial services sector is overwhelmingly beneficial to our nation – it provides the critical mass to draw business to this country; offers diversified sources of capital to our small businesses; makes huge contributions to the Treasury's coffers in terms of tax and employment; and supports a wide range of complementary industries from law to leisure. It is also one of the few areas where we might envisage significant growth in the decades to come. Tens of millions who join the ranks of the global middle class annually from India and China have a greater cultural propensity to save and will seek expertise in investing their savings. Indeed it seems evident to me that the entire drive for the West is directed towards capturing the growth of the developing markets. Here in the UK we have *already* secured such a competitive advantage – in financial services. Why now throw it all away? Aside from this, there are several reasons to believe that the task of rebalancing might prove trickier than we might wish.

It is time that we changed our attitude towards the City from one of punishment to one of realism. How we treat our nation's most valuable economic resource in the years ahead will be the litmus test for international businesses when it comes to determining how serious Britain is in its wish to be a dynamic, open economy which embraces global talent, promotes aspiration and welcomes business.

As the banking crisis was in full swing back in 2008, it seemed almost overnight that the financial sector became the useful scapegoat for all our economic ills.

Many of the criticisms levelled at the banking fraternity have been legitimate. That failure in this sector of the economy exposed the domestic taxpayer to such mindboggling sums was scandalous and seemed to confirm suspicions that the wealth generated by the City was simply a mirage. Irresponsible risks were taken, debt instruments became too complex, money was lent to those who could ill afford the repayments (that incidentally is one of the difficulties when policymakers seek out 'socially useful' banking), regulators (if not regulations) proved ill equipped for their job.

The City's dominance in the domestic economy over the past two decades also had wide-ranging social consequences. For a large proportion of British people working outside the gilded corridors of the financial services industry, the growth of the City's power increased the cost of living and reduced to a wistful dream any prospect of getting on the housing ladder (except via colossal personal debt). It could also be argued that the City precipitated a brain drain from other professions and industries, with our brightest and best graduates tempted away by the unrivalled starting salaries in banking jobs.

But in some respects the City's success merely masked, until its failure uncovered, some more fundamental problems that had developed in Western economies. Governments had been spending too much money. As individuals, we had racked up too much debt. And we found it cheaper and easier to buy cheap goods from abroad, import migrant workers and pay our own citizens off with welfare than confront the difficulties of either finding sufficient employment for blue-collar workers losing ground to Eastern competition or tackling the dearth of skills amongst the indigenous population.

Rather than openly confront some of these issues post-crisis, the implicit – and all too easy – assumption has been that had the banking sector not collapsed through the profligacy and greed of some of its employees, we might have continued as we had. There is also an assumption that to solve our current problems, we simply need to return to what used to be our strength a couple of generations ago by rebalancing the economy back towards 'making things'.

The intensity of the rhetoric that has now built up around the role of banks in the economy is such that politicians and even bankers themselves have been unwilling to stand up for this sector. Alas, this rhetoric has not subsided as time has passed. In fact, it will likely intensify in the months ahead as the cuts bite and questions are asked as to how and why government money can be found to prop up the banks and pay out this year's bumper bonuses whilst public sector jobs, services and benefits face the axe.

In response, governments approach the financial services sector as something to be outwardly chastened whilst privately recognising its importance to the wider economy and relying on the continued income and jobs it provides. In public, banks are told to lend to inherently risky start-ups, small businesses and first-time buyers at the same time as being required to meet stringent new capital requirements. A new £2 billion bank levy is announced with a fanfare and the 50 per cent income tax rate remains in place and yet the Treasury quietly acknowledges that it cannot place any further pressure on balance sheets whilst storms are still gathering in the eurozone. So we witness the public baying for more blood after banks post healthy profits (a combination of low interest rates, a lack of competition and a cut in corporation tax) and yet are bemused when government restrictions lead to increased customer bank charges.

Governments have also failed publicly to make the distinction between different parts of the financial services industry. In order to articulate a complex situation to a baffled public, it has been easier simply to blame all parts of the financial services industry for the turbulence of the last few years. Parcelling up the public whipping boys of Northern Rock, RBS, investment bankers and their bonuses with sectors such as fund management, bond markets and insurance that have played little or no role in the crisis, has been deeply harmful. Indeed we are now at risk of regulating areas that are in no need of regulation with many businesses spending huge sums to second-guess what regulations might be coming over the horizon.

This confused strategy is of no benefit to the government, the banks or the public. In essence we are penalising our most competitive sector whilst fooling ourselves that a miraculous rebalancing of economy will occur by default. In truth, rebalancing will only be threatened by any diminution of the financial services sector. Let us not forget why – on the whole – a thriving City makes for a successful Britain.

Since time immemorial, the City of London has enjoyed an international reputation as a bastion of commercial certainty and reliability. It has promoted financial innovation, provided an international market to global merchants and in commercial affairs has rightly been seen as a watchword for justice, neutrality and fairness. It also has a number of innate advantages that ensure that companies' loyalty to London runs deeper than its tax regime. These include a time zone between North America and Asia which make it an excellent base for international company headquarters, as well as lifestyle assets – culture, an excellent educational offering and a population so diverse that all can feel at home. As a result London has emerged as *the* global financial centre. Indeed so successful has the financial services sector been that it alone now contributes 10 per cent of Britain's economic output.

It is not just banks that benefit from our financial sector but complementary industries such as law, insurance, retail and entertainment. So too do top-flight universities and the arts and social charitable sector gain, the latter two from cultural funds or corporate responsibility grants often provided by the City's top banks and bankers. The presence of our large financial sector gives London the critical mass to attract the best professionals from across the globe.

The banking bailouts notwithstanding, the financial services sector contributes massively to the Treasury's coffers in terms of tax revenues (with an estimated contribution of £61 billion in 2008/09) and employment (with over 1 million people employed directly in financial services across the UK). The financial services sector also plays a critical role in supporting business, whether that be in drawing huge inward flows of foreign capital to help build our infrastructure and prop up our companies or in providing British companies access to diversified sources of capital to enable them to invest and expand.

Even if opposition to City dominance is practical rather than ideological, I suspect that it is unlikely that any other sector will be a world beater anytime soon. The industries in which we are hoping to diversify are ones where competition will be stiff. The Chinese, for instance, are as keen to develop their manufacturing capacity when it comes to green technologies as we are.

We should not assume either that developing countries will start to spend their savings as the Western world weans itself off debt and consumption. Britain is just one nation that has been pinning some of its hopes on export-led growth. But despite the 20 per cent depreciation of the pound, the UK's trade deficit has continued to widen. Meanwhile, with uncertainty infecting the financial system, British corporations have shown little appetite for expansion any time soon as they accumulate cash cushions instead of investing.

Put simply, our financial services sector is a massive asset. With vast numbers of developing-world employees entering the middle classes each year and earnestly looking for new ways to save and invest, it is also one of the few sectors in which we might confidently predict significant growth in the coming years. A nation of only 60 million people should be grateful to have one world-beating industry that is, in normal times, incredibly lucrative and feeds a wide range of other sectors.

By all means, we should build up other sectors if we can and reduce the exposure of the taxpayer to risk. But economic diversification will be no easy option and should *not* lead to the neglect or diminution of the City – indeed if it does, the task of diversification will be far harder. Global businesses and their highly skilled work forces do not necessarily have an innate loyalty to the UK. They will go where the legal, fiscal, regulatory, physical and social environment works best for them. The continued rhetoric of hostility towards banks and regulatory uncertainty serves only to deter. Why stay and put up with ever more grief?

In this respect, more pressing than diversification must be the need to make the UK a place of possibilities, enterprise and entrepreneurship. It is not for the government to pick winners and losers or indeed to prop up losers and penalise winners. The continuing attacks on our financial services sector no longer serve any purpose. Four and a half years from the next general election, the government should have the confidence to say so. So long as we get regulation right, we should not be fearful of confidently articulating the benefits of a robust and expanding financial sector. Let us draw a line under this period of uncertainty and hostility whilst we still have this fantastic springboard to ensuring that the UK still has relevance in a fast-changing global economy.

‡

Rules and Rhetoric are Strangling the City (*Daily Telegraph*), 18 November 2010

I took the opportunity in an article I wrote for the Daily Telegraph, *to highlight some of the threats on the horizon to the City of London's pre-eminence as a global financial centre both from coalition policy and fresh encroachments by the European Union as it sought to create new pan-European regulatory supervisors.*

These days it is rare for a week to pass without my receiving a dismayed email blast or two from a financial services or commercial constituent.

As the City's MP I detect that the UK's tradition as a mercantile, outward-looking nation with a reputation for fair dealing seems increasingly under threat as the ugly rhetoric of banker bashing leads many foreigners to question whether we are truly 'open for business'.

Here in the City the benefits of globalisation over the past two decades have unleashed untold wealth, some of which has trickled down to every imaginable part of the capital's service industries.

A German industrialist put it to me last month that the entire export impetus for the West today is directed towards capturing the growth of the developing world markets. Here in the UK we have already secured such a competitive advantage – in the financial services sphere. My German friend was bemused that we now seem intent through rancorous rhetoric and restrictive regulatory policy on throwing this away.

Yet how we are seen to treat our nation's most valuable economic resource in the years ahead will be the litmus test for international business when it comes to determining how serious Britain is in its wish to be a dynamic, open economy which embraces global talent, promotes aspiration and welcomes new business.

The most prevalent specific complaint from businesses large and small in recent months is over the increasingly inflexible immigration rules. Highly skilled, non-EU nationals must now chance their luck on getting here via a monthly quota. Even intra-company transfers often take such an inordinate amount of time that it is easier to do the work (and pay the taxes) abroad. Three times in the past fortnight alone I have learned of rainmaker law firm partners from the US who had wanted to spend two or three months heading up a team of lawyers from London, but have not been granted the urgent short-term work visa required. Fees running into millions of pounds have been lost from these shores and with it not just tax foregone but lasting damage to our nation's reputation as a global trading outpost.

I have always treated with some scepticism the more hysterical claims about vast numbers leaving the UK following the imposition of the 50 per cent higher rate income tax band. Whilst I suspect those escaping these shores have to date been relatively small in number, what is invariably far more difficult to quantify is the opportunity cost of higher individual payroll or capital taxes. In this respect, the anecdotal evidence is now overwhelming. The perceived uncertainty, bordering on outright hostility, in UK taxation policy has curbed the expansion of many businesses already located here and dissuaded others – and their prospective employees – from setting up shop in the City. Steadily and determinedly London's financial services rivals are gaining ground. Companies, including many beyond the financial services sphere, are seeking to hedge their bets by choosing other more welcoming global financial centres as their locations for future growth.

Meanwhile, the imminent creation of pan-EU supervisors for banking, securities and insurance presents further challenges. One key opportunity is that London will host the European Banking Authority – a body enjoying extensive supervisory powers over firms if a national regulator (in the UK's case, the FSA) fails to implement its recommendations.

By contrast the European Securities and Markets Authority (ESMA) is to be based in Paris. It will enjoy power of investigation over financial products, such as credit default swaps, the derivative innovation whose vast expansion in the real estate field precipitated the banking collapse of 2007/08. ESMA will have the ultimate authority temporarily to outlaw the marketing and sale of such products.

The key issue for the City is to ensure that the EBA, being London based, claims not only full authority on prudential regulation and conduct but also over those institutions that are deemed to have the potential to be a systemic risk to the entire financial system. As such, it is essential that the UK government pushes for all key EU-wide decisions on investment banks, insurance, hedge funds and private equity funds to be made by the EBA. If one takes the view that systemic risk requires proper oversight then it is vital to our interests that these matters are handled out of London.

In its negotiations with the EU, government must now focus its attention on promoting the core business of UK retail and commercial banking, encouraging it to undertake its overriding tasks of providing capital for business and offering day-to-day services for the individual consumer. As far as practical, the innovative, more wholesale, international markets should be left to the market,

subject to ensuring institutions are properly capitalised and regulated. This stands in stark contrast to the continental approach to
heavily regulate the major banks, which would be the fate awaiting
us if ESMA's powers were to be expanded at the EBA's expense.

It is all too easy to dismiss much of this negotiation as an esoteric
'European issue'. However, London's place as a leading financial
centre is increasingly regarded from both Asia and the US as weak-
ened. If we cannot effectively argue our corner in the stagnant EU
zone, what hope to compete with Hong Kong, Singapore, Shanghai
and emerging financial centres in India?

Observers of the European political scene felt as recently as early
October that the French desire to expand the EU budget might
prove a useful bargaining tool for the UK government in negotiating a better deal for the City. We have now contrived to leave
ourselves with less room for manoeuvre. If the coalition is to hold
its line on a 2.9 per cent annual rise in the EU budget for each of
the next four years, I fear that it is our financial services industry
that might have to take the slack.

‡

The True Cost of the UK's Liabilities, 23 November 2010

*As the eurozone crisis spread beyond Greece, attention turned to Ireland
as analysts questioned whether it was likely to have to tap the emergency
rescue fund set up by the European Union in May. Under terms of a
deal agreed by former Chancellor, Alistair Darling, the UK was liable
for 13.6 per cent of the fund, meaning that the British taxpayer would
potentially have to stump up £7 billion to bail its neighbour out.*

Despite the imminent possibility of the UK contributing billions
of pounds to help shore up the Irish economy, Prime Minister's
Questions instead focused on police numbers.

It was an episode symptomatic of our increasing national immunity to big figures. The more we have read about 'billions' over the

course of the financial crisis, the more intense our focus seems to have become on waste or impropriety on a smaller scale. When in the middle of last year we were shovelling cash into the banking system, quantitative easing barely touched the public consciousness when compared to parliamentary expenses claims lodged for duck houses and dog food. When RBS owned up to Britain's largest ever annual corporate loss of £24.1 billion, it was Sir Fred Goodwin's annual pension of a relatively trifling £693k that stole the show. Last week, as crisis in the eurozone threatened to suck more British billions into stabilising the European financial system, the Prime Minister's £35k photographer hogged public outrage.

Anyone partial to conspiracy theories might be inclined to wonder whether politicians contrive such scandal to divert attention from wider, scarier reality. I suspect the sadder truth is that none of us, politicians included, is able fully to comprehend the scale of what has happened to our financial system any more, let alone assess the long-term consequences.

This might explain why the £200 billion worth of payments we still collectively owe under PFI contracts fails to elicit much interest. Some of this colossal bill will not be paid off until 2047 and sits atop a motley collection of other horrors (unfunded pensions, net debt, bank guarantees and more) that take the UK's overall liabilities to an estimated £3.8 trillion. If any of my generation is interested in taking the hit now to remove this burden from our children, how does the prospect of paying 30 per cent more in tax sound?

There is perhaps no better symbol for the nation's financial attitude over the past decade than PFI. The mechanism of the Private Finance Initiative was designed as a means of bringing finance and development expertise from the private sector to public infrastructure projects – schools, hospitals, roads and so on. It was an idea with great promise, designed to make up for a dearth of practical knowledge in the public sector. Instead, it became perhaps the greatest gravy train of them all, heaping colossal debt on the next generation through 'buy now, pay later' deals. But worse than that, it played its part in insulating yesteryear's politicians from tough discipline on public spending and having to educate the public on the limits of the national bank account.

So what went wrong? In essence, in his bid to ensure the Labour government took the kudos for sparkling new schools and hospitals whilst avoiding current accounting of its cost, Chancellor Brown used PFI as a means of keeping infrastructure investment off the public balance sheet by entering into long-term deals. Whilst the capital value of PFI contracts was only £55 billion, the vastly higher sum that we will eventually pay reflects the huge mark-up costs of lengthy maintenance contracts. It was a political masterstroke by the erstwhile Chancellor, allowing him to boast of prudence by keeping the headline proportion of public debt to GDP below 40 per cent, as promised, whilst at the same time generously 'investing' in public services for immediate gratification.

He (correctly) calculated that by the time his trick was revealed, it would not only be someone else's problem but would prove too complex a manoeuvre to capture the public's imagination. After all, what is the more terrifying prospect to politicians? Telling their constituents that the last government has given the country thirty-seven years to pay off a £200 billion bill or that the current government is cutting the number of police patrolling their local neighbourhood? The other smart strand to his ruse was that the other chief beneficiaries of these flawed PFI deals were middle-class professionals (consultants, lawyers, architects, accountants, building contractors), normally the most vocal and articulate critics of public sector waste.

Unfortunately the true cost of the UK's liabilities now presents the sternest of challenges for the coalition government at a time when huge infrastructure investment is still required. Big decisions on energy and transport infrastructure were ducked by the last government and it is calculated that we ideally need £500 billion of infrastructure investment by 2020 on energy (£300 billion), transport (£130 billion), ICT (£30 billion) and water (£40 billion). Much of the money for this will, of course, come from the private sector but the government will have to make its contribution too – indeed it will prove essential to economic growth. The Comprehensive Spending Review recognised this but shelling out for these essential projects will nevertheless divert money from other, less critical infrastructure and maintenance tasks, such as regenerating our increasingly shabby suburbs.

Earlier this year I highlighted on this blog our increasingly shabby suburban districts. One of the unsung triumphs of the past twenty-five years has been the regeneration of city centres in places like Glasgow, Birmingham, Liverpool and Cardiff which have become attractive places to work and live. The same, unfortunately, cannot be said for many formerly prosperous suburban areas. In many of these areas, potholed roads and tatty looking street furniture make way for tired high streets where, in the aftermath of the credit crunch, many shop units still lie empty. It will fall to a group of relatively inexperienced Conservative council leaders to revive our suburbs and local transport infrastructure at a time when funds for regenerating them will be scarce. Keeping political control of these districts will be an increasing challenge, not least as they are likely to play scene to entrenched youth unemployment and swift demographic change.

The blame for PFI's consequences will not be kept from the coalition's door for long. Only briefly will there be any interest in our laying the blame squarely back at Labour's feet. That's politics. But we can at least learn some lessons.

Never again should ministers proudly pledge a new hospital, a new road or revamped school without being transparent about the true cost. In halting the desperately poor-value Building Schools for the Future programme, the coalition has gone some way to recognising this already. It is also vital that we devise a stable, long-term policy framework to attract private sector investment to ensure that critical infrastructure can go ahead. Above all, of course, government, whether national or local, needs to be far more aggressive about the deals we strike.

Just as the credit card and easy mortgage finance gave individuals the chance to consume beyond their means, PFI satisfied the desire for instant gratification by politicians, allowing them to break out of the straitjacket of economic prudence without anyone at the time fully appreciating the mirage. So a generation broke the link between work and reward and fed a culture of indifference to the future. However, it should have been the duty of government to take greater responsibility, to have some consideration for the interests of younger generations to come.

In an age of unprecedented global mobility for our brightest and best, too many of those whom we now rely upon to drive this nation forward in the decades ahead may rationally conclude that better opportunities and possibilities await beyond these shores.

‡

The Next Financial Crisis is Upon Us (*City A.M.*), 30 November 2010

Last week a few unpalatable home truths began to become apparent to the UK political class. Nevertheless, the acute financial woes in Ireland are likely to prove a side-show to a much more serious sovereign debt crisis that threatens to engulf European financial markets in the months ahead.

Outside the single currency the UK may smugly stand, but as this drama unfolds it is clear we will be directly affected. Some 55 per cent of our external trade is with the eurozone and our exports are likely to become considerably less competitive as the euro depreciates against sterling. As William Hague never quite put it, 'We are out of the euro, but not free from the influence of the euro.'

In truth for the financial markets the Irish crisis is now almost history. The show has now moved remorselessly on to more central players – Portugal, Belgium and Spain (the latter's economy being four times the size of Greece, bailed out in May) and before long perhaps even to Italy (twice the size again).

For some months leading European bankers here in the City of London have been telling me of their alarm at the prospect of sovereign default by the turn of the year. Much of the debt of many struggling eurozone countries – unlike the UK – needs refinancing over the next couple of years.

As Ireland's economic woes became critical over the past ten days, so the recriminations have begun. The present panic, so we are told, was precipitated by the German Chancellor Angela Merkel's unilateral announcement that bondholders should take a share of the responsibility for the costs of restructuring sovereign debt, rather than leaving it to European taxpayers, present and future. Yet to place all blame for the escalation on German shoulders is a classic example of shooting the messenger.

For without a mechanism for sovereign-debt default, investors enjoy a perverse incentive to pump ever more money into the riskiest economies. That is precisely what we have seen in Greece and Ireland. This will only stop when bondholders take an enforced haircut as part of any future financial rescue plan. The stark reality is that to date the European sovereign bailouts have been an expensive failure. By nationalising the Irish banking system, governments have across the continent protected not only depositors (unarguably essential in preserving trust in a market economy) but also corporate creditors.

At the time of the September 2008 crisis this was essentially a political gambit – much of the banks' borrowing had been funded by institutional investors and the risk of contagion in the event of their collapse was deemed too great. Yet bondholders, as lenders of capital, are supposed to take risks (and receive ample rewards by way of interest payments). In a grotesque inversion of traditional capitalist practice when all has been turned to dust investors have demanded – and continue to receive – a taxpayer-funded bailout. This cannot go on. In reality, if further sovereign default in the eurozone occurs, European governments will soon no longer have either the financial capacity or political stock to let investors off the hook in this way.

The UK's own participation in the Irish rescue is driven by a hard-nosed assessment of our own banks' exposure to Ireland and the importance to us as an export market.

Meanwhile, Eurosceptic MPs regard the Irish bailout as the siphoning off of £7 billion of scarce UK taxpayers' money in a misguided effort to save the euro. In spite of all the commentary to the contrary it is probably unwise to conclude that we are witnessing the demise of the eurozone. It is difficult to see how, outside the euro, Greece or Ireland would ever again be able to finance their debt by selling bonds in the global capital markets. The lack of any mechanism to expel recalcitrant nations from the single currency have – and will continue to – persuade the most indebted nations simply to soak up support from the emergency fund for the European currency. Debt will only be properly priced when creditors take on some of this burden.

Moreover, the pan-European fiscal and economic squeeze designed to correct the sovereign debt crisis runs the real risk of promoting a renewed banking crisis. The truth is that in this near-zero interest rate environment, many banks, both domestically and in mainland Europe, still have huge unquantifiable toxic 'assets' on their balance sheets and no incentive to crystallise these holdings. Other sovereign nations faltering would most likely precipitate a renewed credit crunch. Then it is difficult to see how the British SME sector can play its crucial part in the export-led, private sector recovery on which all our hopes for economic growth are pinned.

Conservative backbench critics of the Irish bailout are consoled by their clear understanding that such assistance would not have been offered to Portugal, Belgium or Spain. Perhaps this faith will soon be put to the test.

If only the storm raging off the Irish coast were containable. The fear now must be that sovereign default elsewhere in Europe will destroy trust and confidence as it did during the collapse of September 2008. If so, this will have a profound psychological effect on global economic prospects for the years ahead.

‡

Safe as Houses? Why Savings Should Not Always Be in Bricks and Mortar, 15 December 2010

Solve the underlying causes of the West's failure to save adequately and the global imbalances that lie at the heart of the current financial crisis should then correct themselves. Yet, as the events of these tumultuous past two years show us, this is far easier said than done. Populist measures to chasten the banking sector are simple enough to devise, but the underlying deep-seated structural problems facing our economy require tough strategic analysis, potentially divisive policy changes and a harsh dose of reality.

Housing is the classic policy issue urgently requiring fresh collective thinking. Home ownership has blossomed in successive generations from a dream to a goal to an expectation for most Britons. Either in response to or as a direct driver of this trend, successive governments have willingly, indeed aggressively, encouraged the expansion of a 'property-owning democracy'. But this has been a near universal aspiration by necessity underpinned by debt. Most recently, this collective borrowing has become colossal yet so socially mainstream almost to be considered unrisky. However, with debt must come risk, and the dangerous overleveraging of the individual, as we now know, has perilous consequences for the general economy. So we must ask ourselves: is the British love affair with ever-increasing home ownership either desirable or sustainable for the future?

For much of the past decade the availability of mortgage finance went hand in hand with the increased availability of cheap and easy money (the causes of which I have discussed before). The stronger the competition in mortgage provision, the lower mortgage rates fell and the more open the market became to a wider range of borrowers. Alongside exceptionally low central interest rates, a housing bubble began to inflate without limit as property came to be seen as a safe (sometimes, 'the only safe') and lucrative investment. Swiftly rising prices sucked in more buyers anxiously convinced that they would never save as quickly as values would appreciate. Similarly, lenders calculated that appreciating assets outweighed the risk of defaulting borrowers. A diverse array of financial products followed, including the interest-only mortgage, designed to draw in a constant stream of new market participants. As homeowners borrowed against their flourishing equity stakes to fund holidays, cars, home improvements and general consumption, so the perceived gap between renters and homeowners widened to the extent that to rent seemed almost to become a new yardstick of poverty.

The UK economic downturn began when the household debt and housing bubbles simultaneously burst. UK house prices had risen by 88.5 per cent in the decade to 2007, with average household debt leaping from 105 per cent to 177 per cent of disposable income over the same decade.

As we have sought to understand the roots of the ensuing financial crisis, focus has rested upon the role of bankers – their manipulation of and disregard for risk, their short-termism, their failure to respond to public anger and their apparent unwillingness to change. But there is another powerful group that has vigorously defended its vested interest in maintaining the status quo: highly leveraged homeowners. Just as bankers were broadly protected by the bailouts from the consequences of the risks they had taken, so too did policymakers move quickly to protect deeply indebted homeowners with even lower interest rates and mortgage protection plans once the financial crisis hit. The mortgage market may indeed appear to be 'too big to fail' but these measures are unlikely to be sustainable. At some point, I believe we shall have to create an entirely fresh approach to home ownership.

Worryingly, in the meantime policymakers seem anxious simply to return as quickly as possible to the way things were. Excitable predictions suggest that once these past dismal years are behind us, we shall see house prices rising again. Indeed, there have been short-term rallies after the major falls of 2008 which many point to as evidence. But the unravelling of a market is not always linear. After any fall, it is hard to assess the bottom of the market, which is why many were tempted into entering the fray soon after the crash by apparent bargains and low interest rates. A temporary squeeze in supply as large numbers of homeowners wait out the decline, and a longer-term one caused by Britain's restrictive planning laws, give further fuel to those convinced of the inevitability of rising prices.

In reality, I suspect the British housing market will remain vulnerable for some years. The IMF suggests that UK house prices are still overvalued. Higher interest rates, perhaps driven by inflationary pressures as the economy recovers (I have spoken before about the temptation of inflation to any government looking for a speedy and politically palatable way of bringing down public debt) have the potential suddenly to make mortgages much less affordable for the majority of borrowers. For once we should not count on a plentiful and willing stream of new market entrants to shore up existing ones.

This exposure of the wider economy to mortgage holders' risks is only one reason why we should look again at our addiction to home ownership. Ever-increasing house prices have made an older generation complacent about the cost of retirement – with some justification. With the plundering of pensions, the lack of trust in the banking system and markets, and pitifully low interest rates, people understandably feel a sense of both physical and financial security in property. Equity release on a home increasing exponentially in value has become a popular means of funding long retirements. But this mechanism is unlikely to be able to sustain the length of retirement so many may need to anticipate. Indeed, if it does, it will once again widen the grim generational divide that is fast emerging.

The boom years saw a massive transfer of wealth from young households to older ones. Older people with property assets were able to realise the gains of house-price rises and reinvest in other products. Younger households, on the other hand, have simply taken on a very long-term debt or now pay high rents to (generally older) landlords. The stacking of odds against the young is already beginning to convince some of our brightest and best to leave these shores. This trickle may turn into a flood...

For many of those twenty- and thirty-somethings tied into the conventional property market, meanwhile, home ownership has proven in many cases to be a millstone. Whilst it has most commonly been praised for its ability to give people a stake in their community, buying a house often comes at the price of economic flexibility – one of the great sadnesses of negative equity is that it traps people at a time when they may most need to move to find employment.

Finally, houses have become increasingly expensive relative to disposable income. Mortgage debt has not only put householders at an enormous financial risk but it has diverted their disposable income from other sectors of the economy.

But reducing economic dependence on the housing market will be difficult for a nation that has come to consider home ownership an almost inalienable right. It may well come about without the need for government intervention. I wonder if we are now at a tipping point. Many would-be market participants are now concluding that the financial risk of a property many multiples of their salary, that rises in value only sluggishly, is no longer worth it. It will take many others a considerable amount of time to accrue the vast deposits now required to secure a mortgage. It may prove that the younger generation drives a psychological shift that levels the playing field between renting and home-owning which will help to smooth out the current disparities between the two.

But the government has tools at its disposal as well. Given the reliance of so many people on increasing house prices for future wealth, and the sense that it is the only route for the aspirational, this is a tricky subject for any government to tackle with honesty. Perhaps it would be desirable for house prices to remain stable for some time, with a return to the view that property's primary value is in providing homes rather than sure-fire financial investments. The government is keen to increase supply not through national house-building targets, but by devolving more planning decisions to local communities under the 'New Homes Bonus' so that they will feel more engaged in the decision-making. At a time of austerity in local government finance and continued council tax capping, the New Homes Bonus is the only available source of income that most local authorities can create (it will give councils the first six years of new council tax receipts from new house building).

We must also strive to focus the mortgage market on the long term. Before the financial crisis of 2008, the UK market was commended for its diversity. In fact, whilst there was a variety of operators and the short-term deals they offered, very few sold attractive medium- to long-term products. It was merely a mirage of choice for consumers who were often baffled by complexity into some pretty unattractive deals. The FSA is trying to smooth out some of these problems through its current Mortgage Market Review (MMR), but has already been subject to a barrage of criticism for trying to solve the causes of the last housing crisis, making borrowers jump through an interminable number of hoops and failing to take into account new storms that are likely to brew. The real prize must be to promote a more vibrant and sought-after quality private rental market, so that house building can thrive again after a decade in the doldrums.

Either we face up now to the new challenges left by our old dependence on residential housing or, as the Governor of the Bank of England has warned, 'we shall bequeath to future generations a serious risk of another crisis even worse than the one we have experienced'. But it will not be a comfortable ride. Some conventional assumptions of recent decades over the desirability of home ownership need urgent questioning.

2011

The Economic Mission for 2011 – Growth, 10 January 2011

Just before MPs returned to parliament after Christmas, David Cameron gave an interview to the BBC's Andrew Marr. Marr introduced the New Year as '2011: the year when austerity really starts' in reference to a hike in VAT, fare rises, a planned fuel duty increase and rising inflation. He pressed the Prime Minister on these issues as well as the subject of banking reform. Whilst Cameron insisted that banks should be more 'socially responsible' he made clear that micro-managing them was not the answer and warned against banker bashing and the use of banks as scapegoats for the recession.

Forget national sovereignty or control orders, it is the thrust for economic growth that has pride of place in January's grid for government action.

At its heart must be a restoration of the UK's traditional reputation as an outward-looking trading nation and the liberation of our businesses from red tape. Somewhere in a globalised economy that is proudly 'open for business'.

Most of the UK's economic competitors are desperate to break into developing markets in China, India and south-east Asia. Financial services and its vast array of associated professions has provided this country with an enormous competitive advantage in this regard, not least as the increased wealth and propensity to save from people in these new markets will ensure that this sector will continue to grow rapidly in the decades ahead. Whatever the distaste for bankers' bonuses, it is firmly in the national interest that the City of London and the UK maintain its global pre-eminence in this highly mobile sector.

After some weeks of 'banker bashing' and idle threats about draconian regulation from some quarters of the coalition, it was tremendous to hear David Cameron yesterday make a robust defence of the UK's financial services strength. In the heat of a general election it was forgivable not to hold back in joining the public criticism of the banking industry. Now, however, with over four years until the next general election, the government is right to show leadership on the issue, even if the general public are still to be won round. David Cameron was also spot on in his balanced analysis as to why these strictures should equally apply to Lloyds Banking Group and RBS, in which the taxpayer still holds sizeable stakes.

Looking ahead, what the financial services fraternity now need is greater certainty that we truly are moving beyond the 'to bash or not to bash' debate. The City broadly accepts that things cannot be the same as they were – indeed many bankers would point to the concrete changes that have been made to their organisations since the tumultuous events of 2008, particularly with regard to the levels of capital they hold. Unfortunately with the Banking Commission (whose work will include an examination of whether to break up our biggest banks) not due to report until September, and the debate still not settled over the 50 per cent top rate of income tax, there is the perception that the banks are still fair game. Many financial businesses are now spending huge sums trying to second-guess what regulations might be coming over the horizon in this environment of damaging uncertainty. When such uncertainty encourages the holding rather than lending of capital, regulation becomes a problem not just for the banks but for the wider economy.

Naturally, free trade is promoted best by a competitive, certain tax system. We have already done some good work on corporation tax (which will be reduced in each of the next four years) and entrepreneur's relief, but the same must also apply to our income tax rates which are now amongst the highest in the developed world. It is encouraging to see that the case for economic efficiency and maximised tax-takes is being made strongly, even when most of us can appreciate the political difficulties in reducing higher-rate taxation levels at a general time of austerity and rising living costs.

Open trade applies to human capital too. I understand why some of this is an unpalatable message for many Conservatives – and flies in the face of our (in my view unwise) manifesto commitments. However, sustained growth in this difficult era will only be promoted by private sector commerce and global businesses based here will want to recruit the most talented people. This should be encouraged, not restricted, if the UK is to be truly open for business.

The same applies to students who come to study here will return to India, China and elsewhere as lifelong ambassadors for this nation. Similarly if the UK is to be home to global leaders in all business sectors it needs to be open to the brightest and best talent internationally. The sad corollary is the threat of a brain drain. Indeed I take little pleasure in being proved right in something I said several times in parliament in 2004 and 2005 as Shadow Minister for London. I predicted then that the emergence of an access regulator interfering with university admissions would turn what had hitherto been a trickle into a flood of the UK's most talented school leavers deciding to study for undergraduate degree overseas (predominantly in the US). This has now happened and it will be sobering to see how many (or few, perhaps) of these bright, ambitious Britons return to these shores…

Closer to home, it is worth mentioning some of the concerns from business people coming through in my constituency postbag. Alas, many lament that whilst the government talks mistily about support for SMEs and the expansion of Britain's trading links, politicians have no real understanding of the risks and sacrifices taken by business people in trying to generate wealth.

Of imminent concern is the Bribery Act 2010 which is due to come into force in April. No one would dispute the importance of inculcating an ethical dimension to the conduct of British companies trading overseas. However, this little poison pill from the last government does rather more than penalise corruption – it reverses the burden of proof in any legal proceedings arising from international trade dispute. In essence the potentially draconian penalties that will surface when a business deal goes wrong are likely to dissuade many highly respected British businesses from trading abroad, particularly in the developing world.

One constituent, who works for a 300-year-old wine and spirits business, is keen to take advantage of the growing interest in the Far East for whisky but is fearful of the risk. As he advised me,

> I have plans for Board approval to set up a joint venture in China. The non-executive directors are challenging me not on the business case or on the opportunity but on whether we should risk the venture because of inadvertently breaking the law under the UK Bribery Act. Despite Mr Cameron's advice to expand into the new and growing markets of the East, I cannot recommend to the Board that we expand because we cannot prevent our partners doing business in the country in the 'normal' way.

Similarly, a number of dentists have written to me in despair at another new 2011 regulation. On 1 January, a requirement for dentists to register with the Care Quality Commission (CQC) came into force. At a sweep, one constituent in the profession advises me that his small practice will now have to find £40,000 per annum to meet the costs of compliance – 'including £26,000 to pay the salary of an extra member of staff employed solely to ensure our business is abiding by the new rules'. He suggests he will have to stop taking on NHS patients so that he can meet the huge bill through his more lucrative private practice.

Most businesses are not interested that the Bribery Act and the CQC regulations are Labour in origin. They will reserve their anger for the government that has brought them to bear.

We must be mindful too of the unintended consequences on small businesses when, in a bid to reduce the deficit, government contracts are cancelled. A constituent operating a small financial services business recently advised:

I have faced a ruthless, largely unintelligent and exceptionally unpleasant series of demands from the Inland Revenue for tax. This has drained my energy, wasted my time and severely hampered my ability to restore my business to profitability as well as exposing the Inland Revenue as incompetent. The underlying problem was this: the IR, part of the government, was demanding a large sum of money, which I could not pay, because another part of the government had reneged on one contract, cancelled another and delayed payment on a third.

He had been left fearing that the coalition's pro-business promises might be hollow.

In short, our rhetoric on the liberation of businesses must be grounded in reality. They must not just be told we are on their side – they need to feel it with demonstrable action. In this regard the government's review of the tribunal system, as well as the other progress I have mentioned, is a welcome start down this road. But we must relentlessly pursue our task of giving British businesses, large and small, all the tools they need to repair our confidence-battered economy. Politicians must never forget that it is only the energy and innovation of the enterprising in the global marketplace that will provide the growth essential to recovery.

‡

This Year's Economic Headache – The Rising Cost of Living, 18 January 2011

All the upbeat talk is of the UK economy being 'out of the danger zone'. Credit is certainly due to the Chancellor for recognising the serious state of the public finances and setting out a long-term deficit reduction plan.

However, the sombre truth is that for so long as Central Banks maintain a virtual zero-interest-rate policy, UK and European economies will remain on a taxpayer-induced life support machine.

There is little sign of this changing in spite of dark inflationary clouds gathering. The Treasury and Bank of England are well aware that we are entering a very dangerous period. By rights given its express inflation targeting obligations, the Bank should already have raised interest rates well beyond 0.5 per cent some months ago. Whilst it also has a less high-profile duty 'protecting and enhancing the financial system of the UK', the inflation we are now witnessing comes as some of us feared as a direct result of the prolonged policy of quantitative easing (printing money).

At the end of last year Lord Young controversially observed that for the overwhelming majority the recession was 'happening to someone else'. By contrast, nothing will bring home more to the majority of Britons that their own economic reckoning is underway than a marked rise in their mortgage repayments. The extra £20 or so taken up by the weekly shop or filling the car with petrol will be as nothing to the impact of rising interest rates and the cost of borrowing returning to normal. Remember this would already have happened if the Bank of England was obeying its inflation targeting responsibilities to the letter.

So the story of 2011 as the year unfolds will almost certainly be one of a rapid rise in the cost of living as both global commodity prices and taxation spike upwards. The cost of oil has been highly volatile in recent years, but the 50 per cent rise in price over the past six months may prove more difficult to reverse. The exponential growth in demand from emerging economies (also affecting copper, steel, cotton etc.) may be compounded if political unrest in the Arab world spreads beyond Tunisia. Then there is a global shortage of wheat as a result of failed harvests in eastern Asia, whilst the effect, for example, of the Queensland floods on the price of iron ore, coal and other minerals will only be clear in the months ahead.

This impact will be compounded if interest (and mortgage) rates were to rise to 'proper' levels. Understandably policymakers are fearful both of stoking up inflationary expectations or choking off early signs of sustainable economic recovery if they raise interest rates.

The prolonged near-zero interest rate environment has enabled banks to continue holding toxic assets without realising their losses. Similarly there has been no incentive for banks to foreclose on many struggling businesses and indebted individuals. The impact of even relatively modest interest rate rises would undoubtedly be for creditors to cut their losses. The Council for Mortgage Lenders calculates that the impact on homeowners already perched on the edge of insolvency of a rise in base rate to 2.5 per cent would be devastating to some 3 million borrowers. It would also lead to a confidence-sapping depression in both house prices (and more accurately still, house values, for those who have become accustomed to borrowing against the rising value of their main asset).

In truth, the continued failure to raise rates is an implicit recognition by the Bank of the underlying weaknesses of UK plc after three years of patchy or negative growth. Yet the political pressure to keep rates down may test to breaking point in the year ahead the independence of the Bank of England over monetary policy.

The coalition government's policy of a dash for growth (another reason why the rapid rise in imported commodity costs is so worrying) reflects the fact that the deficit remains uncomfortably high, especially as tax receipts plunge. Indeed it now looks quite likely that we shall collectively borrow more in 2010/11 than in the final year of the Labour government. Moreover, in the first six months of the coalition government, current spending has risen by 7 per cent year-on-year, such are the upfront costs of the radical reforms we seek to make to the public sector.

The key challenge now is to tackle inflation without adversely choking off growth or economic confidence. As you may have gathered from the foregoing, I believe that in current circumstances it is impossible to see how we can achieve both.

But I am also pretty confident that the Treasury and Bank have made their choice. Despite its effect on savers and those on fixed incomes, my prediction is that interest rates will not stand higher than 1 per cent by year-end. The calculated gamble by policymakers is that a little inflation in the system is now more desirable than the alternatives.

History teaches us that once in the system, inflation is difficult to control.

The Treasury has skilfully succeeded in persuading the markets of the government's intent to control the deficit, in spite of public spending projected to be higher in 2014/15 than in the last financial year. If there is any element of Gordon Brown's legacy that is worth emulating it is his record of consistently low inflation (admittedly achieved in far more benign economic conditions).

The financial markets may soon need convincing of the resolve to keep the cost of living down, especially as the biggest beneficiaries of inflation are debtors ... and government is the biggest debtor of them all.

‡

A Fresh Look at the Banking Bailouts, 2 March 2011

One of the curiosities of the global bank bailout process since September 2008 has been the consensus that this episode symbolised courageous, decisive government action at its best. The nation's economy teetered over a precipice, mere hours away from a refusal by cashpoints to dole out any more banknotes. The conventional wisdom now, almost regardless of their terms, is that the bailouts were an essential life-preserving shock to the domestic economy.

Unfortunately whilst this version of events contains some truth, it has diverted us from asking searching questions over the deals struck during those whirlwind weeks. As the public distaste for bankers' remuneration and bonus payments reaches fever pitch, correspondingly little attention has been paid to the terms demanded by the erstwhile government in return for propping up the banks. It is still not clear what thought was given during the bailout process to the long-term goals of government; what commercial and political principles, if any, were followed in those early days; whether this emergency action was dictated by tactical considerations alone; and if there was ever a clear strategy for the future.

In truth, the Labour government appeared to lack any coherent vision as to the route ahead. It chose rather to pursue a confused path of unconnected policy announcements dictated by the whims of public opinion, the electoral cycle and the media – a grim foundation upon which the coalition has strived to build a credible alternative since last May.

In fact, some of the inherent flaws of the deals from those fraught weeks in autumn 2008 may help to explain why there remains to this day an overriding sense that the bankers 'got away with it', with the taxpayer picking up the tab. Indeed I would contend that history will view the banking bailouts as a missed opportunity – a moment when moral hazard might have been sewn into the heart of the regulatory system by making recapitalisation a deeply unattractive option.

This issue requires forensic examination and a more thorough analysis than I can provide here. I accept that I write with the tremendous benefit of hindsight about a period of unprecedented strain, when the breath-taking speed of events made mistakes inevitable. It may also prove that only the passing of a greater period of time will reveal the true worth of the deal to the taxpayer and the bailouts' success in deterring another financial crisis of equal gravity.

Nevertheless, it is worth posing some broad questions about the negotiations that preceded this colossal intervention in Britain's economy:

1. Strategy
   Whilst the banks undoubtedly presented the government with a crisis on a huge scale, the Treasury was nevertheless in a position of enormous strength (as is any organisation about to spend such colossal sums of money), and should have recognised immediately that the status quo no longer existed. The fact that RBS's former Chief Executive, Sir Fred Goodwin, walked away with a pension pot of £16 million when his organisation would otherwise have been bankrupt, suggests that the government did not appreciate this.
   Naturally the first priority in formulating a plan should have

been to prevent systemic risk and the eventual strategy ultimately guarded against this. But beyond this task, Ministers should have asked, 'How much money can we make out of this?' In short, rather than view the negotiations as a bailout, they should have been looked upon as a business transaction. But instead of treating the situation as a corporate turnaround, and charging accordingly, the government provided the banks with guarantees commanding a negligible rate of return.

2. Rate of Return

The simple rule of investment is the greater the risk, the greater the return. Back then it was abundantly clear that prospects did not come much riskier than the Royal Bank of Scotland. It announced the largest loss in UK corporate history on the very same day in February 2009 that the government increased its holding in the bank from 58 per cent to 70 per cent.

Putting the terms of the October 2008 rescue package for RBS and Lloyds Banking Group (the product of Lloyds TSB taking on HBOS) in front of an experienced investor associate of mine, he immediately asked three questions. First, why was the most money put into the more risky instrument (with ordinary shares favoured over preference shares)? Second, why did the government pay more for the higher risk share? Third, why did the government not seek to appoint more board members?

In the case of the Lloyds Banking Group deal the government, announcing its rescue package, advised that it would purchase:

Up to £13 billion in newly issued ordinary shares, priced at 182p, and

Up to £4 billion in preference shares, priced at 38p.

Even though preference shares do not typically carry voting rights, my associate was surprised that the government favoured ordinary shares over preference shares when the latter shore up the balance sheet as effectively as ordinary, are less risky and were priced more cheaply. Compare this bailout to experienced investor, Warren Buffett's investment in Goldman Sachs during the same period. In September 2008, Mr Buffett's company,

Berkshire Hathaway, agreed to purchase $5 billion of preferred stock with a 10 per cent dividend, with the option to purchase $5 billion of common stock at any time over the following five years. That stake is now paying his company $500 million annually.

In return for the government's investment in LBG, potentially representing 44 per cent of the proposed merged bank, it was given the opportunity to appoint two independent board members. The board, however, comprised thirteen seats, giving the government a representation of 15 per cent for its 44 per cent share.

Similarly, the terms of the rescue package announced in October 2008 as they applied to RBS were that the government would purchase:

Up to £15 billion of ordinary shares and

Up to £5 billion of preference shares.

In return for that investment, the government would appoint three independent board members out of twelve, i.e. 25 per cent of an organisation in which they owned 63 per cent. No doubt the political imperative of being seen to take a hands-off approach was assumed to be of greater import than being able to hold greater sway over RBS's overall direction. It might also be asked who controlled the other 37 per cent of RBS and how much was paid for that stake when the government only got 63 per cent of a bank which, had it not been for state intervention, would surely have imploded.

3. Advice

It is worth examining who was advising the government during this fraught period. Did they hire experienced investors with a track record of driving hard business deals and did they consider who would pursue the best return for the taxpayer?

It seems instead that the 'usual suspects' made hay. Since Northern Rock faltered in late 2007, the government spent £107 million on professional fees for the banking bailouts. Lawyers Slaughter and May picked up £32.9 million for commercial legal advice, Credit Suisse £15.4 million for financial advice with PricewaterhouseCoopers, Ernst & Young, KPMG and Blackrock taking an aggregate of £35 million for advice on the

Asset Protection Scheme. Understandably the National Audit Office has called into question some of the Treasury's practices in employing professional advisers who were awarded retainer contracts without any clearly defined criteria for success.

4. Criteria for Success

Since the bailouts took place, politicians have defined success as 'returning money to the taxpayer'. This is almost unbelievably unambitious. As I have described, we should have approached the bailouts as a business agreement with our aim, beyond preventing systemic risk, to strike as good a deal for the taxpayer as possible. Had this happened, and the taxpayer was aware year-by-year of the forecasted value of its stake, the debate on the future of banking would surely have been shaped entirely differently. Instead, there has been a sense that the biggest risk takers extricated themselves from the crisis scot-free with the rest of the banking fraternity being able to carry on as before.

The result has been for politicians to try to placate the public with a potentially damaging PR campaign against the financial services sector and its employees, grandstanding on bonuses, cash/share splits and the efficacy of the 50 per cent higher rate of income tax. In essence, the previous government had no coherent strategy on banking after the bailouts, laying a foundation upon which it has been difficult for the coalition to build a credible alternative.

5. Lessons Learned

I doubt any institution would wish happily to go down the path of recapitalisation again. Yet the fact remains that the government stands ready as the lender of last resort to depositors at the very least. History demonstrates that the terms of any bailout should not be as unattractive as they might be.

Had a hard bargain been driven by the government, with no option of a golden goodbye for the most discredited Chief Executives, the fear of bailout could have served as a far better regulator of behaviour than reams of new laws and fresh bodies in place to police the system.

Beyond the prevention of systemic collapse, in future the

government's negotiating teams might ask a few simple questions: what are our guiding principles during these negotiations;
what long-term goals are we pursuing; what are our commercial,
economic and (as ever) political objectives? In short, how do we
want the financial system to look in the future?

The last government's success in preventing an immediate collapse
in the banking system should not disguise its failure to articulate
any overarching strategy for our financial services during and after
that time of economic emergency. Its insistence on pursuing a weak,
ill-defined and ad hoc path left only a bitter taste in the mouths of
banker, businessman and taxpayer alike alongside a messy inheritance for this coalition government.

Whilst no one should anticipate with too much relish the *next*
economic downturn, we should at least hope that today's problems
and the path to their solutions will be in the minds of many who
are charged with fixing it next time round. Nothing can change
the original terms negotiated during those 2008 bailouts, but they
really must hold lessons both for now and the future.

Beware the vested interests or entrenched mindset of the expert.
Be sure to exact terms in line with the risks taken. Most importantly, robustly and continually define the strategic objective in the
general national interest.

‡

Our Economic Missions Needs an Explicitly Stronger Moral Dimension, 17 March 2011

*With the departure of Gordon Brown as both Prime Minister and
Labour leader, a contest ensued which saw three main candidates –
Ed Balls, Ed Miliband and David Miliband – compete for the Party
leadership prize. By late September, the Labour Party had crowned Ed
Miliband as its new leader, and he subsequently brought in former
Home Secretary, Alan Johnson, as his Shadow Chancellor. By January,*

Johnson had resigned his position following difficulties in his personal life and Brown bruiser, Ed Balls, was appointed in his place. Between them, the two Eds developed a narrative that the coalition was cutting public expenditure too rapidly, putting economic recovery at risk. In the meantime, in the aftermath of the autumn Spending Review, the coalition had been forced into embarrassing u-turns over plans to sell off national forests and cut spending on school books and sports.

As the Budget looms, Labour's slogan that reductions in public spending go 'too far, too fast' has regrettably developed resonance. Not simply because it has been repeated ad nauseam – though the discipline with which it has been should also act as a salutary reminder to the coalition.

The reason this soundbite strikes a chord is because it seems plausible. Whether Conservatives like it or not there is in truth an alternative to the immediate cutbacks in public expenditure (after all if there were not, it would have been impossible for the coalition to perform the u-turns it has over controversial items earmarked for savings such as forestry, school books and sports). The Treasury's colossal borrowing over recent years probably means that the odd additional £5 billion or so in annual public spending really is neither here nor there. The benefit derived by the coalition government from its deficit-reduction strategy from the international capital markets has been hard-fought, richly deserved, but in truth relatively marginal.

Unlike the Irish and Greek governments (whose strict spending programmes for years to come have been drawn up under the watchful eye of the IMF and EU) here in the UK we have had and continue to have some choice over these matters. It would, in the short term, be possible to revert to the last government's policy of delaying the day of financial reckoning. But it would come at the expense of the next generation.

As a result it is essential that Conservatives make the unashamedly moral case for an urgent restoration of stability to the public finances. It simply cannot be justifiable to saddle future generations of taxpayers with the debt created by over-consumption by those of us who have been British electors and beneficiaries of public spending in recent decades. This intergenerational conflict will very shortly become the clear dividing line in Western politics.

We should not flinch from making the case that there is an alternative to an urgent deficit reduction – but taking that choice is a path that does not bear contemplation.

The coalition faces one other rhetorical hurdle. Soon it will face deep unpopularity as spending cuts begin to bite – yet simultaneously it lacks any explicit electoral mandate for its actions. In contrast to the increasingly stark economic pain being felt by millions of Britons 'in the real world,' the coalition may come to be seen by many as appearing a little too comfortable. The risk in preaching to the public that everything government is doing is firmly 'in the national interest' is that voters may feel progressively cheated that they no longer have a say in these matters. As a corollary, they may even begin to suspect that 'in the national interest' is little more than a device to close off any reasonable debate about the real choices we collectively face.

Whilst the notion of consensus has hitherto been regarded positively by a general public tired of politicians' synthetic dividing lines, it might easily come to be despised either as a conspiracy against the expression of choice by the voters or as a convenient mechanism for the jettisoning of manifesto commitments. That sense of democratic illegitimacy when compounded by a Labour narrative of coalition economic recklessness could prove compelling.

The economy faces rocky waters ahead. We should not underestimate the power of rhetoric in keeping a disorientated public on board. Warning them repeatedly that there is no alternative to the course we have chosen will not be enough – indeed it may be seen not only as increasingly implausible, but as little more than a conspiracy against the electorate by the governing class. Instead, we require a convincing moral purpose as the backdrop to our actions.

Even in a coalition, politics remains fundamentally about choices. Conservatives make those choices not because they are unavoidable but because we believe them to be right.

‡

Popular Capitalism Reborn, 7 April 2011

Observers of global economic trends will have noticed the paradox that whilst size of national markets is perceived to bring with it unmitigated potential benefits, there is increasing public hostility to large global institutions and corporations.

Hot on the heels of the BRIC group of nations, has emerged the CIVETS amalgam of developing countries (Colombia, Indonesia, Vietnam, Egypt, Turkey and South Africa). It is these nations enjoying critical population mass, and a demographic skewed strongly towards those under the age of twenty-five, which are near universally regarded as locations of likely optimal economic growth in the decades ahead.

Yet there is a contrarian trend in respect of global banks (which 'need to be broken down lest they are too big to fail') and international corporations (witness the recent travails of BP and General Motors to name but two). I suspect that internet transparency will result in greater public hostility towards large, multinational corporations, which have been able to exploit their complex network of international subsidiaries in order to minimise tax and regulatory obligations. Accordingly small remains beautiful in the eyes of countless consumers in the commercial sphere.

The political challenge that awaits government is to distil these two apparently conflicting trends into an effective and populist strategy for competition. Conservatives should be at the forefront in standing up against the power of monopoly, not by pandering to anti-business rhetoric but in an authentic spirit of consumer and individual protection. Promoting the interests of the 'little man' has perhaps too frequently been regarded as a 'left-wing' preoccupation. However, we should not forget the honourable tradition of right-of-centre politicians grasping this nettle.

Arguably the most notorious 'trust-buster' was US President Theodore Roosevelt who at the outset of the twentieth century led his own crusade against the overwhelming power of Big Business. In the era of Rockefeller, J. P. Morgan and US Steel, Roosevelt at the White House stood up against the making of monopolistic profits in virtually unlimited quantities. Closer to home and far more recently, the government of Margaret Thatcher liberalised middle-class monopolies ('Big Bang' in the City in 1986 alongside widescale reform of the legal and accountancy professions in the same decade).

Today's Conservatives also recognise the necessity of open competition as the ultimate safeguard to consumer interests. Reform to the structure of the banking industry, for instance, will amount to little unless the financial sector provides considerably more choice to its retail consumers. Similarly a robust economic crime policy needs to place the promotion of commercial competition at the heart of its enforcement in order to deter fraudulent and anti-competitive activity.

I have written before about the role in this regard of the Serious Fraud Office, an organisation whose investigative function is set to merge with a new National Crime Agency. The government's current proposal asserts that such an Agency should rest within the Home Office's control. Yet a beefed-up National Crime Agency umbrella will do little to ensure that competition policy is properly business oriented. The truth is that the Home Office understandably tends to look at its constituent agencies through the lens of organised crime alone. In a National Crime Agency dealing with child protection and serious organised crime, it is also not hard to imagine fraud slipping down the ladder of priorities.

Nevertheless, pursuing companies who seek to undermine the notion of a level playing field will be crucial to restoring the reputation of and confidence in our seemingly discredited free market system. The bringing of the SFO's functions under the auspices of the Department of Business, Innovation and Skills instead, working alongside a more robust Office of Fair Trading and Competition Commission, could, I believe, prove fundamental to the success of this task.

The continued public debate over the banking and finance

industry, whilst understandable, has been a great distraction in constructing a robust, populist competition policy. It is a great shame for it has always been competition, rather than rules and regulation, that has best served as a restraint on unbridled capitalism.

As the banking crisis unfolded in the autumn of 2008, it was always my fear that the unravelling of the financial system would all too easily be presented as a crisis of capitalism. Bank bailouts would then be perceived as the ultimate reward for failure in a dysfunctional marketplace that had ceased to benefit the consumer. Since that time, we have seen a plethora of quick-fire solutions and superficially attractive regulations. Yet the sense persists that our problems have not really been solved; the anger towards banks and big business lingers rather than dissipating.

This is not because the fundamental principles of capitalism are bust. Rather we have so far failed to restore a moral dimension to the market and resurrect the link between work, talent and reward that had become so warped at the height of the boom. Popular capitalism, by which I mean a capitalism that places the interests of the consumer at its heart, can be retrieved. But only by weaving competition into the very roots of our economic policy.

‡

Banking Reform – Never a Cost-Free Revolution, 27 April 2011

The Independent Banking Commission was established in June 2010 to consider reforms to the banking system that might prevent a repeat of 2008's crisis. Chaired by Sir John Vickers, the Commission released its interim report on 11 April, recommending that banks' retail operations be ring-fenced from their investment banking arms.

Now that some dust has started to settle on the Independent Banking Commission's interim report on reform of the industry it would be wise to recognise this as merely the opening salvo in what promises to be a prolonged battle.

Amidst the smooth consensual tone of the IBC's report no one should be under any illusions that this reflects merely the starting point in the reform process. Negotiations between the Commission (and by extension the UK government) and the banking fraternity alongside their public affairs advisers will now begin in earnest.

Let me stress again what I have observed many times – the most remarkable aspect in the three years since the global financial crisis began is the complete absence of agreement amongst policymakers as to a desirable future shape of the international banking sector. Whilst the ICB may in its recommendations desire to influence this debate, there are clear dangers ahead. Unilateral British action risks diminishing the competitiveness of domestic financial services in the only sizeable sector where in the foreseeable future the UK can really boast global leader status.

The long path towards rebalancing the domestic economy needs to begin with measures that promote UK participants in growth industries of the future. It is sheer fantasy economics to imagine that we will be collectively better off by shrinking the UK banking sector any time soon.

Yet for all their good intentions, the ICB's capital adequacy proposals risk doing precisely that. By gold-plating the Basel III requirements, our own retail banks risk under EU law being placed at a severe competitive disadvantage to European players who would be able to operate here without such stringent capital requirements.

It is also difficult to see how insisting upon a 10 per cent capital buffer is compatible with broader government economic policy on consumer protection and bank lending to SMEs. I fear that the understandable desire in a future crisis to protect the taxpayer from the colossal costs and economic disruption that we have witnessed since September 2008 brings with it plenty of unintended and potentially undesirable consequences. Higher capital requirements will almost certainly increase the cost of banking to the many millions of retail accountholders. 'Free' banking will soon be a thing of the past. It is also difficult to see how meddling in the regulations on holding capital will do anything to alleviate what most MPs in their correspondence regard as the number one pressing problem with the banks, namely their perceived reluctance to lend to the sort of growing businesses that should be the vehicle for private sector employment growth in the years ahead.

The ICB quite properly identifies that in any future crisis the bondholders must not be allowed to get off scot-free. George Osborne has been similarly lucid in recent months on this issue. Indeed the entirely rational banking response to each consecutive eurozone bailout over the past year has been to pile in to risky but lucrative Greek, Irish and Portuguese bonds, knowing full well that EU taxpayers alone will carry the can in event of default.

Nevertheless the new arrangements both on the continent and as proposed here by the ICB should not be seen as a panacea for all problems on the financial markets.

From 2013 a precondition facing any stricken nation needing to borrow from the European Stability Mechanism is a restructuring of its debt in the event that its finances are deemed as unsustainable. Superficially this might seem unobjectionable in the extreme. However, two rather less desirable consequences flow. First, until the ESM comes into force there will now essentially be a moratorium on *any* attempt to restructure debts of struggling eurozone nations. The interconnectedness of the financial system would otherwise trigger a catastrophic wave of debt write-offs amongst banks across the EU.

Second – and this is where the ICB's silver bullet may not prove to be such a good idea after all – the effect of penalising debt-holders in any future banking collapse will undoubtedly have an effect on the pricing of risk. In short, the cost of servicing UK government debt in future may rise substantially. As ever, it is the unpredictable outcome of new regulatory initiatives that has the potential to lead to a host of unintended consequences.

Much of the press coverage prior to publication had focused on the likelihood of Barclays Bank, in the event of 'draconian measures', to relocate their HQ outside the UK. Unsurprisingly such speculation is now more muted. Indeed the Treasury may have been rather relaxed at the prospect of no longer needing to be the ultimate guarantor to a bank whose balance sheet stands at over 100 per cent of the UK's GDP.

A more salient question might be to ask where Barclays (or indeed any of our other retail banking giants) would go in the event of relocation. In truth the size of their loan book makes the only plausible alternative HQ the United States, although whatever benefits might accrue to Wall Street's status would most likely be outweighed by additional taxpayer risk at a time when the Obama administration is trying to wean itself off its own perceived vulnerability to the financial services sector. That might feasibly leave Japan or mainland China as domicile options, but would either of these regulatory options really be what Barclays would want for its business?

My hunch is that we may not have heard the last of banking reform as a bargaining chip between coalition partners if, as expected, the 'NO' campaign prevails in the AV referendum. The conventional wisdom is that such an outcome would necessitate the Liberal Democrats being given a 'quick win' in order to placate its disappointed supporters.

House of Lords reform will be both difficult to deliver (many Conservative politicians in both Houses are utterly unbiddable on the issue of a largely or fully elected Upper House) and time consuming. As a result, I wonder whether the implementation (and even gold-plating) of the IBC's agenda might be seen to provide the Liberal Democrats with a populist cause, which in view of our Party's traditionally strong links to the City, might also be felt to be more expediently delivered by the junior partners in the coalition.

‡

These Bailouts are Appeasement by Another Name, 1 July 2011

As the stricken eurozone continued to be pulled under by the ailing Greek economy, EU leaders agreed to launch a fresh aid package for

Greece on the condition of further austerity. David Cameron argued that the UK, in being outside the eurozone, should not have to contribute to the rescue funds but as a contributor to the IMF, would likely be liable for €1 billion in loan guarantees.

The economic appeasement of the Greeks will soon be over. For in sanctioning a second bailout to Greece, last week's hapless EU summit served only to embolden politicians and protesting populations in Ireland, Portugal and elsewhere that they can continue living beyond their means indefinitely.

It is the abject failure of the European political class to face up to stark economic reality that makes the latest stage of the eurozone financial crisis potentially so very dangerous. This latest episode has served only to buy several more months before the next solvency crisis becomes evident.

I observed a year ago this week that any sovereign default in the eurozone risked being economically as profound as the collapse of Lehman Brothers in September 2008. Such an outcome now appears inevitable and the UK economy, with its continued reliance on the financial services sector, cannot hope to emerge unscathed.

Amidst all the talk of the UK successfully facing down German and French demands during last week's negotiations, I fear the ECB's bailout fund is something of a sideshow in all this. The UK taxpayer is now ever more exposed via the IMF to any sovereign bailouts in the eurozone. Unpalatable though this may seem it is also probably in the UK's best interests. After all, if Greece's banks collapse the EU sovereign state then most immediately on the critical list is not one of the 'Big Four', nor even Portugal or Ireland. It is Cyprus. For the economy of that small nation has historically been even more closely interconnected with Greece than other eurozone nations.

Let's not underestimate the number of UK citizens in North London and beyond, part of the Cypriot diaspora here, whose financial affairs are inextricably bound with Cypriot banks. The UK's exposure here can only be tempered by an urgent strategy for an orderly restructuring of Greek – and in time other sovereign – debt.

Even such an initiative will not get the UK off the hook. For the impact of penalising debt-holders in any future eurozone banking collapse (already agreed from 2013) or restructuring also stands to have a profound effect on the pricing of risk. In short, one of its unintended consequences is that before long the cost of servicing UK government debt may rise substantially.

George Osborne frequently retorts that, 'The UK has Portuguese levels of debt and German rates of interest.' Most commentators regard this as a ringing endorsement of coalition government economic policy. Rightly so – for the coalition government's avowed policy, after a decade of uncontrolled debt and credit, to eliminate the structural deficit within a single parliament has reassured the financial markets. However, it would perhaps be wiser to see this statement of economic fact as an urgent warning of potentially troubled times ahead.

‡

Hobbling the City will also Hobble the Country (*Daily Telegraph*), 13 July 2011

Addressing the annual Lord Mayor's banquet at Mansion House, Sir Mervyn King, Governor of the Bank of England, warned that Britain was in the middle of 'seven lean years' and faced another three years of pain before the economy started to stabilise. At the same event, George Osborne announced plans to sell Northern Rock and fleshed out propos-als to ring-fence banks' retail arms from their investment operations. In addition, he resisted increasing calls for a Plan B on deficit reduction and outlined how he would tear apart Labour's tripartite regulatory system by returning responsibilities to the Bank of England. I wrote this article for the Daily Telegraph *to highlight some of the concerns of the banking fraternity about how the new regulatory regime might work in practice.*

'When the crunch came, no one knew who was in charge.'

It was with those words, at last year's Mansion House dinner, that

George Osborne laid to rest the tripartite system of financial regulation: Treasury, Bank of England and Financial Services Authority.

At the same banquet last month, the Chancellor set out further details of this 'new settlement' between Britain and its banks – and more recently still he has published a White Paper containing the draft legislation that will bring this brave new world into being.

Yet as the City's great and the good have digested the details, there is unease bordering on alarm that the coalition's proposed framework will simply muddy the waters further. The reforms, which involve transferring the FSA's powers to the Bank of England and creating three new financial authorities, are the product of painstaking, innovative analysis. But the predictable series of compromises, designed to keep the main players happy, risks creating another system in which it is impossible to see where the buck stops.

The plan to entrust financial stability to the Bank of England, under the guise of an independent Financial Policy Committee (FPC), has come in for particular criticism. Professor Willem Buiter of Citibank speaks for many who see this as an essentially political area, best handled by the Treasury. Whatever the apparent safeguards for independence, it is difficult to see how the FPC would not be influenced by the government's broader priorities in the run-up to an election – or worse, find its considerations overruled by a Chancellor with a decidedly short-term horizon.

Questions of independence also shade into questions of expertise. The Treasury Select Committee has refused to endorse one of the FPC's 'external' appointees, on the grounds that his forty-year career had been spent entirely at the Treasury and Bank of England. Indeed, there is persistent criticism that the architects of the new system – Treasury civil servants – are too generalist in their experience, given how complex and specialised financial services are today.

Naturally, none of Mr Osborne's new regulators will come cheap. A tougher, more intrusive approach to compliance will require extra resources – a phalanx of risk experts to judge the viability of fresh financial products; burgeoning numbers of new administrative staff and relationship managers; the cost and bureaucracy of annual inspections and so on. The Financial Conduct Authority – which will replicate many of the Financial Service Authority's powers – has been singled out over such fears. Even senior figures at the FSA have suggested that closer supervision of firms could cost an additional £200 million a year, an increase of around 50 per cent of the current organisation's budget. This bill will land at the feet of the taxpayer. But consumers will inevitably bear an additional brunt as financial institutions seek to recoup higher compliance costs. Innovation will diminish.

Many argue that an increased cost burden is a price worth paying for stability in financial services. But intrusive and costly regulation may in fact prove no more effective than that which has gone before. We will only get reform right if it is accompanied by a crystal-clear vision of the preferred place and role for the financial sector within the UK economy. To date, such clarity is notable only by its absence. Instead we seem to have fallen into the perennial trap of creating a system designed to solve the last crisis. In truth, our problems owed more to the impact of an unchecked, old-fashioned debt and credit bubble, accentuated by the impact of globalisation within the banking sector, than flaws in the regulatory model. Yet it has remained politically expedient for the Chancellor to pin much of the blame on Gordon Brown's removal of supervisory responsibilities from the Bank of England.

The refreshingly independent-minded Chairman of the Treasury Select Committee, Andrew Tyrie, has expressed concern 'that we are going down a route which in the long run will stifle competition. We should use the opportunity to make sure there are pressures to cut away otiose regulation rather than a one-way ratchet.' Worryingly, the impact on the competitive position of the City and the UK will no longer be regarded as a relevant factor in interpreting the impact of new legislation.

In short, whilst the government signals its urgent desire to dash for economic growth, its new regulatory regime could do little to help, and much to harm. Most of the UK's economic competitors are desperate to break into the developing markets of the East, where financial services and its vast array of associated professions provide this nation with an enormous competitive advantage. Moreover, the increased wealth of the middle classes in these countries will ensure that their financial sectors grow rapidly in the decades ahead.

Whatever the distaste for bankers' remuneration, it is firmly in the national interest that the City maintains its pre-eminence in the highly mobile world of financial services. The response to the coalition's draft legislation suggests that the battle over the regulatory landscape will be fiercely fought. But it is vital that the right decisions are made to secure Britain's future.

‡

Things Can Only Get Worse Before They Might Get Better, 26 July 2011

The coalition government inherited a catastrophic economic legacy. Unlike those heady days of 1997 things surely can 'only get better'? I am becoming used to reading economic reports from every business sector and special interest groups acknowledging the seriousness of the economic situation, but there still seems to be a common refrain that says '… but please don't cut government spending in our area.'

Well, this morning sees the release of a fresh and uncompromising report into the state of the UK economy, aptly entitled 'Project Armageddon – thinking the unthinkable', that says that failing to address the real problem is now not an option. Tullett Prebon's Head of Global Research Dr Tim Morgan gives an authoritative, detailed and independent account of why the UK is 'mired in debt', 'our economy is flat-lining', and what as a nation we have to do to kick start growth. In short, we need to do much more practically to assist the UK's small and medium business sector to grow and prosper.

Dr Morgan starts by telling us the economic situation is far worse than we think or many are willing to accept. Official figures suggest public debt is 60 per cent of GDP, but this excludes the net present value of unfunded public sector pension commitments not to mention the obligations under PFI contracts. Once aggregated this amounts to £1.35 trillion, lifting the total public and quasi debit to £2.46 trillion or 167 per cent of GDP. Add in the debt held privately by individuals, families and business which is estimated to be £1.2 trillion, and we really are 'all in it together'; and this is before continued government borrowing (running at £140 billion this year) further expands the national debt.

Dr Morgan doesn't pull his punches. His conclusions make exceptionally painful reading for those responsible for leading us into the abyss, but he also fires more than a warning shot across the coalition's bow.

He identifies numerous 'disastrous mistakes' by what he describes as 'Team Brown & Co' that led us to where we are now. The expansion in public spending resulted in an economy distorted towards sectors driven by debt or by public expenditure. He goes further arguing that fuelling this debt created a falsehood throughout the public sector that borrowing more money (or printing more) was the answer. Under Labour, the civil service never had to worry about balancing budgets as more money would be magically on its way.

An interesting dimension to Dr Morgan's thesis is the social impact the public spending spree has had on UK society as a whole and if left unchecked the likely damage it will wreak on future generations. He says the political desire of the Left to 'financially feed' certain social groups with the ideology of entitlement has not only fuelled a 'state of denial' about the true condition of the economy, but consequently hindered social mobility and muddied society's understanding of 'fairness'. This denial is mentioned on numerous occasions and its political implications should resonate strongly with Conservatives.

Dr Morgan's prescription for the coalition is a simple, yet controversial one. So Ed Balls can forget about his 'Plan B'. Put simply, it isn't going to work as it would be more of the same, and place the UK in far deeper trouble.

All of us are now paying for the catastrophic mistakes of the past decade, and will be for many years to come. Dr Morgan recognises the coalition's plan to reduce the deficit must be a priority, but this can only hope to be successful if more is done to promote growth in some key business areas of development in the British economy. This means challenging huge amounts of stifling regulation and burdensome legislation.

Large scale, macro-economic reforms aren't working and nor will they be of any long-term benefit. As a matter of urgency we need to start implementing micro or supply side initiatives designed to free up small and medium-size business. Only such reform will act as the true drivers of the British economy. To get it right we have to 'think the unthinkable' and cut the regulatory and taxation framework which hinders many SMEs.

Stimulating the engines of economic growth is the real key to helping the British economy back on the road to recovery. Like him I fear that this will be too difficult a pill for the coalition to swallow as it requires harsher spending reductions to pay for it. More's the pity for us all.

In 1979 the incoming Thatcher government signalled unashamedly that the UK was open for business by abolishing foreign exchange controls. For modern Britons it seems almost unbelievable that until then wherever travelling abroad you needed to take your passport to be franked at your bank when taking foreign currency abroad. A similarly iconic message is needed today about our commitment to promoting a new entrepreneurial spirit amongst SMEs. Tax rates needs to be sharply reduced for genuine wealth creators. The coalition may have made progress in starting to reactivate our economy after the disaster of three Labour terms, but with Greece facing default, Ireland and Portugal being supported by the European Central bank, and now Spain and Italy hitting turbulent times, Dr Morgan's report is a stark reminder that for a heavily indebted nation the road ahead will be a very long and difficult one. The faster we deal with it now, the quicker we can repay our children's generation, rather than saddling them with unsustainable levels of debt as a result of our overconsumption.

‡

Banking Can Never Be a Risk-Free Activity (*Daily Telegraph*), 7 September 2011

Memories in the world of banking are notoriously short. It was just three years ago this month with the collapse of Lehman Brothers that the global financial system came close to imploding. As time has passed, recollections of this near-catastrophe have rapidly dimmed and the international momentum for fundamental reform has stalled.

Nevertheless the City of London's size and global reach continues to make the UK economy especially vulnerable to turbulence in the financial markets. This is the backdrop to Sir John Vickers' Independent Commission on Banking (ICB) report, which will be published next Tuesday [12 September].

The ICB has been charged by the coalition with proposing structural and non-structural changes to make Britain's banks safer. In the absence of international action, we have decided to go it alone and Vickers seems set to opt for a ring-fencing of high street banking from investment banking. It is worth stressing that irrespective of the hugely interconnected community of global finance, if enacted, these proposals will only apply to banks domiciled in the UK. Moreover, there is nothing in the ICB report that will challenge the more pressing public concern about banks' profits or bankers' remuneration.

I fear that its work also flies in the face of the two overriding insights of this financial crisis. Since time immemorial everything in banking has hinged upon confidence. Talk about 'safe' levels of capital is in the final analysis just that – talk. Raising capital thresholds up to and beyond 10 per cent (as proposed successively by the Basel 3 Accords and in the ICB's interim report) will act only to make the UK banking sector less internationally competitive. Splitting the banks will leave them short of capital and risks cutting off cash-flow to the SME sector that it so desperately requires at this stage of the economic cycle, thereby triggering a renewed credit crunch.

Fundamentally, banking is a daily confidence trick – the only institutions truly safe are those which hold on to every last penny of their depositors' cash. As we saw with Northern Rock in 2007 no bank can survive without confidence. Once it is forced to deny that it is in trouble, the game is up and nothing short of an explicit government guarantee to depositors will save it. The ICB report, however, is predicated on the notion that sufficient safeguards can protect against such a collapse in confidence. Yet contagion is not a rational process. If there is a belief in the banking sector that the travails of any particular institution will spill over to others invariably this becomes a self-fulfilling prophecy.

The Vickers' template for ringfencing banking activities is based on an outdated and simplistic division between what amounts to wholesale and retail banking. There are numerous transmission mechanisms between the two that make a hard and fast split between high street and 'casino' investment banking difficult to achieve.

The coalition government's goals are laudable. Ideally, incentives for excessive risk-taking should be curbed and the process for sorting out banks which get into difficulties should be streamlined substantially to reduce potential liabilities to the taxpayer.

However, banking is a global business. Even the perennially activist EU Commission recognises that it can do nothing if, following implementation of Vickers' proposals, banks simply re-domiciled to the EU and set up subsidiaries in the UK. This raises the more fundamental question – if only UK banks are obliged to sign up to the Vickers reforms then surely the contagion risk from any future global financial crisis will be exactly the same? Small additional amounts of capital being held in a dwindling number of British banks is unlikely to make any difference when the next crisis is in full flow.

The benefits of breaking up the banks are probably being oversold in any event. In practical terms will this much heralded split make banks better at absorbing losses? A failing investment bank which falls outside the ring-fence is still likely to share its name or at least reputation goodwill with the retail bank from which it has been cast asunder. Does anyone seriously believe that there will not also be a run on the retail bank and huge potential liabilities falling back to the taxpayer via the depositors' compensation scheme? Ring-fencing may sound like a neat solution designed by the ICB to ensure banks' support. In truth it is a hopeless fudge – when put to the test it will surely fail.

If we go down this route we would need to enforce a full, legal separation splitting UK banks and create a divided domestic financial sector unique in the developed world. This cannot be in the interests of the UK's financial services sector. Similarly the impact on likely profitability would act to increase the incentive for greater risk-taking.

History shows that tougher regulation in the banking sector is a driver for new, innovative and riskier off-balance sheet vehicles – indeed the explosive expansion in hedge funds over the past decade came about in the aftermath of imposing new regulatory measures following the collapse of Enron and WorldCom.

Before the coalition government becomes too enthusiastic in its endorsement of everything that Vickers and the ICB propose it should be careful what it wishes for. The potential of a renewed credit crunch if lending dries up, choking off hopes of renewed economic growth in order that stringent capital requirements are met, coupled with an outflow of capital from the UK if our banking system goes out on a limb, makes for a miserable prospect.

No one should envy George Osborne as he navigates his way through the recommendations of a Report he commissioned himself. The political pressure from the Liberal Democrat wing of the coalition could hardly be more intense. Following Vince Cable's vindication (as he would see it) over Murdoch and the BSkyB bid, the rhetoric, outlook and interests of his Party favour the Vickers recommendations being instituted in full and without delay. The national interest may not be served so easily.

‡

The Vacuum of Vision and Leadership at the Heart of Europe's Economy, 26 September 2011

By September, concern was once again brewing over the state of the eurozone as Greece rapidly ran out of money. George Osborne famously declared that we had only 'six weeks to save the euro' and at the time of writing this article, G20 leaders were locked in urgent talks, hoping to pressure eurozone members into enacting a plan that would ensure the establishment and sufficient funding of a European Financial Stability Facility in time for the G20's next summit in Cannes that November. Global financial markets were in jittery mood and the Chancellor impressed upon the nation that the breakup of the currency union would spell real trouble for the British economy.

Conventional wisdom dictates that we are imminently reaching high noon for the euro. The assumption then is that the single currency will either collapse or the eurozone will be forced to move rapidly towards full fiscal union.

Recent experience suggests the road ahead may not be so straightforward, whatever assurances we hear about sorting things out 'within six weeks'. It is quite feasible that we shall experience many more months of tottering along from market crisis to emergency meeting to fully-fledged conference and half-hearted bailouts to weaker euro economies. Indeed, provided – and it is becoming the overwhelmingly big 'if' in this whole saga – the global bond market remains stable then the cheap price of government debt provides little incentive to create a viable long-term structure for our ailing continent's economies. With the cost of borrowing this cheap why not continue to appease the Greeks, Portuguese et al.? Let's just avoid the day of reckoning with yet another quarterly Elastoplast 'solution'.

Purists may (rightly) bemoan that politics is being allowed to outweigh economic realities … for now. What is so dangerous about the utter lack of leadership or vision amongst Europe's leading politicians is that the longer this crisis continues the more private sector confidence drains away and global markets discount the entire region. More crucial still is the risk that the two distinct problems that face struggling European economies, solvency and liquidity, become conflated. The Greek issue is simply one of solvency – or more accurately insolvency. It must be allowed to default, from within the eurozone. Their creditors (predominantly EU banks) will need to take a substantial haircut. They lent the money at attractive interest rates (implicitly recognising the risks) and must now take the consequences. Although perhaps having hedged their position, the banking fraternity can spread the burden by triggering the exercise of those notorious credit default swaps. The IMF will need to take control of the Greek economy and in all probability we shall need to be on alert if order breaks down as the pain of extreme economic austerity takes effect.

The prospects for other struggling euro economies are not, at the moment, so bleak. However, for so long as the nettle is not grasped by European leaders and finance ministers there is a real risk that the liquidity problems faced by Portugal, Ireland, Spain and Italy, will become more deep seated. Difficult as it is for Angela Merkel in Germany, the EU's economic powerhouse needs to cede control of this deepening crisis to the European Central Bank. The ECB's mandate must now be to provide market intervention to maintain and restore confidence on behalf of all solvent eurozone economies.

However, the twin lessons of the 1930s economic depression are that avoiding catastrophe requires swift action and once a process is underway not to worry unduly about overkill: better to pump too much, rather than inadequate amounts, of liquidity into the system. A financial system in free fall requires active central bank intervention, however irrational the collapse of market confidence. For all their faults Gordon Brown and Alistair Darling understood this three autumns ago.

Before the UK government becomes too enthusiastic in its promotion of a headlong move towards fiscal union in the eurozone, it should perhaps be careful what it wishes for. Such a development (not that it is on the immediate agenda) would embolden the eurozone to embark upon a rapid and radical political power-grab throughout the EU. Alarm bells should be ringing in the City of London, for whom this almost certainly spells bad news.

The complacent view from Whitehall is that any such emergency development in the eurozone borne out of necessity would act to ring-fence its weaknesses. History teaches us that an economic crisis is often regarded as too good an opportunity to waste for ambitious statesmen and bureaucrats who then impose a far-reaching political agenda. Recent talk of a transaction (Tobin) tax to be imposed throughout the EU to help underpin the eurozone's finance will only be the first such salvo.

As we are well aware dark economic clouds now hang over the EU and the eurozone. For those of us whose instincts support the invisible hand of the market, there must also be recognition that financial markets are peculiarly prone to irrational panic. It is for this very reason that we have central banks, whose remit transcends Party politicking. However, the onus must now be with politicians, from whom vision and decisive leadership is so sorely required.

‡

New Labour's Narrative Still Lives On (*Daily Telegraph*), 30 September 2011

Almost eighteen months ago the Labour Party plunged to electoral defeat. At 29.8 per cent its share of the British vote was its second lowest since the war and smaller still than the Conservatives had achieved in our 1997 and 2001 debacles. Normally such a drubbing represents a seismic shift profoundly shaking up the direction of British politics.

Strangely this has not happened. Indeed the new Labour narrative still predominates amongst the media and vast tracts of the UK population. Speak to most people under the age of forty and their world view goes something like this: the 1980s was a decade of industrial strife, privation outside southern England and poorly thought-through service cuts. The 1990s was a period of economic incompetence (Black Wednesday), sleaze, corruption and moral decay. From 1997 the Labour Party rode to the rescue, invested in public services and ran the economy 'for the many, not the few'. By 2010 it was time for a change as the greedy bankers and international corporations (the beneficiaries of the 1980s Thatcher reforms) caused a colossal recession in which those working in and reliant on the public services are innocent victims.

This commonly held analysis emphasises the magnitude of the task ahead for Conservatives in persuading the electorate of the right route out of the national economic crisis. In part this has been self-inflicted. Responding to the previous decade in which political discourse had become a relentless public relations exercise, for much of the last parliament we offered change (only of personnel) alongside continuity in policy ('sticking to Labour's spending plans' and 'sharing the proceeds of growth').

The entire elite political class colluded in a failure during the last election campaign to level with the British public on the tough economic choices that lay ahead. For Labour's part they are now able to sit happily on the side-lines and blame the coalition government for everything they postponed addressing.

However, even now domestic politics continues largely to be defined by New Labour's rhetoric, with any commitment to cutting public spending being sold on the grounds of necessity rather than natural Conservative instincts for a smaller, more efficient state. Too seldom do we hear the moral case that it is wrong for today's generation of Britons to over-consume and rely upon future generations to foot the bill for this profligacy. The government has yet to challenge conclusively the contention that devoting huge swathes of taxpayer cash to tackling 'social inequality' through a lumbering welfare system is more caring than one which believes in empowering the individual. Nor has it sufficiently defended itself against its opponents' class war politics. Instead we acquiesce in higher taxes on the wealthy without making clear the practical reasons why, in an age of global mobility, the brightest and best of our people will simply leave these shores if their plans to create wealth and promote enterprise are stifled.

Near-zero interest rates in the West have enabled Alice in Wonderland economics to persist. For now. Here in the UK we must now swiftly end this state of denial over the true state of our national economy. The most destructive delusion that threatens to undermine future prosperity is the keen sense of collective and individual entitlement which was fostered under the last government. This has resulted in every departmental expenditure cut announced during the past year being portrayed by vocal interest groups as unconscionable, unworkable or immoral. Meanwhile, the politics of envy has returned with a vengeance to domestic political discourse. The urgent task of any government serious about rapid economic recovery is to effect a sea change in these attitudes.

In truth the UK and its citizens have an automatic entitlement neither to relentlessly higher living standards nor an ever generous welfare state. The latter was created as a reward after the huge communal efforts of winning a world war, but must now adapt to the rigours of a highly competitive global economy. Lifestyle improvements must be earned if future generations of Britons are to enjoy the opportunities and possibilities that we have for too long taken for granted.

Nor does this apply solely to the economy. Following this summer's riots, David Cameron returned to one of his earliest (and most authentic and passionate) themes, 'The Broken Society'. However, much of his ambitious programme of welfare and community reform is unachievable without the repeal of the Human Rights Act, one of the most toxic pillars of the Blair/Brown legacy.

Finally, if one believes much of the media coverage, the spirit of this age is uncompromisingly ugly for those of us who instinctively support capitalism, free markets and global trade. There remains an open hostility (all too frequently expressed by coalition representatives) to banks, bankers, big business, the wealthy, private education, private health and the profit motive. Changing this mindset requires clear-sighted political leadership. As a matter of urgency government needs unapologetically to make the case for individual empowerment, promoting responsibility, efficiency and living within our means.

‡

The UK's Contribution to the IMF (*City A.M.*), 9 November 2011

As the eurozone crisis rumbled on, G20 leaders reached an agreement in Cannes to increase the resources of the International Monetary Fund (IMF). The British government indicated that under the deal, the UK might have to contribute up to an additional £40 billion in guarantees although the Prime Minister insisted that the money ought to be available to all countries, not just those in the eurozone, and that the IMF money should not be seen as a substitute for the eurozone dealing with its own problems. A number of MPs demanded that the increased contribution be put to a vote in the House of Commons. I wrote the following article for City A.M. *to explain why I supported the underwriting of additional funds.*

Without stable financial markets there is little hope for the sustained growth so essential for economic recovery.

The UK economy is a global leader in the financial services sector but as a consequence finds itself especially prone to the adverse impact of uncertainty on worldwide financial markets.

No UK taxpayer stands by and watches unimaginably large sums of money or guarantees in order to bailout the banking system with any sense of satisfaction. Indeed our own Prime Minister and Chancellor have repeatedly pledged that there will be 'no further bailouts of the eurozone'.

Regrettably, however, the seventeen-nation eurozone lacks a central bank with the political clout – or, more important still, sufficient funds – to provide comprehensive cover in the event of a liquidity crisis of similar severity to the credit crunch of 2008. This is partly an issue of design when the euro was set up as well as a

reflection of the historical reluctance of Europe's economic powerhouse, Germany, to surrender control of its financial destiny.

The European Central Bank's mandate should now be to provide
market intervention to maintain and restore confidence on behalf
of all solvent eurozone economies. But it is clear that Angela Merkel
in Germany, whose domestic political position appears ever more
precarious, will not cede control of this deepening crisis to the ECB.
Politically this would require – as ever within the EU – bypassing democratic safeguards and potentially involve unfathomably
vast quantities of central bank support with potentially hazardous
medium-term economic consequences.

In short, whilst the ECB and EFSF (the dedicated fund set up to
rescue struggling economies in the eurozone) is sufficiently capitalised to keep smaller eurozone economies such as Greece, Portugal
and Ireland afloat, it is woefully inadequate to provide the same
security in the event of a market run on economies the size of Italy
and Spain.

This is the problem that will imminently confront the eurozone,
the EU and the global economic system. If Italy is close to default
the only institution capable of bailing it out is the IMF.

In the event of such a collapse in market confidence for Italy or
Spain, the UK as a founder member of the IMF will almost certainly
need to increase both its absolute funding and its guarantee facilities
to the fund. This is an extremely unpalatable prospect. Nevertheless
a failure to act by the UK would not only have immediate serious
consequences to the financial services sector globally, but would
amount to abdication of our responsibilities as a mercantile nation
in the international field of trade and commerce.

As MP for the City of London I accept reluctantly, in the absence
of German backing of the ECB, that I have little choice but to
support a proposal by the UK government to underwrite further
funds in this way to the IMF.

Nevertheless I also regard this as a matter that must be addressed
not by the Executive alone but in parliament. If the UK taxpayer is to
be further exposed to IMF loans and guarantees this must only happen

following a Prime Ministerial statement outlining why such a cause of action is in the national interest; after a full parliamentary debate and finally as a consequence of an affirmative vote in parliament.

‡

Why the Battle for St Paul's is a Challenge for Us All, 11 November 2011

On 17 September, Occupy Wall Street, a protest movement which campaigned under the slogan 'We are the 99 per cent' in protest at economic inequality, descended upon New York's Zuccotti Park. Occupy's aims were unclear but the movement was widely perceived as a physical manifestation of the anger many ordinary people felt towards the global financial elite. On 15 October, in solidarity with Occupy Wall Street, Occupy London emerged and, after failing to camp outside the London Stock Exchange, took root outside St Paul's Cathedral in my constituency. Legal attempts to evict the campers were complicated by the reaction of clergy at the Cathedral who were perceived to have welcomed the encampment on its doorstep.

When the Occupy London movement descended on the City of London, it was perhaps naïve not to fear that the 5,000 protestors might leave behind a core of campers. After all, bedding down for one's beliefs is now de rigueur. That the campsite of choice was in the shadow of the iconic and glorious St Paul's Cathedral has caused an almighty headache both for the City Corporation and, particularly, the Church.

Enormously conflicted between its pastoral duties to churchgoers, the protestors themselves and the local City finance community (the source of much of the £40 million recently raised by St Paul's for renovation work), the Cathedral, its Chapter and even the wider Church of England have struggled to unite. Rummaging for the right moral message, St Paul's is acutely aware of the practical need to keep visitors flowing and protect its status as a global treasure.

But, clergymen have asked, does that need trump all else? In other words, should the Chapter's primary duty be to a building and its supporters or the disaffected on its doorstep? Fearing that the debacle was fast descending into a modern-day parallel of Jesus at the temple, the Cathedral has suspended its eviction bid against Camp Occupy.

I have no such internal conflict about the practical aspects of Occupy's protest. To me there is a clear boundary between the right to demonstrate (an essential cornerstone of our democracy), and a semi-permanent protest village which presumes to annex for itself a communal space designed for the enjoyment of all. No doubt the protestors would argue that everyone is welcome in their pungent parish. Nevertheless haven't those who dislike it – local businesses, visitors, residents – the collective right to object?

That is not to dismiss the message behind the encampment, however. For amidst the pandemonium, I have said for some time that the Occupy movement are onto something.

It is not just the usual suspects on the anarchistic left of politics, but increasingly a lot of middle class, Tory-voting people who feel that the rules of capitalism have become skewed against them. Take an email I received after supporting the eviction in a television interview. The correspondent sympathised with the encampment and signed off 'No protestor me, by the way. Small business owner, ten employees, married, two kids. But shafted by the banks just like everyone else'.

The protestors' message taps into a deep sense of unease, impotence and frustration amongst people who, despite having got themselves educated and then worked and saved hard, now view themselves as the losers of the globalised, capitalist system. As a result, as we all face the economic reckoning over the next couple of years, I suspect we shall see more and more of these protests and they will resonate amongst a much wider audience, even if that audience disagrees with the method of expression.

Here lies the political conundrum. We are reaping the rewards of decades' worth of debt accumulation, implicitly supported by a generation that enjoyed an expanded welfare state, cheap goods, never-ending lines of credit and inflated house prices. All this has quietly torn massive rifts – between young and old, debtors and savers, East and West (I have written many times before about these generational and global gulfs). Profiting from and exacerbating those canyons have been fervent financiers whose passion for light-touch government appeared to slip away when the roof caved in.

Now that it is sovereign debt unravelling, politicians have found themselves at a loss. In a more transparent and fast-moving 24/7 media age, they are given neither the space nor time to work through serious solutions, which is why we have seen a sequence of sticking plasters. In addition, the rapid action required to shore up immediate economic problems necessarily lacks democratic legitimacy. No national leader has an explicit mandate for committing such huge sums of money – and, in some cases, transferring national sovereignty – when there is no guarantee of success. But unless they do, economic pain will be meted out ruthlessly on their people. At some point, therefore, the economic reckoning will turn into a political one.

Yet when both elements are brought together, they boil down to an unavoidable truth – that there is no way of painlessly or equitably untangling a culture of debt and credit built up over decades. The friction between the old structure's beneficiaries and its hapless young inheritors is sure to define the West's story for some time.

In the years following 2008's financial crisis, politicians attempted to dodge that reality, freezing imbalances and even running up further debt in a bid to maintain the status quo. The political context of Britain's 2010 general election campaign reflected that – politicians sensed that the electorate craved security, not a dose of reality.

But things are changing. Alongside governments, which are cautiously beginning to unpick entitlements, the Occupy Movement is starting to articulate a discontent that suggests people are slowly grasping the need for change, even if there are divergent opinions on its ideal form. Whilst I think it highly unlikely, therefore, that the encampment in my constituency will achieve anything coherent, history may well view it as part of a momentum that grew and ultimately created the conditions for the economic restructuring. In truth, however, much of this new thinking may well come from the emerging economic power of the East.

‡

Those Deficit Reduction Plans Revisited (*Daily Telegraph*), 28 November 2011

In advance of the Chancellor's Autumn Statement, the Prime Minister warned for the first time that there was a danger they would not be able to tackle borrowing within the timescale the coalition had set itself, admitting that bringing down the debt was 'proving harder than anyone envisaged'. As such, it was widely expected that George Osborne would cut his forecasts for economic growth for the next two financial years. Meanwhile, shares tumbled as fears spread about US government debt levels and the ongoing crisis in the eurozone, the Chinese government warning that global economic conditions remained grim. I wrote the following article for the Daily Telegraph *as a preview to the Autumn Statement.*

It was not supposed to be like this.

Only twelve months ago we were assured that the government's spending plans for the entire parliament had been conclusively settled.

Instead George Osborne will attempt with tomorrow's Autumn Statement to kick-start UK economic growth beyond its recent anaemic levels. Not that the Chancellor will admit his admirable strategy for deficit reduction has already been blown off course. But it has – as confirmed by his Downing Street neighbour last week.

So whilst Plan A notionally stands intact, lest the markets take fright, we are likely to see the Chancellor present an aggressive series of initiatives promoting industrial intervention and enhancing growth on a scale not witnessed since the 1970s.

If there was a problem with the UK government's goal of wiping out the structural deficit in this parliament it was that it relied on some highly optimistic assumptions.

There have been three main planks to the UK government's deficit reduction plan. First, continued low interest rates. This has been the big success story of the past year. Indeed the cost of servicing the UK government's borrowing has been lower than the Chancellor hoped last autumn.

Nevertheless the astonishing low interest rates on UK gilts in the bond market may prove a temporary phenomenon. I suspect that Chinese and Middle Eastern sovereign wealth funds would be investing in corporate growth if they could find such a thing in UK plc. Instead by investing their vast surpluses into government debt, the cost of UK gilts has been depressed since the eurozone travails make us a (relatively) safe haven. For now...

This is good news as the US, UK and German governments service their huge, and growing, borrowings. But is this really sustainable? UK ten-year bonds are currently priced at just above 2 per cent. This is at a time of above 5 per cent inflation – in short the institutions buying our bonds are doing so at negative real interests. Common sense, yet alone economic theory, suggests this is an unsustainable bubble. In the meantime I fear that the UK government and its debt-laden electors are being lulled into a desperately dangerous sense of security.

This comes at some cost, however, for if we persist in keeping interest rates at near zero we simply delay the commencement of the economic reckoning. The sombre truth is that for so long as the Bank of England maintains a virtually zero-interest-rate policy, the economy remains on a taxpayer-induced life support machine. Our underlying economic problems remain unresolved. This is only delaying the point at which sustainable economic recovery can commence.

In truth, the continued failure to raise rates is an implicit recognition by the Bank of the underlying weaknesses of UK plc after four years of patchy or negative growth.

The second element of the UK government deficit reduction

involves its much vaunted austerity programme – reducing public expenditure from its boom-time levels with a relative squeeze in public spending not seen since the 1920s.

The coalition plan to eliminate the structural deficit requires the gap between revenue and expenditure to be narrowed by £159 billion in 2014/15. Tax rises are expected to contribute £31 billion and spending cuts £44 billion to this total. However, the economic costs of unemployment, which has risen more quickly and to markedly higher levels than envisaged at last year's spending review, have already upset this equation. It is clear that the assumption that UK unemployment would peak in 2010/11 has already been surpassed by events.

In view of the increasing public disquiet about perceived 'savage cuts in public spending' the government risks the worst of all worlds – receiving relentless criticism for harsh austerity measures, and at the same time failing to follow through with the political will to execute the necessary level of savings. The facts are stark. Over the past twelve months UK government current spending has totalled £613.5 billion – the highest figure in history. Borrowing this year is likely to be around £125 billion – the coalition's 'austerity plan' means we are all now borrowing £1 in every £5 we spend collectively rather than £1 in every £4 that UK taxpayers borrowed in 2009. In truth we are digging that cumulative debt hole just a little less slowly than before.

Moreover, one of the biggest challenges that the coalition government faces in getting growth on track is that over the past decade and a half roughly three-fifths of domestic expansion in the economy has arisen courtesy of either financial services, the public sector or in the property/construction field. These are three activities in which the present squeeze will be most profound (notwithstanding the recent announcement to provide an adrenalin rush to the first-time buyer housing market), especially as these areas have been largely funded by borrowing. Yet if we discount these key drivers of the last boom it is difficult to predict the type of economic activity in which the necessary super-charged levels of growth can be achieved in future.

The anxiety now for the Treasury is that plummeting levels of business confidence accompanied by the ongoing stagnation and drift in the eurozone will awaken the markets to some harsh realities.

It will prove mighty difficult to sustain our 'safe haven' status if spending and the overall public debt continue rising inexorably. Only the restoration of the UK's reputation as an outward-looking trading nation, unashamedly 'open for business' can save Plan A now.

‡

It's Not All Doom and Gloom, 2 December 2011

Recently at lunch in my constituency, I found myself seated next to a native partner from one of the two Chinese law firms now operating in London. During our conversation I made some passing reference to the 'global economic downturn'. This was greeted with a wry smile. 'Back home', he said, 'we call it the North Atlantic recession.'

What we so easily forget amidst the West's doom and gloom – where the euro teeters, the United States drifts and the OBR's predictions of sub-optimal UK growth are widely considered optimistic – is that across much of Asia, Australasia, South America and Africa, economies are growing at a steady pace.

Thank goodness. For where there is growth, there is opportunity.

Unlike the 1930s when the global economy was shrinking, here in 2011 economic growth worldwide is likely to exceed 4 per cent. Yet aside from a few vague nods to the desire to increase our exports, we still lack any overall strategic vision and message about the UK's role in the new world that unfolds before us now with frightening rapidity.

I appreciate that in the face of colossal economic difficulties, it sounds almost naïve to talk with wide-eyed optimism. But all too often the political class seems to be in the business of managing decline rather than looking through the darkness at what Britain has the potential to become.

The OBR's figures suggest that some elements of our economy have contracted permanently. Over the past decade and a half, roughly three-fifths of domestic expansion in the economy has arisen courtesy of either financial services, the public sector or in the property/construction field.

Discounting these key drivers of the last boom, it is understandably difficult to predict with any confidence the precise type of economic activity in which the necessary super-charged levels of growth can be achieved in future. Lip service is paid to boosting traditional manufacturing, where we face enormously fierce competition. But what is our strategy when it comes to an area in which we continue to maintain a distinct reputation and competitive advantage – the export of intellectual property?

Let me take a seemingly small example. Both the last government and the coalition have pinpointed the creative industries as a sector that offers the prospect of future growth. Yet for the two years that I have been trying, as Patron of Animation UK, to negotiate a tax credit for the animation industry, I have come up against a brick wall. The televised animation sector may appear only a small slice of the national economic cake but almost every other nation with an animation industry deem the rewards of government subsidy well worth the initial outlay. As such, British animators are losing work from these shores at an alarming rate because they cannot compete with the lure of government-backed incentives which make it so much easier to put together the necessary funding packages for programme-making elsewhere.

Over the past two years the Treasury has been intransigent, seeing only the upfront cost rather than the longer term, revenue-positive outlook. Most critically of all, it ignores the key reason why, as a believer in free and open markets, I am supportive of a targeted tax credit. Naturally it would be good if a tax credit helped keep animation jobs on these shores but the real golden egg is the retention in this country of intellectual property rights. The money generated annually worldwide from unimaginably successful franchises such as Thomas the Tank Engine, Wallace & Gromit and Peppa Pig

– especially when it comes to secondary branded products – massively exceeds the money brought in by, for example, films like *The King's Speech*, which was helped along by the film tax credit. To give some perspective, Thomas the 'Bank' Engine tots up worldwide sales in excess of £1 billion every year, with his tales broadcast to more than a billion households in 185 countries each and every week. *The King's Speech*, hailed as the most successful independent British film *ever*, grossed just shy of £374 million.

Instead of tinkering with little pots of money here and there temporarily to boost shrinking sectors, it is time we started thinking strategically about how we can promote, not only via the tax system, the sectors of our economy that actually have potential future growth. The market for much of our creative industry output are those territories which are growing fast – well outside the area of our North Atlantic downturn.

Oh, and one last thing – if we are properly to exploit those Chinese, Indian and South American connections, we urgently need to commit ourselves to one more piece of infrastructure improvement. A new, Estuary airport for London fit for the twenty-first century is something that has had its supporters even before Boris became Mayor!

‡

We May Be No Nearer to Solving This Economic Crisis, 7 December 2011

As the year drew to a close, European Union leaders prepared for yet another key summit in Brussels to save the euro, billed as a 'do or die' moment for the seventeen eurozone nations.

So here we go again!

Yet another 'last chance saloon' eurozone crisis conference. Maybe, just maybe, this Friday's summit will be the game changer that financial markets so earnestly desire.

In truth, I am still not convinced, in spite of coverage to the contrary, that Angela Merkel has the domestic political capital to drive forward fiscal union. Her electors may warm to the imposition of Germanic economic discipline on southern Europe, but the inflationary consequences of ECB money-printing provide a profound psychological road block. I also suspect her view of 'fiscal union' may be markedly different to that of Nicolas Sarkozy.

A brake on this headlong rush towards fiscal eurozone union, however, may not be such a bad thing for the UK's national interest. It also stands to make life easier for the coalition government, which is already trying to finesse demands for holding a referendum insofar as these eurozone developments necessitate the drawing up of a new EU treaty. A fiscal union amongst the seventeen eurozone nations, even if created at a time of crisis, would almost certainly impose radical economic reform throughout the EU. The skirmishes between the UK and the Franco-German axis over the proposed financial transaction tax would be merely the foretaste to a long battle over London's pre-eminence in European financial markets.

Moreover, the bypassing of national democratic safeguards implicit in making the eurozone a single economic unit would surely act as the genesis of severe future strains on the whole structure. Indeed the clear democratic deficit with what is being proposed as the quick-fire solution to the EU's economic travails unarguably represents the seeds of its future destruction.

More pertinent for the UK in the near term would be the prospect of a superficially more stable eurozone becoming an apparently safer haven for investors. This would almost certainly lead to a consequent and substantial rise in the cost of UK government borrowing on our ever increasing public debt as this decade proceeds.

The stark fact is that the UK's craving for stability in the eurozone is probably better served by an orderly and relatively rapid realignment of the eurozone. Naturally neither of these essential conditions can be easily achieved. However, the departure of Greece and Portugal – to name two – from the eurozone (presumably accompanied by an ongoing commitment to support the sale of their gilts for a future period) would send us into unchartered territory in the immediate term. The optimistic scenario is that the eurozone as a whole would then become more stable, whilst the economies of the departing nations would, courtesy of a massive devaluation, be allowed to become competitive once again. Elusive economic growth returns quickly throughout the EU.

Adopting this path would certainly not come without risk; nevertheless I suspect that opponents of a break-up are considerably exaggerating the Armageddon scenario that might follow from a relatively orderly fracturing of the seventeen-strong eurozone.

Sadly the frenzied continental summitry this week is unlikely seriously to turn its mind to options other than fiscal union (whatever that term may mean). It is not the first time we on this side of the Channel should be uneasy that the activities of core eurozone members are so manifestly at odds with the British national interest.

2012

Fred Goodwin Commentary (*Daily Telegraph*), 22 January 2012

As 2012 dawned, a campaign gathered pace to strip failed RBS boss, Sir Fred Goodwin, of his knighthood. The Prime Minister confirmed that the knighthood would be referred to the little-known honours forfeiture committee which would take into account a recent report by the Financial Services Authority into the collapse of RBS and the failings of its management. I was asked to comment on the story by the Daily Telegraph.

Does it really matter if Sir Fred becomes plain Mr Goodwin again? Watching senior political leaders over the past week falling over themselves in casting to the winds the fate of the disgraced former Royal Bank of Scotland Chief Executive you could be excused for thinking that no issue in public life was more critical.

Don't be fooled by the grandstanding. Messrs Cameron, Clegg and Miliband know in their hearts that the dispute over the award of a knighthood to an erstwhile Master of the Financial Services Universe is little more than a sideshow.

After all, if they truly cared about the sanctity of the honours system they would have long since found a way of booting out convicted expense fiddlers from the House of Lords.

I should declare that I hold no brief for Sir Fred Goodwin. I have never met the man, but everyone I know who has speaks of an arrogant, dismissive individual whose comeuppance seemed long overdue. That said I do not like the way he is being made a convenient scapegoat: it seems all too easy to kick a man when he is down.

A better plan, as they insist in all the best thriller movies, is to follow the money.

In 2004 when Fred Goodwin was awarded his knighthood there was not even the faintest murmur of disapproval. No one realised then that in common with many other financial services institutions, RBS's breath-taking success had been built on foundations of sand.

By contrast, in February 2009 as Sir Fred's retiring pension package was being finalised by the last government, we were all well aware of the illusory nature of his, and his bank's achievements. In the very week that the Brown government brought the taxpayers' investment in RBS to £45.5 billion (the value of our collective holding has since fallen to around one-third of that sum) Sir Fred was an awarded an eye-watering £693,000 annual pension for the rest of his life.

Twice over the last three years 83 per cent state-owned RBS has reduced this colossal reward for failure, yet Sir Fred still receives an annual RBS pension of £370,000, some fifteen times the average national salary.

I suspect the British public will (and should) be far more infuriated that Sir Fred takes home a huge pension for the rest of his life than whether he enjoys the bauble of a knighthood.

No one should forget that Sir Fred's stewardship of RBS was a monumental failure – catastrophically the worst collapse in this country's corporate history. Had the government not intervened to save his bust bank, Sir Fred – not to mention all the other RBS pensioners – would have had to rely upon some sort of pension protection fund. This would have capped his pension award at around £20,000 per year.

As the economic crisis rumbles on, I reckon we have all become almost immune to shock when we hear of financial losses running into billions of pounds. So it is understandable that public anger today rests on something easier to comprehend. We can all make a direct connection between the hard-earned cash we pay in tax and its destination. When we are directly subsidising Sir Fred's ludicrously lucrative pension deal or as bonus season in the City gets underway, minds naturally turn to the disparity of treatment between top bankers and ordinary workers; our own financial circumstances and the rewards for failure in the FTSE 250 boardroom. This is why the Goodwin saga is so dangerous to capitalism.

As a former small businessman I unequivocally support the promotion of free markets, enterprise and capitalism. I believe in honouring contracts and recognise the key importance of these concepts in the UK's global trading relations. Incentives should rightly be offered for good performance. Businessmen who risk their own wealth deserve to keep the fruits of their success.

Over the past three months the Occupy London movement has made its home the steps of St Paul's Cathedral, in my constituency. I have been struck by the support the protestors have received well beyond the usual suspects on the anarchistic left of politics. Increasingly many middle-class, Tory-voting people have come to the conclusion that the operation of capitalism today has become hopelessly skewed against them. Witnessing unwarranted financial wealth being showered on the Sir Fred Goodwin's of this world taps into a deep unease, impotence and frustration amongst many Britons who despite working and saving hard over the years now view themselves as losers in the globalised, capitalist system.

In short, it is Sir Fred's pension, not his knighthood, that helps undermine capitalism and all that it does to create wealth. For the truth is that we now know that the profits, bonuses and other emoluments for many working in our largest companies and banks have been massively overstated. Where possible shareholders must insist that we restate those earnings to reflect reality and to commence an equitable claw-back of those unwarranted rewards.

This week Vince Cable enters the fray with specific proposals for controlling excessive pay. Unless and until the coalition provides, strong, practical support to those disillusioned by the inequitable rewards for failure, its attacks on crony capitalism and corporate greed will be just warm words.

‡

Executive Pay – Why Capitalism Needs Saving From Itself, 24 January 2012

On 23 January, Business Secretary, Vince Cable, unveiled plans to curb executive pay following concerns about a growing disconnect between remuneration and performance at the UK's top companies. Whilst emphasising that it was not the government's role to micromanage company pay, he announced that the coalition would be taking steps to address 'market failure' by increasing transparency and bolstering the power of shareholders.

Like most Conservative MPs, only a few years ago I cannot imagine that I would have been open minded to the notion of government interference in the remuneration of privately owned companies. However, Vince Cable announced to parliament yesterday after-noon that the coalition government will rapidly move towards legis-lating to give shareholders control over the 'excesses of capitalism' and clamp down on the 'rewards for failure'.

Perhaps more than any other, my own constituency, the Cities of London and Westminster, benefited from the boom. Yet I had noticed long before the crisis a growing sense of despair and resent-ment amongst hard-working Londoners. To their surprise, many highly educated professionals working outside the gilded corridors of financial services had started to feel they were losing out, the growth of the City having merely increased the cost of living and reduced to a wistful dream any prospect of getting on the housing ladder. Having then to bail out the financial services sector, which had previously been so keen to keep regulation and government interference to a minimum, was met with disgust by this cohort. It has been a feeling replicated across many Western societies where stagnant incomes have been disguised by an expansion of debt.

What has emerged in the years since is a middle-class revolt over

the unequal rewards to labour and talent that has most recently
coalesced around the issue of pay and bonuses.

The challenge for those whose instincts are for free markets,
enterprise and unequivocal support for capitalism, is whether we
should side with the rich or sympathise with 'our people', the strivers who seem so shut out from the colossal rewards given to the
financial and business elite. For the gap no longer seems between
the richest and the poorest but between the rich and everyone else.

I suspect many Conservatives feel similarly conflicted. Our
political principles make us instinctively suspicious of the interfering hand of government. Yet it sits uneasily that a certain portion
of the population is being remunerated at a level that seemingly
distorts the links between talent, hard work and reward. Normally
this can be reconciled by the fact that to be a top dog is to take on
an extra level of responsibility and, most crucially, *risk*. However
time and again in recent years, we have seen a lack of accountability
through the awarding of financial riches *regardless* of performance,
and frequently for failure or engaging in immoral practices. This has
utterly undermined trust in the system, the ingredient most crucial
to the proper lubrication of our economy. In addition, the rewards
in particular sectors have often been so great as to suck talent from
other productive areas of the economy.

Looking at pay is therefore not about satiating the envy of the left
but a question of whether the remuneration of the richest is starting
to undermine capitalism. Indeed it is a primary reason why capitalism itself has been the big theme so far of 2012. It is a debate that we
are quite rightly embracing as Conservatives and one which, I must
confess, I would not have *dreamed* of touching until the financial
crisis came to light. Nevertheless if we are to have this debate, it
is equally vital that it is framed correctly. That means destroying
some of the popular myths being mooted, such as the crossover
between remuneration committees on FTSE 250 Boards creating a
'you scratch my back' culture or pay rises in a particular year being
linked to share increases for that same year when they are, in fact,
backward looking.

In entering the fray with specific proposals on controlling executive pay, I was a little depressed that Vince Cable's focus was on headline figures for the highest paid, rather than in devising a scheme to ensure failure bears a cost – tackling handsome dismissal packages for ineffective executives, commencing equitable claw-back schemes for unwarranted rewards (Sir Fred Goodwin's pension springs to mind) and making shareholders – particularly large, institutional shareholders who must be more than just absentee landlords – more effective in insisting that earnings reflect reality. Above all, whatever he eventually proposes must be practical, effective and workable.

More important still, it must not detract from the overriding message that the UK is a place that is unashamedly open for businesses and is keen to promote inward investment from the developing world, much of which will regard regulatory tinkering of this sort with suspicion.

No government's role in all of this should be to cap or decrease salaries in general. The success or failure of this policy must *not* be measured by how much FTSE chiefs are taking home year on year. Rather its primary aim must be to restore a sense of integrity and justice to the system so that Britons can once again have faith that talent, hard work and innovation are the fastest routes to prosperity.

‡

Stephen Hester – An Alternative View, 30 January 2012

Awarded a bonus of nearly £1 million as Chief Executive of RBS, Stephen Hester came under intense political pressure to turn the money down after public outcry that the head of a majority-state-owned bank should be so generously rewarded. On 30 January, Hester announced that he would renounce the shares-only payment, RBS Chairman, Sir Philip Hampton, having already waived his own pay-out.

As MP for the City, I have never slavishly defended the level of rewards in financial services which are often disproportionate and, in the current climate of austerity, seem to many as ludicrously out of balance. Nevertheless, the unedifying spectacle of politicians jumping on the banker-bashing bandwagon this weekend, suggests that most cannot resist pandering to the very worst instincts when it comes to debating the bonus awarded to Stephen Hester of RBS.

For sure, such opportunistic grandstanding may reflect the current mood of the general public (at least insofar as collective opinion can be gauged) but I firmly believe the role of politicians must be to lead public opinion rather than to play to the lynch mob mentality that has been whipped up by the media.

Stephen Hester was brought in as a trouble shooter to run RBS after it crashed. Given the mess left behind by Sir Fred Goodwin, and his handsome rewards for failure, it was understandable that Mr Hester might expect a remuneration package that would reflect the mighty challenge of dealing with an organisation that had previously posted Britain's largest ever corporate loss. As a result, the overall financial package was geared to attract someone of his calibre – indeed he had previously been Chief Executive of British Land on a financial package that dwarfed the sums currently the subject of such fierce controversy.

In total, £45 billion of taxpayers' money was sunk into RBS at the time of its rescue in autumn 2008. The share value of the bank is now worth around one third of that sum. We need to protect our investment with the best talent to ensure that RBS is put on a sustainable path towards privatisation.

It is often asserted that because the taxpayers own 83 per cent of RBS that it is effectively in the public sector. Nothing could be further from the truth – the government's share in this bank is held on trust and we have aspired, until now at least, to give RBS the freedom to operate in the highly competitive global banking sector.

Whilst it is true that the share price has fallen by 35 per cent over the past twelve months, this reflects general sentiment towards banking shares as well as the painful process of restructuring that Stephen Hester has led. Whilst this has resulted in significant redundancies, it has also been designed to make RBS far less risky (and as a result less potentially profitable) and put it firmly on the road to recovery.

Whilst I suspect no UK government will be able fully to divest itself of our stake in RBS for at least another decade, it is only through such restructuring that we might not only recover our investment but possibly even enhance its value over the coming years. The lynch mob vilification of Stephen Hester (which has included details of his private life being plastered all over the newspapers in recent days) will only help dissuade potentially talented people from taking on this key task in the years ahead. Indeed I should be surprised if Mr Hester subjects himself to another year of the unwarranted and unpleasant scrutiny that he has had to put up with in recent days.

In short, we have a stark choice here. Either the government leads the way in making the case for protecting our £45 billion investment in this bank, which we so sorely hope to get back in due course. Or alternatively the only other logical option is that we write-off the entire sum pumped into RBS and from now on run it as a public utility headed by a civil servant on an established grade salary. It seems to me that those who have jumped on the bandwagon in recent days may yet win a pyrrhic victory if we are forced down this latter path.

‡

The Real Crisis Today is of Welfarism, not Capitalism (*Daily Telegraph*), 22 February 2012

Forget the breathless pronouncements from Davos. Forget the domestic political posturing of Party leaders desperately trying to convince voters there is much of substance to choose between their economic outlooks. Forget even the furore over the pay, bonus and rank handed out to RBS Chief Executives past and present.

Free enterprise and the market remain the only games in town. As the financial crash of 2008 plays itself out (and it has barely begun to do so) the systemic, existential crisis will *not* be of capitalism. Out of sheer financial necessity the real calamity to which the minds of the political class will soon be forced to turn is the unaffordability of our ever-growing welfare state.

For all the talk of unprecedented austerity and savage public sector cuts the government is still borrowing £1 in every £5 we collectively spend. This current generation of Britons continues to consume recklessly beyond its means. Those of our children and grandchildren who decide not to leave these shores will in due course foot the bill for our profligacy. Three years and counting of near-zero interest rates has helped prolong the era of cheap money, higher borrowing and larger debts in the hope that 'something will turn up'.

In fairness someone, in the form of Work and Pensions Secretary, Iain Duncan-Smith, has turned up. All his instincts are sound. His Universal Credit plan will begin the long path of weaning Britons off their sense of welfare entitlement. He dares to tread where so many of his predecessors have failed in tackling the welfare trap for those in the workplace, who otherwise stand to be better off claiming benefits. But none of this radical restructuring comes cheap. Indeed the annual Work and Pensions departmental budget is likely to crash through the £200 billion mark for the first time in 2012/13 (remember this £600 million daily welfare bill does not include the cost of health care).

One is reminded of probably the most notorious telegram ever from Monte Carlo – 'Cracked the system. Please send more money.'

Prospective reformers' biggest headache is that this addiction to the welfare state extends well beyond the workshy and benefits scroungers of tabloid lore.

This week's headlines may focus on the morality of setting a strict overall annual benefits cap at £26,000, the level of average national earnings. However, there will soon be renewed debate on the rumbling furore over Treasury proposals to deprive child benefit from households with a higher-rate taxpayer.

Paradoxically the government may discover that it is only by depriving middle-class voters in the upper quantile of earnings of their current welfare entitlements that sufficient momentum can be raised to reform radically the entire system.

Created as a reward for the collective national effort in winning the Second World War, the original purpose of our welfare state has been subverted as the UK has become ever richer. Nowadays even well-off Britons regard as an absolute entitlement nursery vouchers for children; living allowance for any disabled relatives; health visitors and carers for the sick, not to mention the benefit gratis of the services of a vast array of local government employees. Meanwhile even the very richest are entitled as a matter of course to free bus travel, substantial rail discounts, winter fuel allowance and free TV licences merely by reaching a certain age.

When it comes to being compromised by the welfare state we are, to coin a phrase, all in this together.

One classic example of an apparently worthy, yet muddled and ruinously costly expansion of the empire of the welfare state came in the early Blair years with Sure Start, an initiative designed to aid pre-school children in deprived areas. My own inner city constituency contains mixed neighbourhoods – as a result 'South Westminster' was designated as a Sure Start pilot area. Disused office space was converted into a state-of-the-art nursery; a children's health-care centre was set up; two sparkling new adventure playgrounds were created on open space. What was unanticipated, however, was that the overwhelming clientele for these services were middle-class Pimlico mums and their offspring's nannies. Years later they became a highly articulate lobby group, as large-scale recipients of (by now) essential welfare provision campaigning against the withdrawal of Sure Start funding.

Naturally, rather than making a blatantly self-interested appeal the prosperous will always seek to justify hanging on to their accustomed benefits on the grounds that such services are an integral part of living in a civilised society.

The recent Dilnot Report on the cost of long-term care for the elderly exposed the confusion lying at the heart of too much policy thinking in this area. Any lifetime ceiling on the financial burden to be borne by the individual (rather than the State) will within a decade be regarded as inadequate such is the rapid pace of life expectancy. The harsh truth is that before long the only way you can be sure to hang on to your anticipated inheritance is to take full responsibility for an ageing relative, in deteriorating physical and mental health. Whatever price-tag the government today wishes to place on these average lifelong costs – £35,000 and £60,000 are the figures doing the rounds – will simply be unaffordable within a very short period.

Long before the financial crisis, welfare reform was no mere academic debate. The expansion of the European welfare model has for years served to make our continent less and less economically competitive. Yet the solution is one we cannot face – to start with a blank sheet and ask ourselves what we *need* instead of salami slicing against what we *want*.

As power shifts eastwards, the Asian economic powerhouses will not be immune from their own demographic problems. Unlike the UK, however, they have an enormous advantage – that blank sheet, the luxury to think afresh and construct a welfare state fit for the twenty-first century without the need to battle against a morass of vested interest. Meanwhile, we cling to an unreformed set of entitlements that has grown like topsy from the late 1940s, when life expectancy on retirement was under three years. It serves to convince me ever more that for so long as we keep clinging, the gulf with our Eastern counterparts will only deepen.

‡

The New Thinking is Coming from the East, 25 February 2012

As we have all learned from the graveyard of failed forecasts, economics is an unerringly inaccurate as well as a dismal science, inextricably bound to the whims of irrational human behaviour. All too frequently it follows that economies develop haphazardly and tend to reflect a nation's collective ability (or otherwise) to innovate and provide conditions in which the experience and aspiration of its people can flourish.

One of capitalism's enormous strengths is its accommodation of human nature by the creation of broadly stable environments that liberate and incentivise people to pursue new ideas whilst casting aside defunct thinking.

Yet those encamped outside St Paul's Cathedral in my constituency argue that capitalism is now itself a defunct idea, fundamentally discredited by the global financial crisis. It is a view that is beginning to have greater traction amongst a wider group of middle-class, thoughtful, responsible Britons, uncomfortable with and anxious about recent economic developments.

My counterclaim to them is that capitalism continues to offer us the best system of delivering prosperity and liberty to the greatest number of people – but it was never meant to be a static framework. Capitalism works because it adapts and adjusts through crisis. The real problem is that we in the West are now subverting its natural processes of correction by clinging to outdated, discredited ideas and institutions.

The US is stuck in political deadlock, seemingly too caught up in partisan wrangling over its budget deficit to provide the global leadership we have expected from it over the past century. Europe has proved incapable of finding a credible solution to its own single currency crisis. Historically low interest rates in the UK reflect an economy still firmly on a life support machine. Across the Western world, continued political compromise and a desperate hope that 'something will turn up' are favoured over taking the immediate term pain of radical restructuring. As a result, the challenges we face appear simply too great to articulate for contemporary politicians at the mercy of short electoral cycles and restricted by conventional thinking.

I suspect this state of affairs will continue for so long as the main beneficiaries of the status quo remain more powerful than its losers. But whilst we appear to have avoided financial disaster turning into economic catastrophe, there will be also long-term costs to be borne largely by future generations.

Firstly, 'Who are you to lecture us?' is a sentiment on the rise, the West's financial woes having led to a comparative loss of global credibility. Undoubtedly developed nations will find it increasingly difficult to maintain their role as directors of the world economy, as the composition and governance of international institutions no longer reflect reality. The G20, the 'permanent five' of the UN Security Council and the IMF may soon seem quaintly dated.

But my greatest concern is this: that the West will no longer seem the place where the world's brightest and best see their future. When societies cling to conventional ideas which disproportionately benefit established generations, inevitably the number of losers begins to increase over time. The largest contingent of these must surely be amongst our young. As we are already witnessing across the European continent, youth unemployment is regarded as a price worth paying if it avoids unstitching the patchwork of entitlements and way of life that the post-war generations of citizens have taken for granted. As power shifts eastwards, the Asian economic power-houses will not be immune from their own demographic problems. Nevertheless, unlike the West, they have an enormous advantage in being able to construct from scratch a welfare state fit for the twenty-first century without the need to battle against a morass of vested interest.

Eighteen months ago, in his book, *Capitalism 4.0*, *Times* journalist Anatole Kaletsky argued that we are witnessing the fourth trans-formation of the global capitalist system. After liberal free trade capitalism in the early nineteenth century, the Keynesian welfare state of the 1930s and beyond and the free market monetarism of the Thatcher and Reagan era, we are likely now to see a change in the relationship between markets and governments.

Writing since about his promotion of the book, he has noted that it is in Asia that it has captured the most imaginations. It has become a surprise best seller in South Korea, where the implications of *Capitalism 4.0* have become a subject of national debate and

Kaletsky's transformative message has been most enthusiastically embraced in Singapore, China and Hong Kong.

As I suggested in a recent ConservativeHome article, many Asians have perceived since 2008 not a global financial crisis but a 'North Atlantic recession'. Yet Kaletsky's experience suggests that it may not just be in hard economics that Asia is overtaking the Western world, but less expectedly in new ideas too. He observes:

> the crisis blew away, at least in Asian thinking, the simplistic belief that the market automatically produces the best possible outcomes and that societies must always accept whatever social consequences market forces dictate. [As a result] they can engage in a potentially inspiring debate about the role of politics, as well as of markets, in creating a fairer, more stable and sustainable capitalism.

If it comes to pass that Asia flourishes most economically *and* becomes the region that most welcomes fresh thinking, the contrast will be stark with a Western world that complacently harks back to historical dominance and fudges the important economic and political choices we now face.

Naturally the magnitude of the West's difficulties is intimidating, and it would be naïve for me to imply we face easy answers. After all, a crucial part of our future involves unravelling the past. Nevertheless, for a capitalist system to be successful and enjoy popular electoral support, it must ensure that it creates societies which liberate and incentivise people to pursue new ideas and cast aside defunct ones, not where the group of disaffected losers expands.

As such, it strikes me as essential that alongside the tackling of our structural problems, we begin to articulate and embrace a fresh and positive vision of the future. This will involve a painful acceptance of marked, rapid decline in relative Western influence. However, unless we face up to the challenge, we risk undermining the very compact upon which our capitalist economies are based.

‡

Taxing Times for True Tories, 4 March 2012

As the 2012 Budget beckoned, tensions between coalition partners began to emerge, with the Liberal Democrats proposing £16 billion in tax rises for the rich including a mansion tax and the maintenance of the 50p top rate of income tax.

Conservatives instinctively believe in lower taxes. We believe that individuals are better able to judge where their money should be spent than the State. We support choice and economic freedom.

It came as something of a disappointment, therefore, last week to read virtually daily pre-Budget stories concerning proposals to *raise* taxes. Indeed this has been made worse still by recent careful coalition choreography from Downing Street allowing the Liberal Democrats to showcase themselves as promoters of tax cuts for the less well-off.

As it happens, I am not convinced that a programme of personal tax cuts at the forthcoming Budget would produce the boost to demand and growth the UK economy do desperately needs. More likely any reductions in income tax would simply be saved, necessitating further borrowing for so long as the coalition remains unable to execute significant reductions in public expenditure (despite the incessant austerity rhetoric).

First came the decision by the Treasury to rush through retrospective legislation (invariably an unwise move) to capture tax from Barclays Bank, which had designed a scheme to reduce its tax liabilities by £500 million per year. These days, global banks have little vocal political capital to call upon; nevertheless I was disquieted by the Treasury's precipitate actions. True, all large banks had agreed a detailed memorandum with the Treasury after the financial crisis began to avoid 'unfair tax practices'. However, the scheme in question had been expressly approved in upfront discussions with HMRC. This sets a worrying precedent that will cause concern to corporations as well as banks about the previously rock solid, commercially certain reputation that the UK has diligently built up over centuries of international trade and commerce. Our nation has every reason to be proud of its central role as a bastion of commercial robustness – standing in stark contrast to the arbitrary legal decision-making of many other jurisdictions.

If the Budget is to introduce a general power of anti-avoidance in tax affairs (which I regard as undesirable and probably unworkable) it must do so together with a commitment to pre-clearance. In short it must enable individuals and companies to agree in advance with the tax authorities whether its proposed scheme falls foul of an all-embracing anti-avoidance measure. Anything less will drive business away from these shores.

The other big tax story of the week surrounds the desire – initially led by our coalition partners – to impose higher property levies. In principle there is something in this – in a globally mobile world it will become increasingly difficult to raise tax income and sales, so fixed assets such as real estate are likely to attract higher levels of tax. Indeed I strongly approve of George Osborne's plans to close loopholes that allow very wealthy foreigners from buying property free of stamp duty – although again I suspect it may prove easier said than done and will probably raise rather less in revenue than is hoped.

Where I part company with some in the coalition is over proposals for a mansion tax or increasing the number of council tax bands beyond its current total of eight. At various times Business Secretary Vince Cable has promoted an annual 'mansion' tax to apply for all properties valued at over £1 million, £1.5 million and now £2 million. Amongst other difficulties that such a policy contains is the fact that many of those who live in properties of such value (a considerable proportion of whom are my constituents) are asset rich but income poor. Indeed for many their main – or only – asset is the property in which they live. An annual charge of 1 per cent (i.e. minimum of £20,000) would be ruinously expensive for many of these so-called 'super-rich'.

Likewise the imposition of further council tax bands would run counter to the very idea of the council tax, a part personal and part property charge. It would also largely fall upon people in London and the south-east, who already make a disproportionate contribution to the national tax take whilst living in cramped conditions, incurring expensive commuting costs and generally a lesser quality of life than those living in other regions of the UK. As David Cameron has often said, we need to look to General Well Being rather than simply financial assets.

Central Londoners already more than pay their way supporting other parts of the UK – I reckon it would be inequitable for us to face higher council tax bills targeted directly at those needing to live and work in the capital and its surrounding area.

‡

Greek and Eurozone Salvation is No Nearer Whatever the Bailout Merchants May Say, 9 March 2012

On 21 February, after more tense negotiations between eurozone finance ministers, the terms were finally agreed on a second rescue package for Greece worth €130 billion. Under the agreement, aimed at averting a Greek default in March, Greek private creditors were to accept deeper losses on their Greek debts and it was agreed that further austerity measures would be imposed by Lucas Papademos' coalition government.

There is not much that unites eurozone politicians and the financial markets. But it is undeniably the case that neither trusts the Greek government or its people to stick to their latest bailout deal.

This matters because the real impact of the ongoing eurozone saga is that the opportunity to erect a firewall around the Greek economy is fast fading. Contagion, which by rights should be a pure matter of economics, has now become a product of political interference.

When – and it really is no longer 'if' – Greece eventually defaults on its debts and leaves the euro the real risk is that by then (probably early in 2013) the outlook in Portugal, Ireland, Spain and Italy will have so deteriorated that the markets will turn on these nations, rather than regarding Greece as exceptional.

For several years after joining the euro, the Greek people were to a large extent masters of their own destiny, and this should temper instinctive, natural sympathy for their current plight. However, the stifling austerity now being imposed upon Greece calls to mind the impossible demands made at the Treaty of Versailles of the defeated Germans over reparations following the First World War. What is being proposed for the Greeks today will also assuredly end in tears. Worse still, the resentment as this latest eurozone 'rescue' precipitates a worsening Greek recession, threatens the doing of untold damage to multilateral continental relations.

The most surprising thing to most eurozone watchers has been the vehemence with which German Chancellor Angela Merkel and her finance minister, Wolfgang Schäuble, have recently addressed Greek politicians. Ever since the creation of the Federal Republic it has been an article of faith that German governments would present themselves as 'good Europeans', promoting the EU ideal often at great (financial) cost to itself. It would have been unimaginable that Adenauer, Brandt, Schmidt or even Helmut Kohl would have thrown away patient decades of diplomacy towards European neighbours, especially those with which Germany had been at war in the first half of the twentieth century.

Angela Merkel spent the first quarter-century of her life living under communist rule; what is perhaps less well understood here in the UK is that her politics are far more free-market, low-tax orientated than the typical corporatist outlook of the German centre-right. We should not underestimate the resentment that this hard line will have in Greece for now, but also potentially in other parts of the eurozone if, as I fear, the prolonged crisis cannot be quarantined. Indeed one of the biggest future risks is that any sign of short-term Greek recovery will in all likelihood embolden Portugal, Ireland and Spain (for starters) to attempt to cut their own more favourable bailout deal rather than faithfully repay their debts.

It is worth spelling out just how unfeasibly tough are the terms of this latest Greek deal. Public debt will be capped at 120 per cent of GDP in 2020 after a further eight years of austere recession (the Greek economy has already been in free fall for five years). However, as all previous EU imposed plans have failed in recent years we should not hold our breath. Under the terms of the June 2010 'definitive' bailout deal the Greek economy had been anticipated to contract in 2011 by 3 per cent. In the event it shrank at double that rate with unemployment now at a ruinous 20.9 per cent. Meanwhile, manufacturing output has collapsed by 15 per cent over the past year alone. VAT receipts are down by a fifth as a result of 60,000 small businesses going to the wall in Greece since last summer. To make things worse (as they assuredly will) the latest plan involves cutting back 150,000 public sector jobs by 2015 – no risk of the famed automatic stabilisers applying here.

Even though there has been agreement, for now, in Greece, to delay elections, it is difficult to see how the latest EU programme can possibly command democratic consent. The next government to be elected by the Greek people will almost certainly contain large numbers of MPs from the extreme left and far right, whose first action will be an attempt to repudiate the latest bailout. It is quite impossible to see where the economic growth that Greece so desperately needs will come from. Any default from inside the eurozone will self-evidently do nothing to promote its competitiveness. As a result, Greek departure from the single currency must surely only be a matter of time. The interim will be painful for Greece and grim for both the eurozone and the EU. Whilst it is true that UK banks may not be directly on the line for much of the Greek debt, the interconnectedness of the global financial system means that indirectly UK banks are very much at risk.

Do not be fooled by the present lull – the next few weeks or months of relative calm in the financial markets will most likely be followed by a storm of a ferocity that we have not anticipated.

‡

Some Thoughts Ahead of the Budget, 19 March 2012

'Maybe something will turn up.'

One of the classic stratagems of last resort in politics – and indeed for life in general.

I suspect Chancellor George Osborne's tactical handling of the UK economy owes rather more than he might willingly admit to the Mr Micawber principle. After all, waiting for something to turn up is *not* always the ill-advised course of action. The accretion of time often does alleviate, and sometimes even solves, what seems an intractably difficult situation.

The fragile state of our domestic economy at the time of the May 2010 general election and the indeterminate election result meant that a mandate to take radical action on the economy was neither sought nor won by any political party. So in stark contrast to the first Thatcher government which front-loaded the economic pain, George Osborne – whilst espousing a tough austerity message – has adopted a more pragmatic, steady-as-she-goes path.

His intention now, I have no doubt, is to maximise the coalition's chances of re-election in May 2015 even if this results in the delay of essential longer-term structural reform. Equally it would be unfair not to recognise that the difficulties of coalition-building and maintenance, events in the eurozone and the sheer weakness of the UK economy also persuade against a short sharp economic shock.

Nevertheless, the inability of the coalition to formulate a consistent programme for economic growth is having a chilling effect on our nation's prospects. There is an overriding sense of progress every time the Chancellor declares the UK 'open for business' when in Asia, South America or sub-Saharan Africa. Yet persistent talk of tycoon or mansion taxes, executive pay clampdowns and enhancement of employee rights, and the continued regulatory burden on SMEs, all proceed to run counter to this positive, global message.

So what should this Budget herald? Let's get one thing straight – there is zero veracity in Labour's proposition that the government has cut 'too far and too fast'. In the past twelve months UK government *current* spending has totalled £613.5 billion – the highest figure in history. Borrowing this year will be at least £120 billion, even if a little shy of what was predicted at the Autumn Statement.

However, over half of the deficit reduction plan was predicated on annual compound growth through this parliament of 2.7 to 2.9 per cent. It is clear that for the first half of this parliament we shall struggle to achieve growth at a fraction of this level – which is why we ought to view with suspicion likely forecasts that miraculously suggest growth of over 3 per cent in 2014 and 2015.

Rather than responding to this deteriorating situation by imposing more savings, Mr Osborne has taken the path of ever more debt courtesy of the Bank of England's quantitative easing programme. The real purpose and impact of the UK central bank's intervention has *not* been to ease the path for investment borrowing by small business. Instead it has mopped up a substantial proportion of the gilts being issued. This of course is where Mr Micawber comes into play – the actions of the Bank of England will not be sustainable in the longer term without a real risk of inflation. I suspect global conditions in the years ahead will make it less easy to finance deficits of this size. Which is why, in truth, we should urgently and aggressively be reducing public expenditure further.

In view of the stalling of both health and welfare reform programmes, however, I fear it will prove incredibly difficult to find the political will to execute even the planned level of spending cuts. The expansion of the European welfare model has for years served to make our continent less economically competitive. Unfortunately the solution is one the government and the public still cannot face – to start with a blank sheet and ask ourselves what we *need* instead of salami slicing against what we *want*.

It is for this reason that to date, the fiscal constriction has owed far less to spending cuts than to tax increases, which have squeezed disposable incomes and consumption. However, in spite of protestations from many of my Conservative colleagues, it is by no means clear that tax cuts would boost demand a great deal in the current economic environment. A fiscal giveaway today would in all likelihood be saved by most Britons. Once any economy is as over-leveraged as ours, demand is inevitably impaired. As such, tax cuts now make little economic sense if aggregate demand cannot be boosted.

Yet the process of deleveraging – within the public sector, banks and households – has barely begun. The irony is that of those three, the area boasting most progress – the financial sector – is the one in which deleveraging causes most damage to the economy as a whole. Banks' aggressive strategies in this regard have dried up traditional lines of credit for enterprise and consumption. Yet even here the near-zero interest policy of the past three years has enabled too much toxic property debt to remain on balance sheets rather than losses being crystallised and a sustainable recovery being allowed to commence.

Taking all these factors into account, I firmly believe that the Budget's focus must now urgently rest upon a radical supply-side reform in both the tax system and employment legislation.

It seems a long time ago, but when in Opposition the now Chancellor implored an overhaul of the UK economic model. His big idea then was to incentivise investment over consumption and equity rather than debt (let's not ask savers how they feel right now as rates remain stubbornly below inflation). What this requires in the current environment is forensic attention being paid to the impact of high marginal rates of income tax and the disincentives that have crept into the system as a result of both the poverty trap for the low paid and the removal of some relief for higher rate taxpayers. If the latter process is to be extended to all pension tax relief (which appears the most favoured Liberal Democrat means of soaking 'the rich') we shall move further away from desirable reform.

A more serious potential conflict between the coalition parties is arguably the more urgent supply-side priority – namely legislation over employment rights. Once more the glad, confident morning of June 2010's Budget has given way to starker reality. At that point the increasingly discredited Office for Budget Responsibility (OBR) predicted that unemployment would peak in tax year 2010/11. We now know that unemployment is likely to rise further in the next two years and remain stubbornly high for the foreseeable future. And still the UK continues to gold plate continental employment legislation and grant ever more generous paternity and maternity rights. Precious wonder that many employers are reluctant to take on more permanent staff.

It is instructive to witness how the US has shown signs of turning the economic corner. In simple terms it is easier to hire and fire staff there, which allows flexibility and supports rapid readjustment economically, especially as a recovery phase commences. Closer to home, Germany's micro-businesses (i.e. those start-ups employing ten or fewer) are largely exempt from employment legislation. This type of enterprise is the engine for job opportunities, especially in innovative sectors employing the school and university leavers who have had such a raw deal. If we are really serious about getting people back to work, we in the UK need to allow business to take on and let go of staff more readily. Alas I see only strife amidst coalition players if this is to be rectified, although surely the rights of the unemployed to get back into the workplace should now take precedence over the generous protections enjoyed by those with jobs.

Nevertheless, if the government insists on eschewing regulatory reform, how about we allow SMEs to take on any extra employees over the next two tax years without paying National Insurance? This might help stimulate growth without costing the Treasury too much. In fact better still an NI holiday might even be extended to *all* employees aged under twenty-five. Let's not forget that the UK's SMEs account for over 13 million jobs in Britain and by most calculation two-thirds of all new employment creation.

I should also like to see the government think strategically about how we can promote, via the tax system, the sectors of our economy that actually have potential future growth. Lip service is paid to boosting traditional manufacturing, where we face enormously fierce competition. But what is our strategy when it comes to areas in which we continue to maintain a distinct reputation and competitive advantage such as the export of intellectual property?

The real weakness we need to rectify is the lack of domestic demand and an inability to appreciate that much of the growth in the last decade was illusory ... little more than debt-fuelled borrowing in property, the public sector and financial services, none of which will be drivers of economic expansion anytime soon.

All the traditional macroeconomic levers that governments pull to promote growth have been tried, but all have failed. Interest rates have been near zero for three years, we have had fulsome benefit from being outside the eurozone, the stimulus of QE and a 25 per cent devaluation of sterling. We now need to look at microeconomic reforms.

If the UK can continue to convince the markets we have a serious deficit reduction plan (and a reliable tax base to pay back the ongoing debts in future) a slight relaxation to boost growth by selectively cutting taxes may do the trick. The legislative and regulatory burden on job-creating small and medium-sized enterprises needs urgent reform. My overriding fear is that the Treasury has become complacent about the continued stagnation especially as the political polling figures seem so benign. Paradoxically if we were now 10 or 15 points behind Labour in the polls we might be more inclined to take the radical action I have proposed. Now is surely *not* the time to 'wait and see' how things turn out.

‡

New Property Tax Rules Will Stamp on UK Developers (*City A.M.*), 19 April 2012

George Osborne delivered his second Budget on 21 March. Borrowing for the year was to be £126 billion and the Office for Budget Responsibility revised its growth forecast upwards from 0.7 per cent to 0.8 per cent. Grabbing headlines were the cut in the top rate of tax from 50p to 45p; the removal of age-related tax allowances for new pensioners (the so-called Granny Tax); an incremental fall in child benefit for those earning more than £50,000; and the controversial 'Pasty Tax' on hot

food. Also planned was a tax relief for the video games, animation and
high-end television production sectors, something for which I had been
campaigning for three years in a bid to keep these industries afloat in
the Soho area of my constituency.

From midnight on Budget day, a new stamp duty level of 7 per cent
was to be imposed for homes worth more than £2 million, with any
homes bought through companies paying 15 per cent. I wrote an article
for City A.M. *which outlined my concerns about the unintended conse-*
quences of this change.

I suspect relatively few voters (or even readers of *City A.M.*) will lose
sleep over the Chancellor's decision in the Budget to impose a 15 per
cent Stamp Duty Land Tax (SDLT) on acquisitions of homes costing over £2 million by non-natural persons. After all, why shouldn't
we clamp down on the purchase of residential properties through
companies, collective investment schemes and the like – for so long
the tax-dodging mechanism of choice for super-rich non-doms
hoovering up British homes?

There is some sense in what the government is trying to achieve.
It doubtless ticks populist boxes too. But the Treasury should not be
blind to the potential funding hole this policy is creating.

High-end property developers may not be seen as a bunch deserv-
ing of particular attention from Whitehall, but there is no doubt
that the property development industry in and around Central
London generates significant tax revenues and creates job. Not only
are the profits taxable here, there are often significant amounts of
irrecoverable VAT incurred on redevelopment projects and developers will generate SDLT revenues by buying, and then reselling, the
redeveloped properties.

In the Budget press release, it was noted that the 15 per cent
SDLT charge would not apply to developers as they tend to use
companies for limited liability rather than tax avoidance reasons.
When the draft legislation was published, however, the relief for
developers was limited to bona fide developers who have been

carrying on a residential property development business for at least two years.

Eminently sensible, you might think – a two-year requirement would deter individuals who ultimately wish to use the property from establishing 'short life' development companies as a means of avoiding the levy. Nevertheless this qualifying period will discriminate against new property development businesses which cannot show the requisite track record. Indeed, most prospective new entrants into the market are likely to be priced out because their acquisition costs will be 8 per cent higher than their competitors. The unintended consequence of the coalition's activity here is the creation of an uneven market.

The 15 per cent charge is likely to present a real issue for experienced developers as well. The scarcity of bank finance on development properties at the moment means that much of the funding for high end residential property development is coming from equity investors – who are bridging the significant financial shortfall that now exists since banks started exiting the residential housing market. The requirements of these equity investors will often mean that standalone Special Purpose Vehicles (SPVs) are established for individual projects – so once again the statutory test is not met.

If HMRC wants an alternative policing approach that avoids creating a dual market, it might consider imposing a second charge (another 7 per cent or the balance of the 15 per cent) if the property is used before being sold on by the developer (with SDLT). Alternatively, it could be a time-based charge – a second charge if the property has not been sold after, say, three years.

As ever with intricate taxation policy changes, their success will be determined by whether government gets the detail right. In the case of SDLT, I fear that the unintended consequences of a superficially attractive policy might be yet another funding hole for the Treasury to fill.

‡

A New President in France & the Impact on the City
(*City A.M.*), 9 May 2012

On 7 May, French Socialist, François Hollande, succeeded in his campaign to become the next French President, beating centre-right incumbent, Nicolas Sarkozy, with just under 52 per cent of the vote in the second round run-off on a turnout of 81 per cent. The result was perceived to have implications for the handling of the eurozone crisis since Hollande had expressed his desire to renegotiate a deal on government debt and budget discipline in member countries, presenting the French electorate with a binary choice between growth and austerity.

I was asked by City A.M. *to comment on what an Hollande victory meant for the City of London since throughout the campaign he had expressed his hostility to the banking fraternity, proposing a marginal tax rate of 75 per cent on incomes above €1 million a year.*

François Hollande's victory at the weekend by a majority only slightly larger than Boris Johnson's over Ken Livingstone scarcely provides him with a convincing mandate for radical change.

Constrained by a lack of executive experience and the watchful eye of the international markets, I suspect Hollande will follow in the footsteps of his Socialist predecessor, François Mitterand, who was elected on a radical platform which he was soon forced to water down through his 'tournant de la rigueur' (austerity turn).

Therein lies the danger for the City. With former French finance minister, Christine Lagarde, at the IMF, and Angela Merkel unswerving, Hollande will struggle to overturn the broad thrust of the austerity programme. To detract from his inability to make progress, he may well be drawn to totemic diversions such as a financial transactions tax or a land grab by the Paris-based European Securities and Markets Authority, which may start sabre-rattling when it comes to the question of which financial entities and products pose systemic risk.

So whilst the markets may not yet have cause to take fright at

Hollande's election, the City must be on its guard as a constrained President searches desperately for external enemies.

‡

The Illusion of Prosperity, 16 May 2012

Sarkozy is history, the Greeks are in paralysis, the coalition has for the first time experienced mid-term electoral blues (just wait until May 2013 and 2014). This month has already been one of savage reprimand at the polls in Europe. Yet rather than a definitive judgement on the benefits or otherwise of austerity, I suspect electorates continent-wide are issuing a plague on all our houses.

We are reaping the rewards of decades' worth of debt accumulation, implicitly supported by a generation that enjoyed an expanded welfare state, cheap goods, cosseting employment regulation, neverending lines of credit and inflated house prices (in the UK and US, if not on the continent). Voters are furious that they were sold, and then readily bought into, a lie of prosperity. Nobody, left or right, seems to hold a solution.

As we have sought to understand the roots of the financial crisis, focus has rested upon the role of bankers – their manipulation of and disregard for risk, their short-termism, their failure to respond to public anger and their apparent hostility to change – as well as the apparent willingness of politicians of all parties to give them free rein.

But there is another powerful group that has vigorously defended its vested interest in maintaining the status quo – highly leveraged homeowners. Just as bankers were broadly protected by the bailouts from the consequences of the risks they had taken, so too did policymakers move quickly to protect deeply indebted homeowners with even lower interest rates and mortgage protection plans once the financial crisis hit. The mortgage market had become 'too big to fail'. We still are with the legacy of this after thirty-eight consecutive months of near-zero interest rates – better to keep the economy on life support than risk millions of Britons crystallising unsustainable losses on property 'investments'.

It represented the culmination of a decades-long march towards increased home ownership both in the UK and the US. The conventional wisdom of recent decades is that everyone had the right to own a home regardless of income or personal history, and if the free market could or would not provide this, then the government should be duty bound to step in to assist.

Politicians used various methods to increase lending – mortgage-related subsidies, the encouragement or forcing of lenders to provide mortgages to 'sub-prime' groups – creating an illusion of prosperity that became a deeply persuasive tool to use in any reelection campaign.

Leading up to the financial crisis of 2008, one of the most influential players was the United States' department for Housing and Urban Development (HUD). This government body contributed to the creation of 'affordable housing' (sub-prime mortgages). The HUD had the power to set quotas for lending giants Fannie Mae and Freddie Mac. They dictated minimum amounts of lending to be allocated to the 'underserved population' (those with low incomes, poor credit histories, no deposit etc.). As Fannie and Freddie were government-sponsored enterprises, they had every duty and incentive to abide by government regulation and they did; year after year, targets set by HUD were met.

By 2006, HUD had Fannie and Freddie dedicating 53 per cent of all loans to sub-prime borrowers. It was this debt that was then famously repackaged and sold onto investment bankers. Between 2005 and 2007 Freddie and Fannie took on $1 trillion in non-traditional mortgages and in 2009 the two companies received $238 billion in bailout funds.

Furthermore, as Fannie and Freddie were the largest underwriters of US mortgages and as the two giants were pressurised to take on sub-prime debt, primary lenders were pressurised as well. Prudent, thoughtful lending – or borrowing – was no longer prized as volume dealing was demanded.

In addition, primary lenders felt the pressure directly from the government to achieve their own social 'goods'. The US Community Reinvestment Act of 1977 was expanded so that primary lenders were either encouraged or forced to ignore traditional standards of creditworthiness. As the government actively encouraged 'creativity' in lending, such things as adjustable rate mortgages (ARMs) gained in popularity. ARMs became notoriously problematic when low interest rates began to rise. Other forms of lending, such as 'stated income mortgages' (also known as liar loans) proved to be even more toxic. As the name suggests, stated income mortgages allowed borrowers to take a loan without providing any proof of income. As these types of relaxed lending standards became increasingly popular with primary lenders, less and less was known about borrowers' circumstances. Fannie and Freddie began underwriting large amounts of debt with unknown levels of risk in order to meet quotas and this debt was repackaged and sold onto Wall Street.

These were the building blocks for the financial crisis in which we were all complicit. Although bankers took part in buying and leveraging this debt, it was government obsession with home ownership that created much of the culture of debt to begin with. Even as individuals it seems that we have not learned from our mistakes.

So compelling is the dream of home ownership that in a proposal reminiscent of Fannie and Freddie across the Atlantic, the coalition government has recently proposed to commit taxpayers' money to underwrite mortgages. These mortgages are dedicated to borrowers who do not have enough money saved for a down payment and are intended to encourage lending. Naturally – and with some relief – this new proposal is on a much smaller scale than the United States, but the principle is the same; taxpayers are underwriting loans which the market, through the absence of willing lenders, has implicitly deemed too risky. Yet we should not shy away from the fact that in this way the coalition has made a *political* decision to override the natural *economic* break that capitalism has put in place.

The short-termism borne of electoral cycles makes the temptation to sell unrealistic aspiration over more unpalatable reality too enticing for most politicians to resist. How to tell young, aspiring homeowners that in unravelling the bubble created by previous generations, they are likely to be frozen out of the market for the foreseeable future? How to tell homeowners that an asset that has been reliably increasing in value is overpriced? Rather than precipitate a rapid and painful bust, governments time and again opt for the emollience of long-term stagnation.

In short, whilst capitalism oversees the frequent inflation and deflation of bubbles, the magnitude of the property bubble and its toxicity says more about the weakness of politicians than the viability of the capitalist system.

‡

It's Not Only the Eurozone Kicking the Can Down the Road, 18 June 2012

In the Chancellor's annual Mansion House speech in the City, George Osborne declared that 'we are not powerless in the face of the eurozone debt storm' and launched a coordinated £140 billion emergency funding plan between the Bank of England and the Treasury. This included a new bank funding scheme that would allow high-street banks temporarily to 'swap' their assets with the Bank of England in return for money that could be loaned to customers. There were also signs that the Bank of England stood ready to expand its quantitative easing programme, which at that time already stood at £325 billion.

Whilst it was hoped that the emergency funding plan might kick-start lending and avert a second credit crunch, there was concern in the City that the programme would fail to address the fundamental problem of companies' reluctance to borrow. With storms still swirling over the continent, and a further Greek election due on 17 June, many firms were battening down the hatches.

As the Greek economic tragedy reaches yet another climax, it remains fashionable from these shores to decry the eurozone for its schizophrenic lurching between hapless inaction and spurts of frenetic, if misguided, activism.

However, with this critique in mind, it might also be wise to examine carefully what is happening closer to home.

For so long as global financial markets remain flooded with cheap money, courtesy of government underwritten bailouts, then political consideration will continue to outweigh sound economics.

Conservatives are right to dismiss the Opposition claim that the UK economy currently faces a binary choice between growth and austerity. But nor should the coalition fall into the trap of thinking that preserving historically low interest rates is an adequate compensation for sluggish economic growth.

Last week's Mansion House dinner was notable for the co-ordination in message between the Treasury and the Bank of England over the coalition's emergency 'funding for lending' proposal. In truth the past three years have been characterised by an unspoken bargain between George Osborne and Bank Governor, Sir Mervyn King. Each has provided the other with political cover – the Treasury's increasingly unpopular austerity programme has been underwritten by the Bank's steadfast reliance on monetary tools well beyond a time when conventional wisdom and common sense would suggest undertaking renewed fiscal stimulus (i.e. tax cuts) would be the wisest course.

I suspect that their joint plan now amidst such uncertainty is no more ambitious than to keep the show on this road until the next general election – and that means maintaining ultra-low interest rates to ensure that most voters are not overwhelmed by mortgage and personal debts this side of May 2015. For the stark reality is that any sensible UK government has to soften the electorate up for a decade ahead of diminished living standards, whilst having an eagle eye on the remorseless logic of the electoral cycle.

The Governor has plenty of critics in the City of London where few will mourn his retirement next year. In Mervyn King's defence his voice was one of the few warning of excessive leverage before the crash. At the Mansion House dinners of 2006 and 2007 he observed both signs of overheating (his desire to raise interest rates was outvoted by the MPC) and the deeply compromised role of credit ratings agencies. When the history of this era is written I believe his reluctance to rush into bailouts for Northern Rock and RBS (almost universally derided as 'dithering' at the time) may yet be seen as the correct response of a wise central bank governor, keen to stress moral hazard.

Much more questionable, however, has been King's support for continued quantitative easing. As the economy has deteriorated since May 2010 we have taken the path of racking-up ever more debt, rather than imposing greater savings on the public accounts. Yet the real purpose and impact of the Bank of England's intervention has not (as commonly assumed) been to ease the path for small business borrowing. Instead the Governor has encouraged banks to mop up a substantial proportion of the gilts being issued (currently one-third are now back on the government balance sheet). Whilst this has enabled UK banks to begin the long journey back to prudent recapitalisation, these actions will not be sustainable in the medium term without a very real risk of inflation. Indeed last week's £140 billion emergency scheme is an implicit recognition that global conditions in the years ahead may make it far more difficult to finance our current levels of debt.

Whilst I take the Chancellor's announcement of emergency loan facilities as a welcome recognition that much of the QE has to date failed to reach the 'real economy', it is also a timely step to stay ahead of the game as the eurozone enters a new, dangerous phase.

But will it work? The trouble is that most thriving small businesses are battening down the hatches. The global economic outlook is desperately debilitating to business confidence – for solvent businesses the issue around extending credit is less one of supply than of demand. By contrast those struggling businesses eagerly seeking credit will probably still find it difficult to access funds as (for now at least) the Treasury's new bank loan scheme has *not* been designed to transfer underlying risk from commercial banks to the public purse. Like all too many government initiatives designed to kick-start borrowing, take-up is likely to be derisory.

Yet if there is one thing worse than government presuming to pick winners, it is surely the prospect of the Treasury subsidising known loss-making ventures.

This new initiative was unveiled in the week that the coalition restated its intention to implement the Vickers' review on banking reform, whose centrepiece is the gold-plating of already enhanced capital requirements under Basel 3. One of the causes of the para-lysing strategic uncertainty that has enveloped the UK's big banks is the mixed messages from the Treasury and central Bank alike over the dual requirements to recapitalise (and thereby reduce risks of future taxpayer bailouts) whilst being ready to lend to credit-starved UK plc as if it were 2007 all over again.

The nagging doubt must remain that in these increasingly desperate economic straits meaningful credit will only flow into the veins of the UK economy if it is underwritten by the government. I reckon that last week's announcement was laying the groundwork for whatever eventuality may emerge from the eurozone in the trou-bled months and years ahead. In setting out its plan, the Treasury implicitly recognises that we are all but powerless to prevent the consequences of the potentially perilous next phase of global economic events.

‡

Tax – A Modern Moral Maze, 22 June 2012

On 19 June it emerged that popular television comedian, Jimmy Carr, had been exploiting a legal loophole, channelling money through a company based in Jersey, in order to pay only 1 per cent income tax on his earnings. It caused public uproar and a wider debate on tax avoid-ance and tax evasion. The Prime Minister later criticised the comedian by describing his activities as 'morally wrong'.

It is difficult not to have some sympathy with David Cameron over what I suppose will soon be known as 'Carr-gate'. In today's

24/7 media world there is a constant demand on political figures to provide a running commentary on populist media campaigns.

Nevertheless by personalising his message, the Prime Minister has unwittingly opened up a dangerous flank. No doubt some elements of the press will now feel it is fair game to expose and weigh up the 'morality' of tax arrangements of Tory donors, high-profile Tory supporters and Tory MPs alike.

But here is the bigger picture: the UK's proud, traditional place as a bastion of commercial certainty, attracting investment from every corner of the globe, will be further undermined by high profile rows like this. If investors sense that UK policy over tax and regulation is becoming ever more arbitrary – and governed by sentiment and the news cycle as much as strict rules enforced by the courts – we shall all be the losers.

The furore over Stephen Hester and Fred Goodwin at the beginning of the year also flies in the face of the key coalition message that the 'UK is open for business'. The government needs to nip this dangerous misconception in the bud.

Meanwhile the Treasury is committed within a year to introducing general (tax) anti-avoidance provisions, whilst too often coalition Ministers seem to conflate the concepts of 'avoidance' and 'evasion' in debating taxation policy. It is clear that any such general power of anti-avoidance will result in retrospective taxation; this is wrong in a free society and will further risk damaging our nation's reputation as a free, open, transparent place to set-up, develop and run a business.

As a matter of urgency the Treasury needs to promote a better pre-clearance regime to allow companies, individuals and tax advisers to road-test their proposed schemes. HMRC has to invest time in developing and managing relationships with accountants and tax lawyers. The ideal situation is that aggressive tax avoidance schemes are stopped in their tracks *before* they are marketed to the Jimmy Carrs of this world. That requires constant dialogue and the re-establishing of trust between HMRC and tax intermediaries.

Amidst all the furore of recent days it is worth remembering that the underlying lesson of all this is that the UK tax code and regime remains far too complicated. We need (as we were promised before the election) a simpler, flatter tax system with more transparency, fewer loopholes and as a result less incentive or desire on the part of taxpayers and their advisers to avoid ever increasing headline rates of tax.

‡

The Latest Scandal to Beset British Banking, 2 July 2012

Barclays bank was fined £290 million after investigations by the UK's Financial Services Authority, the US Department of Justice and the Commodity Futures Trading Commission, uncovered attempts to rig LIBOR, the London Interbank Offered Rate.

The daily-calculated rate for the average cost of borrowing for banks, LIBOR is used to price trillions of pounds worth of loans and financial products across the world. The scandal provoked public uproar, sparking a parliamentary review of the banking sector by the Treasury Select Committee and eventually leading to the resignation of Barclays' Chairman, Marcus Agius, and Chief Executive, Bob Diamond. Questions were raised too over whether the Bank of England, possibly at the behest of the Labour government at the time, leaned on Barclays to lower its submissions.

I suspect that today's resignation of Barclays' Chairman, Marcus Agius, will be the first of several high-profile departures in the weeks ahead.

For those who wistfully hoped that Barclays alone was implicated in this LIBOR scandal, the news that RBS had fired four traders following irregularities and that the Bank of England may also be involved (not so much the raised eyebrow of the Governor, more the closed eyes of the Old Lady of Threadneedle Street) comes as a grievous blow.

This is rapidly developing, but I reckon it would be difficult to overstate the potential impact and importance of this latest banking scandal.

The paradox is that this episode may prove to be the moment that public anger reaches boiling point. For LIBOR manipulation arguably has less direct impact on taxpayers than much we have experienced since the financial crisis began. Yet the greatest damage here could prove – and as you might imagine I say this with the heaviest of hearts – to be to the City of London's position as a highly trusted worldwide financial centre.

For key City institutions to be seen as manipulating the London Interbank Offered Rate is akin to debasing ones national currency – consider the sheer number of financial instruments traded in the City of London each and every minute of the day, whose price is set by reference to LIBOR.

I realise that this will very likely lead to a feeding frenzy of class-action litigation most likely originating in the US, but more importantly still risks doing lasting reputational damage to the City of London. It is, therefore, imperative that the appropriate authorities get to the bottom of this fast.

Like it or not our economy is and will remain massively dependent on financial services. There is no comparable sector emerging which will provide jobs or earnings to anywhere near the same extent anytime soon.

Despite all the talk over recent days of criminal sanctions being impossible to sustain, I am not so sure. The manipulation of LIBOR, even if only for institutional gain, is essentially fraudulent activity. It might fall outside the FSA code but the Fraud Act 2006 or most obviously the Theft Act are likely to apply.

However, amidst all the understandable furore, it is also important to nail the understandable misconception that it has been 'business as usual' in the City since 2008. There has been a huge jobs cull alongside falling salaries and bonuses – for the vast majority of workers.

In spite of all the headlines about super-earnings and vast bonuses, they remain assuredly the exception rather than the rule. In addition, the government is committed to further regulation with the Financial Services Bill on its way through parliament and the Vickers reforms to come in a Banking Reform Bill which will be published later this year. Given these potentially game changing developments I hope the Treasury will be open-minded to looking beyond the Vickers recommendation – both to accelerate the long-stop timing (currently set at 2019) and also examine whether a fully fledged breaking up investment banks from retail banks might prove more practicable, publicly acceptable and long-standing than the ring-fence provisions that the Vickers Commission has proposed.

Whatever happens in the coming months it is of overriding importance to restore trust in the financial institutions based in the City as well as confidence in the UK's regulatory framework if the City is to survive as the world's pre-eminent global financial centre.

‡

Will London Survive as the World's Financial Capital?
3 July 2012

Towards the end of June, world leaders gathered in Los Cabos, Mexico, for a further G20 summit at which they hoped to show unity over measures to boost growth across the global economy. However, with the eurozone debt crisis wearing on as talks continued in Greece over how to form a coalition government and Spain's borrowing costs soared, negotiations were tense.

In this context, I was asked at an event sponsored by global law firm, Latham & Watkins, to contribute to a panel discussion with historian Niall Ferguson, banker Jeremy Quin and financial journalist, James Ashton, on whether London would survive as the world's financial capital. The speech below sets out an expanded version of the views I expressed.

As the world's most powerful leaders gathered in Mexico last month for the latest G20 'last chance saloon', each turned to their domestic media to declare that 'something must be done' to stem the descent of the global economy into chaos. Surely no one disagreed. But what and by whom?

When politicians concur only on the gravity of a situation, the seemingly endless rounds of summitry achieve precisely the opposite to their goal – the unnerving impression of impotence. Precious wonder that investors now seek security. With the eurozone's problems deepening, many find it in London.

Some now describe the capital's real estate as being akin to gold – a secure store of wealth as Western economies wobble. In spite of the state of the UK's public finances, the government continues to borrow at rock bottom rates. Our continental competitors are currently too busy stabilising ailing banks and sovereigns to launch power grabs at our capital's expense. Panic that investors and entrepreneurs will flee new regulation and taxes, leading to the inexorable decline of the City, seems not to be shared by those with money to spend. Surely this all adds up to a vote of confidence in the continuing status of the City of London as the world's financial capital?

Perhaps. After all, London's apparent resilience is not a consequence of global volatility alone. One cannot discount how well our capital has been served by its international reputation as a bastion of commercial certainty and reliability. It has promoted financial innovation, provided an international market to global merchants and in commercial affairs has rightly been seen as a watchword for justice, neutrality and fairness.

London also has a number of innate advantages, including a time zone that lies between those of North America and Asia – making the City an excellent base for international company headquarters – and the lifestyle assets of culture, an excellent educational offering and a population so diverse that all can feel at home. We also have the inestimable benefit of the rule of law, a crucial ingredient for investors from all corners of the globe keen to undertake international transactions.

The government has committed itself to key infrastructure projects aimed at boosting London's ability to compete globally. I have already visited Crossrail's headquarters and seen the gargantuan concrete box that will eventually become the new Canary Wharf station. After years of wrangling, it is encouraging to see this crucial transport link finally take shape and provide jobs and training in the meantime. The picture on HS2 and aviation is more mixed. I am not yet convinced the government has properly made the case for a new high speed rail line and HS2 should also not be seen as compensation in the absence of a serious aviation policy. Until the government has a clear strategy in this regard, the inadequate capacity and service at Heathrow will continue to blight London's ability to compete as a truly modern, global city.

But there is no room for complacency. The threats to London's competitiveness, many of which I have long warned about, have not yet gone away. As a place to do business, London is promoted best by a competitive, certain tax system. The government has already done some good work on corporation tax and entrepreneur's relief. I have long said that the same must also apply to our income tax rates and am glad that the government has recognised that the 50 per cent tax rate was sending the wrong message about what Britain and London stand for internationally.

But the recent furore over tax avoidance is not what international investors expect from the Britain. If investors sense that UK policy over tax and regulation is becoming ever more arbitrary – and governed by sentiment and the news cycle as much as strict rules enforced by the courts – we shall all be the losers.

The targeting of Stephen Hester and Fred Goodwin at the beginning of the year also flies in the face of the key coalition message that the 'UK is open for business'. The government needs to nip this dangerous misconception in the bud.

Meanwhile the Treasury is committed within a year to introducing general (tax) anti-avoidance provisions, whilst too often coalition Ministers seem to conflate the concepts of 'avoidance' and 'evasion' in debating taxation policy. It is clear that any such general power of anti-avoidance will result in retrospective taxation; this is wrong in a free society and will further risk damaging our nation's reputation as a free, open, transparent place to set-up, develop and run a business.

Arguably the biggest threat to the competitiveness of London is the gloomy picture of the wider British economy. The capital is the engine for economic growth in the UK and the revenues it generates are redistributed across the nation. Whilst this makes it all the more important to nurture London's competitive advantages, it also leaves open the temptation to milk the cash cow.

The government should also be mindful of the impact on London's image of its occasionally dismissive attitude to financial services. That industry has provided this country with an enormous competitive advantage in exploiting developing markets, not least as the increased wealth and propensity to save from people in these new markets will ensure that this sector will continue to grow rapidly in the decades ahead. Whatever the current distaste for the banking fraternity, it is firmly in the national interest that the City of London and the UK maintain its global pre-eminence in this highly mobile sector. By contrast many of the sector's leading players are now spending huge sums trying to second-guess what regulations might be coming over the horizon in this environment of damaging uncertainty. When such doubt encourages the holding rather than lending of capital, regulation becomes a problem not just for the banks but for the wider economy, as businesses seek to borrow and grow.

It has always been my concern that unilateral British action on bank regulation risks diminishing the competitiveness of domestic financial services. Historically the City of London has benefited from arbitrage with Wall Street from withholding tax under President Kennedy (which precipitated the creation of the Eurodollar and Eurobond markets) to Big Bang in the mid-1980s and the effects of Sarbanes–Oxley (2002) in the aftermath of the Enron and Worldcom scandals. If we are to prevent our competitors benefiting from unilateral action in the UK, we must continue to press for international agreement on the future landscape of the financial services world. Instead the Chancellor has accepted in full the recommendations on banking reform put forward by the Vickers Commission.

It remains crucial that we keep an eagle eye on developments across the Channel. I suspect new French President, François Hollande, will struggle to overturn the broad thrust of the eurozone's austerity programme. To detract from his inability to make progress, he may well be drawn to totemic diversions such as a financial transactions tax or a land grab by the Paris-based European Securities and Markets Authority, which may start sabre-rattling when it comes to the question of which financial entities and products pose systemic risk. The Treasury must be on its guard as a constrained President searches desperately for external enemies. As ever, the City of London's pre-eminence as the only global financial centre in the European time-zone could be under envious threat from across the Channel.

Finally, many City figures with whom I am in regular contact feel passionately that the coalition's approach to human capital is a threat to London's competitiveness. Sustained growth in this difficult era will only be promoted by private sector commerce and global businesses based here will want to recruit the most talented people. This should be encouraged, not restricted, if the UK is to be truly open for business. The Prime Minister has acknowledged some of the concerns over his government's immigration policy by providing assurances that, for instance, those with the skills we require – scientists, entrepreneurs, people with specialist knowledge – will be welcomed with open arms via changes to qualifying criteria. Yet the cap on numbers remains firmly in place and, indeed, stands to be lowered.

To know London's history is to understand that our great city has suffered innumerable breakdowns and revivals. There are many reasons to believe that the capital will once again thrust forward and reinvent itself in an ever more competitive global economy. But we cannot take anything for granted. If London is to maintain its reputation as a premier world city long into the twenty-first century, it must also maintain the characteristic diversity and openness that have been crucial to its former glory. In this regard, tax, regulation (both home grown and European) and the quality of London's human capital loom as clouds on the horizon. The government would be wise to address these quickly. If one thing is for sure, if this ever resourceful city stalls, so too will Britain.

‡

MF Global's Bankruptcy Highlights Perilous Faults in UK Finance Rules (*City A.M.*), 9 July 2012

MF Global, a major international derivatives broker, filed for bankruptcy in October 2011. A number of my constituents had been MF clients and they came to see me in parliament to discuss their worries about the handling of the administration of MF Global UK by the British authorities. Since I felt the case highlighted significant shortcomings in the British financial landscape, I sought to publicise my constituents' concerns and an abridged version of the following article was later published in City A.M..

'Lessons have been learned' – the contemporary platitude of choice for repentant organisations and governments alike in their communications strategy.

All too frequently was it employed when bankers and politicians accounted for the gross regulatory and commercial failings that precipitated the collapse of Lehman Brothers. Lehman was meant to be the event that changed everything. The lesson of all lessons.

So it was with disbelief that I heard a blow-by-blow account of the travails of an articulate group of MF Global clients who came to see me in parliament recently. As the City's MP, I have the privilege of regular contact with a range of professionals who act as an early warning system when it comes to any clouds gathering on the financial horizon. The sorry tale of MF Global's demise seems to suggest that almost four years on, we have failed to heed the warnings of Lehman's collapse.

MF Global was a major international financial derivatives broker until it filed America's eighth largest bankruptcy in October last year. A primary dealer in US Treasury Securities and provider of exchange-traded derivatives, it made an ill-fated $6.3 billion trade on the bonds of some of Europe's most indebted nations that contributed to an internal liquidity crisis. In the chaotic days before bankruptcy was declared, MF seemingly dipped into segregated US customer funds to cover margin calls through its UK operation (MFGUK) as a result of the escalating European sovereign debt crisis. The UK provided a convenient cover for such trades in comparison to the US, where the reuse of clients' collateral on such a scale would not be allowed. Debate continues to rage over whether the misuse of customers' money was intentional, US lawsuits and congressional hearings failing yet to uncover a smoking gun.

As soon as the ship hit the rocks, regulatory authorities from leading financial jurisdictions such as Singapore and Canada acted quickly to get MF clients their money back. Seven months later, Canadian clients have had their investment returned in full, Singaporeans 90 per cent and in the United States 72 per cent of funds have been returned. By contrast, in the UK, the figure stands at 26 per cent (and even the returned funds of those lucky clients come with strings attached).

The MF Global case is important as it highlights two significant shortcomings in the British financial landscape. The first is that of re-hypothecation, a process whereby banks and brokers use, for their own purposes, assets that have been posted as collateral by their clients. In return the client may be rewarded with a rebate on fees or lower borrowing costs (but often clients are not even aware that their money is being used in such a way). The second is the efficacy of the UK's regulatory system and its impact on the City of London's vital reputation as a safe place in which to do business.

Re-hypothecation usually involves a right of a bank or broker to transfer assets held in custody and over which they will usually have a charge to their own account. This 'right of use' allows them to get an enhanced return on the assets and the client is left with a claim to return of the equivalent amount of money but crucially no claim on the assets if the bank or broker becomes insolvent. This is really a form of churning of collateral and typically sees organisations such as banks or brokers using the collateral to back their own trade and borrowing. Crucially, since collateral is not cash, it does not show up on balance sheets, making any re-hypothecation activity opaque. Before Lehman's collapse in 2008, the IMF calculated that US banks were receiving over $4 trillion funding on the back of $1 trillion of original collateral – a churn factor of four. This significantly affected the overall volume of leverage in the system, but only came to light after the collapse.

Frighteningly, this is and remains largely a British problem. In Canada, re-hypothecation is forbidden. In the US, a defined set of client protection rules exists alongside a cap of 140 per cent on the amount a client's debit balance can be re-hypothecated. In the UK, there is no limit unless a client has specifically negotiated one with their broker. Such are the implications of this that Edith O'Brien, Assistant Treasurer of MF Global Inc., has claimed 'Lehman happened in the UK; it did not happen in America.'

Which brings us to the efficacy of the UK's system of regulation. Amongst the Financial Services Authority's myriad edicts sits COBS, the Conduct of Business Sourcebook, which explains how banks and other financial institutions should classify their clients. They can be labelled either Retail, Professional or Eligible Counterparty. Clients classified as Retail have their funds held in a segregated account. But the money of clients labelled Professional or Eligible Counterparty – a precondition for having access to a more comprehensive suite of financial products – can effectively be lent to the business where the client has agreed to the so called 'title transfer' of the cash. Clients have little control over their classification and in practice would often be under pressure to agree a title transfer structure in order to obtain financing on their positions, particularly in relation to derivatives products. In spite of the conflict of interest, this is decided by their financial adviser. This has huge implications for this latter grouping in the event that a broker goes bust. They are considered unsecured creditors and therefore on liquidation find themselves far down the pecking order as the carcass of the insolvent company is picked over.

Such has been the hapless fate of the vast majority of MFGUK clients who took for granted that 'client money was client money' which would be returned in the event of bankruptcy. They now find themselves in a much more complicated situation, jostling with all the other claimants on the client money pool for a share of all the property via a Primary Pooling Event (PPE). PPE entails appointing a trustee, in this case KPMG, whose job it is to determine who is owed what. It is set to be a long, protracted and enormously expensive process. All the while, money is tied up that might otherwise be reinvested by clients in other areas of the economy.

It did not need to be this way. The FSA put MFGUK into special administration at a time when it was technically solvent with sufficient resources at its disposal to give regulators scope for an alternative strategy least disruptive to clients and counterparties. Nevertheless, in the face of FSA failings, the role of the Financial Services Compensation Scheme (FSCS) becomes all the more important. Yet the FSCS is only obliged to compensate clients once an amount is agreed with KPMG and then is granted six months to pay out. In addition, the sum that the UK insures – up to £50,000 – is trivial in the context of a large broker insolvency. To contrast it with some of our international competitors, the US insures up to $250,000 USD for equities, Canada $1 million CAD. After nearly seven months since MF Global was declared bankrupt, the FSCS has paid MFGUK clients a pitiful £130,000 from the $2.5 billion funds owed.

What is at stake here is more than just the return of client funds. The handling of MF threatens the very vitality of the UK economy. International brokerage firms have exploited regulatory arbitrage to transfer an unknown amount of client funds to the UK to be re-hypothecated many times over. That has the potential seriously to compromise the stability of the entire UK financial system. Whilst it may ensure large sums of money come into the UK, clients and taxpayers potentially bear all the cost and none of the benefit.

Second, the speed at which clients' money is returned in the event of bankruptcy is seen as a litmus test when it comes to the attractiveness of the City of London to investors. Not only have clients suddenly realised that their money may not be as safe as they had assumed but re-hypothecation makes sorting out trading positions and who gets what out of an estate very messy. Many of Lehman's clients are still stuck in the courts several years down the line and I have no doubt that the same fate awaits MFGUK's. When our competitor jurisdictions are returning funds to clients in double quick time, it will be no surprise if investors start to turn their backs on the City of London. Ironically if the Vickers reforms are enacted later this year we shall institute a 'ring-fence' yet even now we fail successfully to safeguard segregated funds.

The FSA's remit is to protect clients and maintain confidence in the financial system in the UK. The bungled handling of the MFGUK administration singularly highlights the FSA's inability to fulfil its duties and learn the lessons from the Lehman collapse. To shore up London's reputation before investor confidence drains away, the MFGUK case now requires the immediate involvement of the wider UK financial establishment. We also need an urgent review of client protection rules and the effectiveness of the FSCS as a backstop. Until very recently, the UK could boast that no material client money losses had resulted from broker failures. This is the standard that a leading global financial centre must surely strive to uphold.

Standing aloft these priorities *has* to be an examination of re-hypothecation. I appreciate that the ability for London-based financial firms to manipulate collateral via this mechanism is an attractive means of promoting liquidity to the City of London. Nevertheless, surely this benefit must now be balanced against the opportunity costs of investors overlooking the UK and the potential burden on the taxpayer in the event of systemic failure. I reckon we need either to dispense with re-hypothecation entirely or at least limit the percentage of client funds that can be used in such a way.

The handling by the FSA of the MFGUK bankruptcy could have

been rationalised had its demise been a complete market surprise. Yet the FSA's full awareness of client segregation problems following Lehman's collapse debunks the myth that 'lessons have been learned'. This latest episode of regulatory incompetence risks doing real and lasting damage to the international competitiveness of London as a financial centre.

‡

The Role and Changing Powers of CEOs in the Spotlight, 17 July 2012

This speech to a group of Chief Executives in the City drew together many of the strands consistently running through this book.

When historians look back upon the first decade or so of the twenty-first century, I suspect they will analyse just how and why every one of Britain's institutions (bar the Monarchy) came to be discredited. They will also ponder the demise of leaders in the worlds of politics, finance and business.

The end of the noughties witnessed a breath-taking financial collapse which swept away trust in banking. Simultaneously, a scandal broke over the misuse of MPs' expenses that deepened an historical distrust of politicians. As the 2010s began, a dirty tale of phone hacking sucked media, police and politicians, into a fresh quagmire of shame. Faith in the justice system seemed to be at an all-time low as successive British judgments were overturned by European courts. And as the nation faced its collective indebtedness, the mantra *'we're all in this together'* led to searching questions about whether celebrities, bosses and companies really were paying their fair share.

As a corollary, 21st-century Britons came to feel impotent, disillusioned … and angry.

The upshot of this simmering cauldron of fury will, I suspect, be the emergence of those who instinctively understood that the old ways of doing things were defunct and that a new, tougher world was fast emerging. Most crucially, however, they will be the people who showed vision and leadership. With CEOs facing a level of scrutiny as never before, how does the contemporary business leader get ahead of the curve and avoid potential pitfalls? There are huge opportunities for those flexible, dynamic and imaginative enough to grasp the nettle but they first require an understanding of the unique challenges of the current climate.

1. *Who Are the Disgruntled?*

It is not just the usual suspects on the anarchistic left of politics, but increasingly a lot of middle-class, Tory-voting people who feel that the rules of capitalism have become skewed against them. There is now a deep sense of unease, impotence and frustration amongst people who, despite having got themselves educated and then worked and saved hard, now view themselves as the losers of the globalised, capitalist system.

Here lies the conundrum for today's leaders. We are reaping the rewards of two or three decades' worth of debt accumulation, that have quietly torn massive rifts – between young and old, debtors and savers, East and West. Anyone seen to be profiting from or immune to those canyons, whether fervent financier or top tier businessman, is now a potential target for public outrage.

In a more transparent and fast-moving 24/7 media age, leaders are given neither the space nor time to work through serious solutions, which is why we have seen a sequence of sticking plasters and cheap, anti-business rhetoric. Truth is, there is no way of painlessly or equitably untangling a culture of debt and credit built up over decades. The friction between the old structure's beneficiaries and its hapless young inheritors is sure to define the West's story for some time.

2. *Transparency and Trust*

Growing in tandem with this mood has been a push for transparency as the internet and investigative journalism have shone a light on hitherto shadowy areas and helped focus public anger.

The most obvious examples in business are tax and pay. Take the Uncut sit-ins at top retailers and the campaign against Amazon over tax avoidance, or the furore over pay and bonuses for FTSE boards that seem to be out of sync with share performance.

The political challenge for those of us whose instincts support free markets, enterprise and unequivocal support for capitalism, is whether we should side with the rich or sympathise with 'our people', the strivers who seem so shut out from the colossal rewards given to the financial and business elite. For the gap no longer seems between an essentially equally sized grouping of rich and poor but between the super-rich and everyone else.

Instinctively suspicious of the interfering hand of government, it nevertheless sits uneasily that a certain portion of the population is being remunerated at a level that seemingly distorts the links between talent, hard work and reward. Normally this can be reconciled by the fact that to be a top dog is to take on an extra level of responsibility and, most crucially, *risk*. However, time and again in recent years, we have seen a lack of accountability through the awarding of financial riches *regardless* of performance, and frequently for failure or engaging in immoral practices. Even when a Chief Executive resigns, stories of hefty payoffs and pension deals rather weaken the notion that they have paid a price for their incompetence. This has utterly undermined trust in the system, the ingredient most crucial to the proper lubrication of our economy. Its restoration should be one of the greatest priorities of the modern CEO.

3. *Morality*

As my colleagues in parliament learned to their enormous cost a few years ago, being within the letter of the rules does not mean one operates within their spirit.

The public increasingly demands that leaders, whether in the political or business worlds, apply a sense of morality to their conduct, to make a distinction between legal practice and immoral practice. Not even some of the nation's most popular celebrities are immune, as we have seen from the furore over the financial affairs of Jimmy Carr and Gary Barlow, where legal (if so-called 'aggressive') tax avoidance was seen as morally equivalent to tax evasion or theft in the court of public opinion.

The modern-day CEO should therefore grasp that corporate social responsibility is no longer simply about bankrolling community projects. It is about passing the eternal smell test on pay and tax. It is about being seen to deliver for shareholders not board members as the primary motivation. It is about understanding that 'this is how it has always been done' no longer cuts the mustard.

As our economic woes deepen, we will also likely witness a shift in public worry from how British companies operate in the developing world to how companies serve the citizens of their own country. Most notably, this is beginning to manifest itself in questions over the make-up of the workforce. Over the past decade, companies understandably chose to take on enthusiastic migrants over workshy, low-skilled young Britons. For so long as the welfare bill was manageable, this bargain was sustainable. But as unemployment even amongst young graduates expands, there will likely be a growing demand for British companies to train and employ British workers – see the recent slating of Pret a Manger for employing so few home-grown youngsters.

Hostility and suspicion will doubtless grow as well towards companies that sell out to foreign buyers – see Cadbury's take-over by Kraft – or choose to locate important offices or factories beyond these shores. CEOs will have to balance such calls alongside the demands of operating in an aggressively competitive global marketplace.

4. *Ongoing Political and Economic Uncertainty*

Contemporary CEOs, many of whom will have built a career during the good times, will rapidly have to come to terms with a decade of low or no economic growth and the management of employee and shareholder expectations.

The resolution of the eurozone crisis will not, in my view, come any time soon. Summit after summit demonstrates that the main actors can get away with doing just enough to get through the next phase before markets strike again. It has worked so far in keeping the cart from running off the tracks but the price will be long term stagnation as uncertainty infects the entire system. I suspect that amidst this uncertainty the joint plan of Chancellor George Osborne and Bank England Governor, Mervyn King, is no more uplifting or ambitious than to keep the show on the road until the next general election – and that means maintaining ultra-low interest rates to ensure that most voters are not overwhelmed by mortgage and personal debts this side of May 2015.

On top of the formidable challenge represented by the general economic outlook, the modern CEO may have to grapple with challenges presented by our own government, whether in response to public anger (stamp duty hikes that squeeze London property development, student visa clamp downs that stifle the higher education sector), a desire to court votes (granting new maternity rights) or the simple need to raise taxes to fill empty coffers.

5. *Global Competition*

Western companies have long been used to the notion of outsourcing lower-skilled jobs to the East. But our hope that we can assume continued dominance in the 'knowledge economy' may prove optimistic. I suspect that within the next decade or so, it is quite likely that the intellectual property rights that have underpinned the West's competitive advantage (licensing, patents, copyright protection) are overdue for a radical, philosophical shakeup.

An ever more assertive China will argue that traditional IP structures are no more than the West's attempt to impose its own form of protectionism to suit its particular demographic. We should not assume that the dominance of 'our' values in determining global trade will remain unchecked. If there is to be a longer-term price for our collective indebtedness, it will be for the UK to watch with increasing impotence as it becomes our turn to suffer as the rules of the global trading game are changed. The modern CEO will have to be alive to these changing terms of trade and a fresh army of competitors who may have the backing of governments with far greater global clout than our own.

These are doubtless unnerving times for those wedded to the old ways of doing things. Paradoxically, whilst the public currently believes itself to be impotent, I suspect its anger is levelling the ground for new and improved ways of working – exactly what Britain needs as we wake up to the brave new world before us.

To mark oneself out as a survivor in these turbulent times will require the modern business leader to have an intuitive understanding of the public mood alongside a firm vision and sense of direction. However, they will also need to be fearless about shaping the debate when all around seem all too timid to fly the flags of commerce, enterprise and job creation.

‡

The Fee Pool – London's Essential Export (*Daily Telegraph*), 10 September 2012

Along with the Queen's Diamond Jubilee and the London Olympics, the summer of 2012 also brought with it less positive news stories affecting the reputation of London. Hot on the heels of the Barclays LIBOR revelations came news that HSBC faced a possible fine of $1 billion from US authorities for failing to stop the bank from laundering money for terrorists and drug barons. In a separate investigation, Standard Chartered stood accused of helping Iranian clients avoid US sanctions against Iran, and it also emerged that Barclays, HSBC, Lloyds and RBS faced a bill of up to £6 billion to compensate small business customers who had been mis-sold interest rate hedging derivatives.

I felt it timely amidst all this negative press to issue a reminder of the importance of the City of London to the nation's economic health and had the following article published by the Daily Telegraph.

Fashionable it may be. But banker bashing and public hostility to wealth creation is doing lasting damage to the UK's economy as it rummages for recovery.

The City of London has a proud reputation as a bastion of

commercial certainty able keenly to attract investment from every corner of the globe. Indeed it is for this reason that the recent LIBOR, money-laundering, derivatives' mis-selling and financial assistance to Iran scandals spelt potentially lasting damage to the City as a whole, for they chipped away at the key ingredient of London's success: trust.

Trust that rules, contracts and laws are respected; trust that goal posts won't be moved; trust that the climate will remain welcoming to those who wish to trade and do business here; trust that commercial competitors are treated equitably.

It is the same reason why if investors, present and future, sense that UK government policy is becoming ever more arbitrary – governed more by sentiment and the news cycle than by strict rules enforced even-handedly by English courts – we shall all be the losers. The UK must be 'open for business' or economically it is nothing.

This point was driven home in an article written earlier this summer by David Wootton, Lord Mayor of London, about a business delegation he led to Russia. With its vast natural resources, that country has enormous potential but, Wootton observed, it lacks a developed service industry and, most crucially, a predictable investment environment. Listening to a lecture in Moscow about the importance of the rule of law, he noted that the Russian audience hungrily consumed the message that its application is all about 'creating the stability, predictability and clarity that business needs'.

Here lie two key lessons for the UK that can put us back on the path to growth. First, there are enormous markets for the UK's financial and professional services industry to tap; markets that, to reach their full potential, require precisely the type of expertise we can offer. Second, that the UK's open commercial climate, so carefully nurtured over decades, even centuries, is an asset we can ill afford to lose.

Amidst all the fierce debate about the greed of bankers, it is easy to forget what we mean by 'the City' and 'financial and professional services'. Arguably for too long we have overlooked what banks actually exist for; what social and economic value the financial services sector adds to the UK. Fundamentally, a bank is there to assist companies and individuals in managing their finances. It acts as an intermediary between those who seek capital (businesses wanting loans to expand, governments wishing to fund services now and pay later) and those who have surpluses that they are seeking to enlarge (investors, savers, pension funds). In short, banks circulate money, dispersing it to areas of an economy that require it, and provide the sense of security and stability so crucial to confidence.

The City of London, the centre of the UK's banking industry, has grown to provide that role not just for the domestic market, but more importantly for the global economy. In becoming a hub for the circulation of money, a centre ruled by English law, the City became a place in which people wanted to do business. When deals are being struck and money being lent, people need lawyers and insurers. They need risk analysts, taxation advisers, fund and asset managers, share dealers. With such a concentration of expertise in one compact geographical area, companies (both local and global) want to be headquartered here – indeed more multinational businesses choose to be headquartered in London than any other city. They in turn require accountants, auditors, management consultants and pension advisers. With legally sound deals, insured trading and access to growth capital, businesses large and small have the confidence to expand.

The wealth of professionals and business people in the City spend money on housing, restaurants, culture, education, domestic services. Many engage in philanthropy, to the enormous and lasting benefit of London's galleries and museums, theatres and charities. Indeed the City of London has a proud 1,000-year tradition of charitable giving which sees tens of millions of pounds dispensed each year – often by centuries-old livery companies – for schools, social housing and other good causes. To give some perspective, the financial and associated professional services sector in 2010 contributed 14 per cent to the UK's GDP, comprised 7 per cent of total UK employment (more than two-thirds of it outside London) and contributed £63 billion in tax revenue in 2010/11. The City is not only creating wealth but it is distributing it, principally by directly and indirectly employing millions of people and paying taxes.

Crucially, in financial and professional services, we run a trade surplus of £43 billion and one third of financial services' GDP contribution arises from exports – services provided to overseas clients. So if we want to measure the success of City, we ought not look at the size of bankers' bonuses but instead at the size of the City fee pool – the revenues generated by bankers, lawyers, accountants, insurers, PR advisers, arbitrators and consultants. It is that fee pool which has huge potential to grow.

London's reputation is such that mega-mergers often take place on our shores between two companies that do not even operate here simply because executives want deals done under English law. That creates UK jobs. Similarly, London has become a centre for commercial dispute resolution and is at the forefront of developing new markets and products such as carbon trading and Islamic finance. We have expertise to export in what is a growth industry. Just think of the opportunities. In China, the new rural pension scheme has acquired over 240 million people in only two years – that is more than the number covered by America's *entire* social security scheme. As the Chinese economy matures, there will surely be an ever greater demand for private pensions, wealth management and more dynamic investment products.

Undeniably there is a separate debate to be had about how well our banks have fulfilled their primary function as service providers. The financial crisis uncovered serious regulatory and cultural flaws, but one of the reasons that so many recent scandals seem to have their origins in the City of London is simple: the sheer scale of business conducted here. Regardless, the past four years do not obscure the fact that our economy needs the financial and professional services industry. It is not a necessary evil to be tolerated but an absolutely fundamental cog in the functioning of our economy and an incredibly successful sector ripe for expansion. If we want to know where growth is going to come from, we need look no further than the City's fee pool.

One last thing: when people talk about weaning ourselves off the City, it might well be asked how the Treasury will compensate for the loss in tax revenue whilst continuing to provide the same public services. In all likelihood in this current climate, the money will have to be borrowed – an action necessarily facilitated by the City. Let us not forget either that periods of prosperity in Britain have always gone hand in hand with London occupying a key position in international finance. As London wallows in self-loathing, its competitors eye up the prize. This is not some distant threat and if you don't believe me, maybe this email I received a few weeks ago from a constituent will convince:

> You know this year I have started getting my UK legal work done out of Singapore … they work weekends, they do what you ask, they are never ill and they charge reasonable rates … even the professional services in the UK are in trouble … before it was manual manufacturing … now it's everything. I am happy to offshore.

‡

The Road to Fiscal Union in the Eurozone, 20 September 2012

As September dawned, the eurozone countries faced fresh pressures in holding together the ailing currency union. In anticipation of this challenging month, Mario Draghi, President of the European Central Bank, unveiled plans for a new, potentially unlimited, bond-buying programme aimed at cutting borrowing costs for the most indebted member states and countering speculation by financial markets about a break-up of the euro. His proposals were backed by German Chancellor, Angela Merkel, leaving Bundesbank President, Jens Weidmann, out in the cold after he criticised the plan.

It was in this context that I made the following speech about the likelihood of fiscal union in the eurozone at a conference hosted in Cadenabbia, Italy, by the Konrad Adenauer Stiftung, the German centre-right political foundation.

In spite of the annual August lull, September – with the Dutch election, the troika's verdict on Greece and the German constitutional court ruling on the legality of the European Stability Mechanism – always promised to snap the continent's politicians out of their sun and sangria-induced stupor.

In anticipation of these potentially destabilising events, and the growing storm of unease over the state of Spanish and Italian public finances, the European Central Bank sent markets its strongest signal yet that it is apparently potentially willing to deploy unlimited monetary muscle to save the euro. 'This is your bazooka', suggested the OECD's chief of Mario Draghi's bond buying programme. In this carefully calibrated balance between the economic and the political, the onus now rests firmly with national governments.

Which is why, regardless of this shot in the arm from the ECB, a final resolution of the eurozone crisis is unlikely to come either this month or any time soon. Summit after summit, crisis meeting after crisis meeting over the past three years, demonstrate that Europe's main actors can get away with doing just enough to get through the next phase before markets strike again. To date this has worked in keeping the cart from running off the tracks, but for so long as growth remains elusive then the price will be long-term stagnation. Indeed arguably underwriting Italian and Spanish bonds for the next two or three years only stacks up bigger problems for the future unless almost heroic levels of economic growth return.

This period of flat-lining may buy politicians the time necessary to convince electorates continent-wide that greater political and fiscal union is a price worth paying for economic relevance in a globalised economy.

But the whole structure of EU economic health could unravel much faster, perhaps beyond even Germany's power to control, as markets lose patience with successive failed attempts by European leaders to deliver a lasting solution. At its most extreme this might lead either to the breakup of the euro in the event that Germany repeated refuses requests to do 'whatever it takes' or the rapid introduction of more credible and lasting solutions such as the collectivisation or mutualisation of historic and future debt. How the people of Europe react to the latter scenario, when they wake up to the political illegitimacy of fiscal union, is the great unknown. Responding to the ECB's bond-buying programme, *Der Spiegel* this week concluded: 'The euro may be irreversible, but apparently democracy is not.'

What would such fiscal unity mean for the European Union as a community beyond the euro of twenty-seven member states?

In the United Kingdom – where I represent a constituency that contains the City of London, our famous financial district – there has been enormous complacency. The break-up of the euro – which would undoubtedly inflict significant short-term pain on the City – remains the British government's greatest immediate fear. Forget triumphalism about the UK staying out of the single currency. Britain's key trading partners remain European. If they suffer, so too does the forlorn hope of export-led growth. This summer's dire trade figures already demonstrate just how vulnerable the British economy is to continental storms. Politicians at home have found it impossible to squeeze out any growth in the absence of any real domestic or international demand. Even the Asian and South American economies, which the UK has been so slow to exploit, show signs of a sharp downturn.

Nevertheless, the greater existential threat to the City and the UK surely comes from a successful banking and fiscal union. The complacent view from Whitehall is that any such emergency development would act to ring-fence the eurozone's weaknesses. That might well be the case in the event that there was fiscal union amongst *all* of the euro's current members. It would be very hard to see, for instance, how the fundamental dearth of competitiveness in states like Greece could possibly be addressed if the eurozone remained seventeen 'strong'.

Yet fiscal union in the eurozone would still represent an almighty challenge to an EU member state like Britain. History teaches us that an economic crisis is often regarded as too good an opportunity to waste for ambitious statesmen seeking to impose a wider political agenda. Look at activity around a transaction tax, or the pronouncements from the Paris-based European Securities and Markets Authority. To hope that the UK would have any real clout in an EU with fiscally integrated eurozone members would be hopelessly naïve. The City of London is only too aware of the risk of losing business from regulatory arbitrage, having benefited so handsomely in the past from US regulatory clampdowns on Wall Street. There is also the not insignificant benefit of the UK's 'safe haven' status. The UK's continued colossal public borrowing has been at historically low interest rates. However, a successful eurozone fiscal union would surely have the effect of diluting the UK's safe haven status in the international gilts markets. We can expect a significant rise in our domestic interest rates.

A far greater threat still to the UK – and to all those member states not within the single currency – would be tighter fiscal and banking union amongst a core of EU members. Liberated from the dead weight of Greece and Portugal, for example, it would be hard to imagine that the institutions, supervisory and regulatory rules of a strong core would not begin to impinge on the economies of non-eurozone member states. In the UK at least – a nation always inherently sceptical of the European project – the domestic case for the Britain's continued membership of the Union would become increasingly unsustainable and unpopular, particularly if closer political and economic integration amongst that core came at the expense of the Single Market, not least in financial services. It would surely only be a matter of time until the choice would be put to the electorate that we either join the core in currency union or leave the European Union altogether.

Barely two and a half years into this parliament, Britain's coalition government has already had to address bubbling resentment over a host of EU-related issues. Fierce debate has been waged over the amount the grossly indebted UK Treasury should contribute to bailing out European partners. Hostility to judgments by the European Court of Human Rights, whilst unrelated to the European Union, have nonetheless been conflated by the British media with broader disgruntlement towards supranational organisations. And the Prime Minister scored one of his greatest ever public relations victories when he refused to sign Britain up to the EU's fiscal compact last autumn.

The case in favour of Britain's membership of the European Union will hold so long as the UK electorate perceives its economic interests to be served by it. The moment that the economic case diminishes, we should not be surprised if a clamour for Britain's exit from the EU quickly follows. In the meantime, we ought not be surprised if British domestic grandstanding has a significant impact on diplomatic relations with our fellow member states, risking a self-fulfilling prophecy as Britain's ability to influence in its favour the outcome of the eurozone crisis and the future direction of the Union declines as a result.

And what of the futures of any ejected eurozone members in the event of a smaller, fiscally integrated core? The popular anger that would be felt towards the European project in an ejected Greece, Portugal, Ireland or even Spain would not be salved entirely by generous economic development packages upon exit, even if there was no appetite in those countries for leaving the safety of the Union.

We can conclude only this: that European leaders can decide whatever they wish at summits and conferences. The greatest unknown for us all is the politics. Mario Draghi can provide the bazooka of support from the European Central Bank and appears for now to have the tacit support of Angela Merkel. But will the German people, with their historical, deep-seated fear of printing money, accept the liabilities of a continent? Will the electorates of debtor nations accept swingeing austerity and fiscal rectitude as the price of inclusion in the grand European project? And could a fiscally integrated core of EU member states be reconciled with a broader and looser Union of twenty-seven member states?

For some time, well before the advent of the eurozone crisis, the European Union had been suffering a dearth of political legitimacy, the consequences of which were kept at bay by steady, if under-whelming, economic growth. Putting aside fundamental questions about the Union's economic competitiveness and sustainability, the European project requires belief if it is to survive. Belief from markets. Belief from electorates. The question now is whether each can keep pace enough to satisfy the other.

‡

Lack of Capital and Onerous HMRC Rules Are Restraining Tech Start-ups, 12 October 2012

As 2012 wore on, the government came under increasing pressure to address anaemic levels of growth. Earlier in the year, it had commissioned venture capitalist, Adrian Beecroft, to examine whether reform of employment laws might liberate businesses and stimulate the economy. The Beecroft Report was released in May but caused considerable tension within the coalition between Conservatives and Liberal Democrats.

In his autumn Conservative Party Conference speech, Chancellor George Osborne hoped to get around some of the reservations expressed over Beecroft by proposing that businesses could remove 'gold-plated employment rights' in exchange for handing out shares to employees that would be exempt from tax.

In an article for City A.M., *I suggested a simpler way of stimulating growth via the government's approach to share ownership, an idea which had been shared with me at a City conference by a London businessman.*

Shares for sackability. The Chancellor's announcement earlier this week that employees could get a stake in their company in return for waiving certain employment rights seemed a rare flash of creativity from the Treasury. But as Allister Heath noted in Tuesday's editorial, there are practical barriers to its implementation.

It will come as no surprise if, in a year's time, the Opposition begins mischievously to ask how many businesses have made use of the Chancellor's big new idea. With this in mind, now might be the time to consider alternatives for stimulating growth via the government's approach to share ownership. As ever, the key lies in reducing complexity rather than adding to it.

At a recent City roundtable on intellectual property (IP), I met a former engineer and investment banker who now helps technology start-ups. A few years ago, he had worked as a part-time CFO for a tech spin-out from one of Britain's top research universities. Backed by a quasi-governmental venture capital fund, in the end the technology was sold prematurely to a large French company as it had proved impossible to eke out limited VC funding to expand the fledgling enterprise. Had it not been for the complexity of HMRC's rules and an equity gap in first stage VC, he believed, the UK Treasury would by now have been enjoying the rewards of fresh job and corporation tax receipts.

New tech businesses are typically nucleated when a piece of IP is picked up by a small team of high calibre executives who practically apply and market the technology. Seed funding of £50–250k to get these start-ups off the ground is typically not difficult to come by. The founders' own resources, or those of business angels, can be tapped and new government mechanisms, such as the Seed Enterprise Investment Scheme, incentivise investment in early-stage companies. Instead it is the next part of the corporate journey – obtaining £1–5 million in first-stage venture capital – that represents the greatest stumbling block to expansion.

The structural shortage of this type of funding in the UK is exacerbated by the fact that before these start-ups begin generating revenue, a large share of funds goes towards paying executives' salaries. It is the taxman, therefore, that gets much of this VC money through employer and employee NI and PAYE tax – particularly ironic in instances where a quasi-public source has granted the VC funds.

To work round this problem, many start-ups eke out their VC money by instead rewarding executives with 'sweat equity'. Since many are in the 45-to-60 age bracket, they tend to have an existing financial cushion that leaves them prepared to work for 'free' in return for shares. However, HMRC currently insists that those shares are valued and treated as taxable salary. In order to pay the tax charge associated with the granting of shares for which there is no liquid market (and which may in the end turn out worthless), executives must raid their savings. In short, when a start-up fails, as so often is the case, executives will have paid from their own resources for the privilege of working for free.

Partial work-rounds are in place based on approved share option schemes and the recognition of capital losses on shares in companies that fail. However, these are complex, hard for many SMEs to understand (at least without the services of expensive advisers) and costly to administer. As a result, many corporate mentors simply do not bother to become involved, their wisdom and experience lost in the process.

The government could solve this conundrum relatively simply by allowing qualifying early stage tech companies to reward executives with shares on an ad hoc basis that could be held in 'escrow' by HMRC but would not crystallise any taxation in the year they were awarded. Instead, a tax charge could be levied (on the individual rather than the company) on withdrawal of the shares from escrow, which presumably would only happen once there was a liquid market for them that would establish their fair value.

The downside for HMRC would be the delay in levying tax but the only net loss would be the employer's NI. This would be more than offset by the simplicity of collecting the tax which would eventually be forthcoming. And if VC was used not for meeting PAYE bills but expansion and development, it would be HMRC that would reap the reward from the uplift in economic activity.

If the Chancellor is looking to prove that rejigging HMRC's approach to shares can tick the box for economic growth, this could prove a handy addition to his arsenal.

‡

Child Benefit – Misery Ahead? 29 October 2012

At the Conservatives' 2010 Party Conference, Chancellor George Osborne announced that from 2013, the coalition would be scrapping child benefit for those on the 40 per cent and 50 per cent income tax

rates. The move caused controversy since household income would not
be taken into account. This meant that if both parents each earned less
than the current higher-rate threshold, but their combined income was
more, they would continue to receive child benefit whilst families with
only one main earner over the threshold would have benefit withdrawn.

The plans were watered down in the 2012 Budget, with a tapered
reduction in child benefit for those earning over £50,000. Nevertheless,
by October 2012, the enormous complexity of the new arrangements
was beginning to dawn on HM Revenue & Customs, with half a
million people required to fill in self-assessment returns for the first time.
Controversy remained over the disparity between households of either
one or two earners.

Although first mooted by the Treasury over two years ago, it is only
this week that changes in child benefit will become fully apparent,
as letters drop through the letterboxes of over a million households
where one earner is bringing home at least £50,000 per annum.

Only last month at Conservative Party Conference, David
Cameron made a powerful case for supporting the 'strivers' and the
aspirational in our society. Yet it is precisely this group that stands to
be most adversely affected by the child benefit changes.

Conservatives like me regard deficit reduction as a moral, as well
as an economic, matter. Surely we owe it to our children and grandchildren alike not to pass on huge debts in the decades ahead for our
consumption today.

As a result I shall *always* support measures by the coalition to
reduce public spending.

But on the implementation of these child benefit reforms let's for
once be wise before the event.

Tax collection should invariably be efficient and certain. Yet I
fear that much of the £2.5 billion per annum that these changes are
expected to raise will either need to be written off as too difficult to
claim or be swallowed up in huge administrative costs. This is my
core concern.

Ideologically my fear is that the scheme acts as a penalty on aspiration. Certainly in my own central London constituency, earning £50,000 p.a. does not place you within the ranks of the super wealthy. It is also the case that many people who earn just below the threshold will regard it as being a promotion away so these changes will therefore act as a significant disincentive to earn more, not least as the tapering arrangements for those earning between £50,000 and £60,000 results in marginal tax rates of 65 per cent for families with three or more children. This just seems perverse. After all the (correct) justification at March's Budget for reducing the top rate of tax for those earning more than £150,000 p.a. was that a 50 per cent tax rate was acting as a strong disincentive to further effort.

The other glaring problem with this scheme as currently constructed is that a couple where both parties are earning £45,000 (an aggregate household income of £90,000) will lose not a single penny of their child benefit, whilst a family with a single earner of £60,000 will lose it in full. Surely the tax system and society as a whole should respect and support households choosing to have a 'stay at home' parent?

There are also some stark practicalities about the way in which many modern Britons live nowadays. Many people work on a consultancy basis – indeed this has been one of the big success stories for the coalition as this level of flexibility has helped add over 1 million people to private sector employment since 2010. However, working on this basis means that many will not know at the beginning, or even quite near to the end, of any tax year whether they will be earning as much as the £50,000 threshold. We run the risk of some perverse incentives to delay invoicing and many will likely seek the services of an accountant in order to find ways around the changes such as making additional pension contributions or adopting other means of tax avoidance. Separated and divorcing couples may also find themselves lumbered with big repayment bills after the event. The lesson of the community charge two decades ago is that many such liabilities will end up being written off by the government as uncollectable.

I have long been a critic of universal benefits, especially in this era of economic austerity. However, the full panoply of non-means-tested old-age benefits (many of which were only introduced during the last Labour administration) seem to be regarded as sacrosanct. Given the well-mobilised efforts of pensioner lobby groups to commit Party leaders in the teeth of a general election to protecting 'their' benefits, I reckon it is unlikely there will be any action to pare back this type of universal benefit.

Yet it is worth remembering that the child benefit came into being in the mid-1970s to ensure that 'stay at home' mothers had some disposable income for children they were bringing up. Until then there was a system of tax allowances for parents to reflect – properly in my view – the notion that the time, effort and financial outlay involved in bringing up children was a 'social good' that should be reflected in the tax system.

Conservatives rightly accept, to coin a phrase, that we are all in this together and must recognise the need to live within our collective means. However, my fear is that this child benefit policy as currently constituted will bring a lot of pain for relatively little gain.

‡

Why the Vickers Ring-fence is No Panacea (*International Financial Law Review*), 12 November 2012

The City of London's size and global reach continues to make the UK economy especially vulnerable to turbulence in the financial markets. In a bid to reduce that vulnerability and avert future crises, the UK's coalition government, soon after taking the reins in 2010, tasked an Independent Commission on Banking with proposing reforms to Britain's banking system.

Last autumn the Commission, under the chairmanship of Sir John Vickers, released its much anticipated final report, its centrepiece a plan to ring-fence domiciled banks' retail arms from their investment ones. Based on the notion that 'less risky' retail operations required protection from the 'casino excesses' of investment banking, the reforms aimed to reduce the burden on the British taxpayer in the event of banking failure. To the relief of many in the financial fraternity, the reforms fell short of a return to full-blown Glass-Steagall, the US legislation which had separated commercial and investment banking for seven decades until 1999. In addition, the big banks would now need to raise capital and loans equivalent to 20 per cent of the part of their balance sheet for which UK taxpayers would be liable in a crisis.

The coalition government was swift to accept the Vickers recommendations without reservation, giving British banks until 2019 to install their ring-fence. Yet a year on from this blanket acceptance by the coalition, the question about the separation of banks' retail and investment arms has still not been successfully settled here in the UK.

Fears have been raised that the Vickers reforms will tie up billions of pounds in additional capital and impose upon banks a requirement to overhaul compliance and corporate affairs, a burden that will be met by the public in higher interest rates and a sharp reduction in the amounts banks are willing to lend. One of the causes of the paralysing strategic uncertainty that has enveloped the UK's big banks is the mixed messages from the Treasury and central Bank alike over the dual requirements to recapitalise (and thereby reduce risks of future taxpayer bailouts) whilst being ready to lend to credit-starved UK plc as if it were 2007 all over again.

Meanwhile, as the government prepares to legislate for Vickers in a Banking Reform Bill scheduled to be considered by the UK parliament early in the New Year, at EU-level, the Liikanen Report has recommended to the European Commission a similar, Vickers-style ring-fencing of retail from investment banking. This has given a small crumb of comfort that the UK may not now be going down this path alone. However, Liikanen's proposals are sufficiently different from Vickers' to heap further uncertainty upon financial services providers here in the City of London. Since there is likely to be precious little consensus between the EU, UK and US authorities any time soon as to whether the structure of banking is best under Liikanen, Vickers or Volcker, how should banks now prepare? Once again, the cost of uncertainty will be borne by the consumer and the wider economy, not to mention heavy job losses in the financial services sector. In this regard, it is important to nail the understandable public misconception that it has been 'business as usual' in the City since 2008. Over the past two years volumes of business have collapsed, state financial support has been largely withdrawn and there has been a huge jobs cull. Couple this with falling salaries and bonuses for the vast majority of workers and it has been bad news all round, as Treasury receipts from financial services have plunged to a new norm.

Aside from the issue of commercial uncertainty, there are question marks over whether the ring-fence will actually work. I believe the Vickers template is based on an outdated and simplistic division between what amounts to wholesale and retail banking. There are numerous transmission mechanisms between the two that make a hard and fast split between high street and 'casino' investment banking difficult to achieve.

The Vickers model also implicitly assumes that retail banking is 'risk-free'. Part of the genesis for the 2008 financial crisis, however, lay in the lending of money by retail banks to poorly-risk-assessed clients, particularly in the US. After all Northern Rock, whose decline famously sent the balloon up for what was to come in the UK, did not have an investment arm.

In practical terms, it is questionable whether the much-heralded split will make banks better at absorbing losses. A failing investment bank which falls outside the ring-fence is still likely to share its name or at least reputational goodwill with the retail bank from which it has been cast asunder. Does anyone seriously believe that there will not also be a run on the retail bank and huge potential liabilities falling back to the taxpayer via the depositors' compensation scheme?

Unilateral British action over bank regulation also risks diminishing the competitiveness of domestic financial services since non-domiciled banks would be able to escape the ring-fence. This raises the more fundamental question – if only UK banks are obliged to sign up to the Vickers reforms then surely the contagion risk from any future global financial crisis will be exactly the same? Small additional amounts of capital being held in a dwindling number of British banks are unlikely to make any difference when the next crisis is in full flow. In any event, what is to stop banks simply re-domiciling to the EU and setting up subsidiaries in the UK?

Historically the City of London has benefited from arbitrage but if it is to prevent its competitors benefiting from unilateral British action along Vickers lines, it must continue to press for international agreement on the future landscape of the financial services world.

There is a danger now that the UK Treasury and EU regulators are viewing ring-fencing as a panacea – and are selling it as such to the general public. Instead, in light of the pitfalls of the ring-fence options, the UK Treasury should be open-minded to looking beyond the Vickers recommendations. In this vein, it might prove more effective to look at an alternative dual system when it comes to ordinary deposit accounts, allowing those who desire a risk-free place to store their money to place it in savings banks, whilst those willing to take more of a risk can have an account with a fractional reserve bank, as used to be the case in the UK until the mid-1980s.

The UK's coalition government has faced an unenviable task in reforming Britain's banking system without placing the UK's vital financial services sector at a competitive disadvantage. It has been brave in wholeheartedly accepting the Independent Commission on Banking's reforms. But before it becomes too enthusiastic in its endorsement of everything Vickers, it should be careful what it wishes for. There is the real potential of a renewed credit crunch if lending dries up. We would then see the choking off of hopes for renewed economic growth in order that stringent capital requirements are met, coupled with an outflow of capital from the UK. In short, I fear that if the UK financial services system goes out on a limb over an unworkable banking ring-fence, we risk a perilous prospect ahead for the real economy.

‡

The Summit that Lies Ahead (*City A.M.*), 22 November 2012

On 22 November, Prime Minister David Cameron travelled to Brussels to take part in a critical summit on the EU's budget from 2014 to 2020. On 31 October, the government had been defeated in a vote on an amendment calling for a real terms spending cut in the EU budget, as Labour joined forces with Tory rebels. Whilst the amendment was non-binding, it heightened tensions between the Prime Minister and Eurosceptic factions of his Party in the run-up to the Brussels summit. I wrote the following piece for City A.M., *published on the morning of summit, warning that Party management issues should not distract the government from forming a coherent strategy over Britain's relationship with the EU, particularly given the importance of that relationship to the future of the City of London.*

Short-term tactical expedience continues to outweigh longer-term strategy in the coalition's approach to both the UK's relationship with the EU and the future of our single most important global industry, financial services.

As a consequence, our ability to dictate the terms of trade in either area is fast eroding.

Historically there have tended to be two potential models for a successful financial centre. The first, an onshore version, is based around the notion of a hub city servicing a sizeable domestic market – think New York and the US market. The alternative approach, offshore, depends upon attracting business primarily via competitive tax rates, regulatory arbitrage and other distinct selling points such as a respected system of law, privacy and a skilled workforce – the most obvious example here being the Swiss niche in secret bank accounts.

Until 2008's financial crisis, the City of London had pragmatically been enjoying elements of both models and benefited handsomely. Prominent first as the epicentre of the British Empire, servicing the

UK's great global trading market, since the 1980s the City had taken on the role of offshore/onshore financial centre to the European continent – more recently still as a member of the European Union outside the eurozone. As a pan-European capital market, the City flourished and alongside that role was able to develop a light-touch regulatory approach that attracted huge volumes of foreign money. But the arrival of the financial crisis fundamentally changed the rules of this game.

Almost overnight since 2008 the eurozone has demanded greater oversight of its financial infrastructure. Awkward questions have been raised about the ability of London and UK financial services regulators to prevent the system silting up; whether it is sustainable (or desirable) for euro-denominated risk to be cleared offshore in the British capital. In turn, the City has questioned how long it might feasibly avoid being infected by the numerous directives churned out by the EU to create common financial standards without its global competitiveness being fundamentally damaged.

The invoking of a British 'veto' at last December's EU summit was billed as an aggressive demonstration of the UK's intention to retain its offshore/onshore model, protecting the City as its vital interest. To much of the EU it was perceived as an unrealistic and petulant attempt to maintain an unsustainable status quo. The UK's demands for safeguards would have given the UK an effective veto over European financial regulation, a request that was never going to be acceded to.

In reality, that veto was less about the future of the City and more a political gesture to a domestic audience aimed at keeping Eurosceptic wolves from the door ideally until well beyond 2015. The backdrop to that last summit, it is important to recall, was the unexpectedly large 'rebellion' in support of an EU referendum. It was perhaps naïve ever to suppose that this would close off debate on the issue. Instead the Prime Minister's superficially popular move delighted the media and hardened Eurosceptics' resolve to extract further concessions.

Over the past year, of course, matters have moved on apace.

The EU, under the leadership of European internal markets Commissioner, Michel Barnier, is finalising work to set up a single bank supervisor. Next month the EU's executive and the European Parliament will be agreeing a legal framework. Meanwhile, the coalition government has failed to see off a further rebellion on the UK's relationship with the Union, this time over its budget. Another summit showdown is surely inevitable.

The uncomfortable truth fast facing the Prime Minister is that there is no third way in the UK's relationship with Europe. His understandable instinct is to play for time, trying to placate Eurosceptic passions with aggressive talk about repatriating powers from and renegotiating our relationship with Brussels, whilst smoothing relations with European partners behind closed doors. To some extent, this is a challenge faced by all European leaders, whose electorates are increasingly restless at the influence of EU bureaucrats. This approach is, however, no substitute for a clear view about how Britain's economic interests are best served, particularly when it comes to direction in which the City – the nation's only substantial, globally competitive industry – should evolve. Our European partners are entangled in a crisis of continental scale and are fast losing interest in being lectured to accede to the UK's demands.

If the Prime Minister sees our future in the EU, with the City remaining closely integrated into the vast domestic European market, a more collaborative approach with our European partners is now required. This path will involve facing down Eurosceptic sentiment in the UK. He will need to put forward a powerful case for why now is not the time for British belligerence. Time will need to be spent extracting the best deal for the City through careful diplomacy and the building of alliances.

If, however, he truly believes that the raft of EU directives coming this way are anathema to the long term interests of the City of London, with its future best served by adopting an offshore model, a path towards British withdrawal from the EU will need to be sketched out before long.

Talk of fundamental renegotiation is illusory. We may not like it, but for the EU and the City the choice ahead is increasingly binary. This arises out of a dearth of strategic thinking in how we see the City operating in future and the relationship Britain should enjoy with the European Union in the years ahead. As it stands, the UK government has no clear answer on either of these issues. This is a perilous position for the national interest.

‡

Autumn Statement, 10 December 2012

As Chancellor George Osborne prepared to make his Autumn Statement on 5 December, it was becoming increasingly clear that the coalition's economic plans were being blown off-course by disappointing growth figures. In the week leading up to the Statement, the OECD downgraded its forecast for UK growth from 1.9 per cent to 1 per cent and Bank of England governor, Sir Mervyn King, warned of a 'slow and protracted recovery'.

The Chancellor won praise for his sober delivery of the Statement, particularly when contrasted with the poor parliamentary performance of his Shadow, Ed Balls. However his underlying message was unremittingly gloomy. The government was going to miss its debt reduction target, with public debt rising until reaching 80 per cent GDP in 2016 or £1.5 trillion. Instead of taking five years to deliver on the fiscal mandate, as had originally been promised, the government would now need seven to eight years, extending the period of austerity still further.

The coalition's expenditure programme for the entire parliament was designed to have been done and dusted in November 2010. Subsequent pre-Budget reports were expected to feature only the odd tweak here and there.

Last week's Autumn Statement may have had the Westminster village agog with anticipation, but for three reasons it was met with supreme indifference by the large corporates and banks of my constituency. First, a recognition that any government in these acutely difficult times has virtually no room for manoeuvre. Secondly, despite all the continued fire and brimstone of the exchanges between Osborne and Balls, there is in fact vanishingly little to choose between their approaches to economic management. Indeed all the talk of 'austerity' and 'savage cuts' provides the coalition with the alibi to the markets that they have a deficit reduction plan that is being vigorously stuck to (not borne out by the economic facts) whilst Labour can take comfort in playing their familiar 'heartless Tories' card in drumming up support from swing voters, without having any plausible alternative.

Finally, there is now near universal acceptance that the coalition's strategy is to keep interest rates at near zero (as they have been for the past forty-five months) and hope that something turns up. I suspect Chancellor George Osborne's tactical handling of the UK economy owes rather more than he might willingly admit to the Mr Micawber principle. After all, waiting for something to turn up is not always the ill-advised course of action. The accretion of time often does alleviate, and sometimes even solves, what seems an intractably difficult situation.

The sobering truth, however, is that these ultra-low interest rates mean that the UK economic patient remains in a government-induced coma and these historic low returns provide no incentive for prospective investors to take the plunge again in large-scale UK projects.

So what of the strategy for growth?

Essentially the Autumn Statement, via some financial engineering, has reinstated the erstwhile Labour administration's capital programmes for schools and science, which were axed before the 2010 election.

The justification for this additional £5 billion capital splurge (remember this amounts to less than 1 per cent of GDP) is that there will be commensurate current account savings across Whitehall. I await to be convinced if these will ever happen as it will prove incredibly difficult for the coalition as we approach May 2015 to impose the necessary political will to execute the planned level of spending cuts. If they don't, then there really is nothing to choose between Chancellor Osborne and would-be Chancellor Balls on the public spending issue.

Until now the coalition's growth strategy – if you can really call it that – has been to rely on loose monetary policy in the forlorn hope that cheap money alone would encourage businesses and individuals to spend. But with little consumer or business confidence, and fears about employment security and rising household bills, there is scant evidence of new private sector spending. This ultra-low interest rate policy has benefited banks who can continue to delay the crystallisation of bad debts, especially in the property sector. However, the failure to create other forms of debt capital mean that hoarding cash has been the order of the day rather than investment by businesses and individuals alike.

Faltering demand has lain at the heart of the coalition's failure to achieve growth over the first half of this parliament. The superficially more attractive paring back on procurement may be more politically palatable than cutting pay or sacking staff in the public sector. But it has come at a cost – further reduced demand. In short the Treasury implicitly recognises that the 'wrong sort' of spending cuts were targeted in the 2010 Spending Review and stealthily this Statement represented a reversal of policy.

So how is the austerity strategy going? Well, let's look beyond the rhetoric of 'savage cuts in public spending' at the facts. During the debates following last year's Autumn Statement, I observed that in the twelve preceding months, UK government current spending had totalled £613.5 billion – the highest figure in history. So it pains me to confess that spending in the first half of 2012/13 has been 2.1 per cent *higher* still, with public expenditure this September 3.8 per cent higher than in the same month in 2011. Indeed the total spend by the time this financial year is out is forecast to be some £683 billion, with an expected £120 billion added to the government debt pile.

Small wonder that so much now rests on achieving the other pillar of the deficit reduction plan – economic growth. Indeed £83 billion of the planned £159 billion deficit reduction plan hinges upon achieving sustained economic growth up until 2015. These aspirations were predicated in June 2010 on the basis that the UK would achieve compound growth of between 2.7 per cent and 2.9 per cent per annum over the entire course of the parliament. As we all now know, growth over the past year has stalled and predictions for the near and mid-term look similarly grisly.

This is why the UK government invested so much hope, hype and faith in last week's Autumn Statement as the pivotal moment from which recovery could be kick-started through a programme of expansion. Large-scale headline-grabbing infrastructure projects have already been showcased in Lord Heseltine's 'No Stone Unturned' report. In keeping with its author, much of the publication seems like a throwback to a by-gone age with aggressive industrial interventionism with regional planning at its heart.

Funnily enough I had predicted last year that we might then start down such an interventionist path. Under Vince Cable, the sage of the noughties who in Opposition predicted seven of the last three recessions! However, I suspect the current pressure to boost government spending seems based upon two questionable contentions. I have already touched upon the reality that cuts in government spending have been so modest as to have had little impact upon economic growth. Rather counter-intuitively the same can be said for the received wisdom that public sector workers' incomes are being so squeezed that a vicious spiral of declining demand is preventing any growth.

Public sector pay has risen by some 9 per cent over the past three years (so much for headlines about public sector pay freezes – the simple reason is that pay hikes have been camouflaged as promotions and there has been a disproportionate retention of more senior staff at a time of downsizing). However, the overwhelming focus on achieving the fiscal mandates at the time of the June 2010 Emergency Budget meant that the consequences for growth and employment of the spending cuts announced then were ignored.

Much has been made of the *clear* distinction between capital and current spending. In mid-2010 the easier hits, which enabled aggregate spending figures to be reduced most rapidly, were capital and infrastructure project spending. By contrast this mid-term Statement represents an abrupt change of direction as capital spending by function has been established as a clearer indicator of sustainable economic demand.

To the Chancellor's credit, however, he has resisted the superficially easy option of a 'dash for growth' of the type that his predecessor Anthony Barber unleashed precisely four decades ago. On 21 March 1972 Anthony Barber's second Budget was widely, almost universally, well received. The critics of what later became known as the 'Barber Boom' only spoke out in opposition later. At a time of rising unemployment and sluggish growth, the 1972 Budget was unashamedly designed to provide a massive boost to demand. Income tax and sales tax were slashed. A vast array of incentives for industry, including generous tax allowances for machinery and extensive regional investment grants were introduced. As Dominic Sandbrook observed in his outstanding book, *State of Emergency*, it was as if Christmas had come early and several times over for ordinary taxpayers and business folk alike.

Naturally commentators at the time ought to have realised that all this feverish activity brought with it an enormous risk of inflation. In the years ahead indeed this is precisely what came to pass. Yet at the time the dash for growth was justified by the need for government to urge the economy onto faster growth and it was widely assumed that the resulting gains would rapidly allow for the additional public borrowing to be repaid. After all interest rates were at historically low levels.

There are striking parallels with today's outlook. I have spent much of the past three years warning about inflation and diminishing living standards. Frankly it has been Bank of England policy (presumably with a blind eye from the Treasury) over this period that a little inflation in the system is a risk worth taking to keep interest rates at rock bottom levels. For those of us who believe in 'sound money' this is always a mighty dangerous thing as it helps to relieve the burden of debtors at the expense of savers. You may have noticed that government is the biggest debtor of them all.

I suspect the real danger will come if sluggish growth continues and even the OBR's modest deficit-reduction projections for the years ahead turn out to be massively optimistic. The risk then is that the Treasury loses its nerve and allows a dose of inflation to take on the burden of paying down the effective public debt.

In the meantime, there is a continuing need to experiment in order to accumulate; we must innovate or suffer the consequences. Treasury orthodoxy is hostile to granting tax breaks and capital allowances which would bring a flood of 'shovel-ready' investment into infrastructure projects. Yet it is unarguably preferable that we kick-start the construction industry today at a time of economic stagnation even if this somewhat reduces tax receipts from such projects in future years.

In the months ahead as the eurozone crisis unfolds into a new stage, the UK also needs to drive home its 'safe haven' competitive advantage. Provided we talk less of rebalancing and make more of London's unrivalled position as a centre for global finance, the UK stands well placed to benefit from the flight of Italian and Spanish capital. We ought to be ruthlessly targeting this money, but only if the Treasury makes the unreserved case for the City as an open, safe haven for such foreign investment can we hope to harness this flow of imported capital which could kick-start a fresh generation of infrastructure projects.

Needless to say, another government department that needs a sea change in its approach is BIS. Over recent years there has been much talk, but relatively little concrete action, over Export Guarantees, the lifeblood for medium-sized enterprise breaking into new non-EU markets. The UK needs to exploit supply chain finance within the eurozone and recognise the strengths of its position as a distribution hub. To be frank, we are well behind the French and German governments, which are often accused by British prospective exporters of unfairly promoting their own national exporters in new markets in Asia, Africa and South America. Now is not the time for orthodoxy and timidity in the export guarantee field: we need to integrate policies in this area and aggressively market that diminishing but still highly respected UK expertise at the top end of the value chain in the manufacturing sector. Inevitably some export guarantees will go sour, but that is the price any government must pay if we are to exploit the new export markets that will invigorate the UK's traditional role as a global trading nation in the century that lies ahead.

The new conventional wisdom is that whilst the economic outlook to 2015 and beyond remains bleak, the politics for the Conservatives are a good deal more encouraging.

That may be right; indeed given there is so little to choose between the Chancellor and his Shadow, why not stick with coalition economics come the next general election?

However, serial incompetence may prove its undoing. Even in the past month we have seen scathing independent reports detailing the costly failure of the coalition's apprenticeship initiatives, the Work Programme and the West Coast Main Line fiasco. These unforced errors provide ample opportunity for the Opposition to undermine the very real achievement that the international bond markets are continuing to reassert their faith in the government's determination to put this nation's economy back on the right track.

EPILOGUE

Mid-September 2008. The collapse of Lehman Brothers – the moment at which the impact of the West's suicidally debt-fuelled, credit bubble, coupled with the hopeless financial imbalance between US consumers and Chinese savers, finally broke into global consciousness. This implosion sent shockwaves rocketing through the world economy. They wreaked particular devastation on the UK whose magnificent capital, London, suddenly felt hollow after its confident boom into the planet's preeminent financial centre.

Yet arguably the crisis might best be considered to have kicked off one year earlier. In August 2007, the European Central Bank felt obliged to pump €95 billion into markets after it had become uncomfortably clear that the continent's banks were sagging with the colossal weight of US housing debt on their books. If we take that moment as our starting point, we have been living with this unresolved global financial crisis for some five years.

Five years. Half a decade. Watching, waiting for a resolution. Hoping, Mr Micawber-like, for something – anything – to turn up. Lulled into a false sense of security that the worst is behind us. Perhaps, despite the title of this collection of essays, it is. But, to coin a phrase, let's not bank upon it.

It is difficult now to imagine a time when the terms 'credit crunch', 'quantitative easing' and 'pump priming' were not in every-day parlance. When a billion (pounds, euros or dollars) seemed like a lot of money. When the nationalising of banks and the supranationalising of countries was just plain unthinkable. A time when the European and US economies were still presumed to be unassailably robust global benchmarks and investment bankers were privately envied for their wealth, not publicly berated and even ostracised for it.

Indeed in many ways the landscape appears to have changed completely. And yet how far have we *really* come?

The initial drama of wild stock market fluctuations and swift corporate collapses has made way for a monotony of seemingly endless sluggish growth and tough, grinding attempts at reform. Political leaders globally have failed to provide conclusive leadership or indeed understanding that the real threat of this economic crisis is its political impact. The longer the misery continues, the greater the danger to capitalism, globalisation and free markets as a result of consistently diminished living standards.

Even the apparently relevant experience from the 1930s holds few answers. Whether governments should favour austerity or more debt; whether the currency union (now the eurozone, then the Gold Standard) should be saved; how the West might regain competitiveness and retain relevance in the decades ahead; how to maintain democratic legitimacy whilst internationalising ever more economic policy; what role the state should play in the functioning of a healthy economy; how the ideal future landscape of global banking should look; and how, as the backlash to globalisation and the creation of a mobile elite takes hold, to reconcile the super-rich with the rest of society.

Nor is there a sense of any progress in unravelling the colossal trade imbalances that underwrote the crisis. For a decade or more, countries like the US and UK pursued models of growth based on debt-fuelled consumption, the cheap credit and cheap goods provided courtesy of Asia's savings glut. Within the eurozone, it has been the German government and other northern member states that offset the profligacy of their Mediterranean counterparts. China's current account surplus is now dropping, suggesting that the Sino–American imbalance may be very gradually correcting itself. But there is no sign as yet that Germany, as a conspicuous creditor nation, is willing to take on – or mutualise – its neighbours' debt as its own. It is easy to lay the blame for this at the door of

Chancellor Merkel but her task will only get harder in the months ahead as she seeks to convince the increasingly tetchy German taxpayer (and electorate) that it might now need to nationalise a continent's liabilities.

Instead the eurozone staggers from one crisis summit to another. The fingers of central bankers worldwide remain poised on the printing presses to provide fresh stimulus. Political uncertainty across the globe threatens new shocks. Not only have Europe's political elite failed to make much headway, but there remains a sense that a crisis which began half a decade ago still has much further to unwind.

In the UK, 2010 was meant to herald an era of fresh politics as a new coalition government took the reins, signalling its explicit intent to reduce Britain's bulging budget deficit. Perhaps we were all guilty of naïvety at how easy that task would be. At that time UK exporters were reaping the benefits of a 25 per cent devaluation in the pound, the initial lift from quantitative easing and a year-long boost to consumption as VAT rates had been lowered. With the new Office for Budget Responsibility predicting compound growth of 2.7 to 2.9 per cent all the way until 2015, the coalition was lulled into believing that growth would offset the deadweight of the glaring deficit in the public finances. Alas that export-led growth on which so many hopes were pinned has failed to materialise. 2012's dismal trade figures proved that two years on, the task of closing our trade deficit and shrinking our public one, let alone eliminating the structural deficit, during the course of this parliament will be no mean feat.

It is fine to talk airily of growth as essential, but without a consensus for radical supply side innovation alongside tax cuts which actually boost demand, it is difficult to see where this will come from. Meanwhile the clamour for banking reform in the eurozone will be nigh on impossible for so long as a near-zero interest rate strategy of the past four years in the EU and eurozone ensures that so much bad – not to mention toxic – property debt can readily remain uncrystallised on European banks' balance sheets.

Chancellor George Osborne can justifiably be proud that in spite

of doggedly and consistently higher borrowing than anticipated
(with government debt rising by more than £100 billion annually),
the UK has been able to maintain its AAA rating since he has been
at the Treasury, in marked contrast to many of our competitors. Yet
in doing so, he has essentially defied economic gravity. Through
quantitative easing, it is the government itself which currently owns
a third of its own bonds and it remains to be seen if – and for how
long – the UK will be able to convince the markets that it can
service its debt. The lesson of 1931 and 1976 is that once financial
market sentiment turns, all is lost.

For all the good that has flowed from markets' failure to spot
the gap between rhetoric and reality when it comes to UK public
spending, it is rather more worrying that the British public is so
convinced that the government is making 'savage cuts' (in the words
of the Opposition). In spite of all the talk of our 'dealing with the
deficit' and 'sticking to the plan', central government current spending in August was 2.6 per cent higher than in the same month the
year before and spending over the five months April to August was
3 per cent higher than in the same months of 2011. To compare the
coalition to the last administration, in 2011/12 public expenditure
totalled £681 billion compared to the £689 billion that Labour
spent in its last year in office (2009/10) – hardly indicative of a
radical change in tack.

In essence, when it comes to the politics at least, the coalition
now risks the worst of both worlds – the unpopularity that comes
with cutting back the state without the economic uplift that would
be derived from actually shrinking it. In the meantime, this misunderstanding has allowed the Labour Party to erect a false choice,
presenting itself as the neo-Keynesian, anti-austerity alternative.
With the government's 'austerity' programme failing to deliver
the growth that was faithfully forecast back in 2010, the case in
future for essential cuts in public expenditure (and debt) will be
ever harder to make.

Naturally this problem is compounded by the coalition's lack of
real mandate when it comes to reducing the empire of the state.

During the run-up to the 2010 election, Britain willingly partook in a collective delusion. Insofar as the three main parties presented voters with a choice at the general election, it was whether to cut public expenditure by £6 billion now or slightly later. It served us all to skate over the gravity of our economic problems at that time. In truth, voters did not want to hear about cuts to services or entitlements – and politicians were not going to break ranks to tell them, particularly when all parties had supported government spending plans before the financial crisis. Better to present the electorate with a sense of security than level with them about the scale of our challenges.

In reality, £6 billion represented the total that we as a nation had been borrowing every fortnight. Essentially and implicitly we recognised that this was more than just a bank and banker-inflicted crisis. The events of 2008 were merely the crescendo to two or three decades' worth of debt accumulation, racked up in part as a response to our declining competitiveness. This was tacitly supported by a generation that enjoyed an expanded welfare state, cheap goods, never-ending lines of credit and inflated house prices and by politicians who were unable to confront openly the toughest questions of our time as a result of a pathological fear of unpopularity. Yes, our financial brethren had exploited, exacerbated and expedited that debt accumulation. But did we *all* not sense that much of the past decade of economic boom was built on an illusion?

Since the pre-crisis policies of the last government were never fundamentally discredited by the Conservative Opposition, we have led the public to believe that all we need to do is get back to the high spending, low interest rate, high lending days of 2007. The fateful decision in late summer 2007 to 'stick to Labour's spending plans' and 'share the proceeds of growth' reinforced the conventional wisdom that it was the financial elite, rather than profligate government and global imbalances, that lies at the root of the crisis. Economic policy has therefore been designed to park rather than solve our problems. This assists in upholding the living standards of the old system's beneficiaries. But it is also creating an ever-increasing group of disenchanted losers – whether that is the saver whose pot is being eroded by low interest rates and high inflation or the young jobseeker looking for work in a stagnant economy where high house prices and expensive commodities seem to shut the door on aspiration. Unable to cut the debt, I have never doubted that any incumbent government would choose instead to inflate it away.

Those already facing the pain of the new world and its new realities will begin to rub ever more against an established order and vested interests. It will take some time for angry electorates to grasp the changes that will inevitably flow from this and it may be that the moment has not yet come for bold leadership and fresh ideas. Politicians have a tough enough task before them in unpicking the tangle of debt and entitlement that has accrued over so many years. Nevertheless, the dearth of vision and leadership is creating a deepening and corrosive sense of impotence within electorates. Muddling through has been order of the day and it has, in a way, worked. For now. But there is a potential sacrifice for that and the extremes of politics may hold ever more appeal to disillusioned voters as the only symbol of real choice.

Electorates across the developed world need to be convinced that politicians have a plan and that it will be followed; that they have innate confidence in its success and that there is a vision for a better tomorrow that will benefit the public. This requires broad-brush confidence and chutzpah. In times of crisis a political leader must not be the master of detail, but an illusionist.

Unfortunately, however, since we have never before seen a crisis of public indebtedness on this scale, it is not clear in which economic theory leaders should place their trust. The Keynesian spending splurge since 2008 may well have staved off a complete financial collapse but the concept of moral hazard got buried underneath the pragmatism of crisis prevention, with the cost for reckless risk-taking transferred to the taxpayer and normal capitalist safeguards overridden. And for all the money being pumped into the system, it is failing to stimulate growth and jobs. Indeed the notion that such pump priming may well eventually stoke inflation seems not to be the bête noire it perhaps ought to highly indebted governments. Similarly, the austerity programmes being implemented in Greece and now Spain that are stifling those economies and bringing fury to their streets, are bringing into question the limits of a hands-off, Hayekian approach, at least for economies that are unable to restore their own competitiveness through currency devaluation.

I should have liked to conclude this book with my own answer to the great conundrum that now sits before us all. Nevertheless, just as I have confessed my shock at the scale of 2008's crash, I fear I must conclude only that whichever road we choose, pain is inevitable, no matter how much we appear to have been insulated. The racking up of ever more debt cannot forever shield us from reality and the fear that economically the UK is still between the crashes looms large in the minds of many of our fellow Britons. Nor should we forget, however, that intense, passionate conflict between competing visions is often the greatest driver of human progress.

ABOUT THE AUTHOR

Mark Field

First elected in June 2001, Mark Field is a third-term Conservative MP representing the Cities of London & Westminster seat, a central London constituency that incorporates in the West End, Whitehall and City of London respectively the capital's prime cultural, political and financial districts.

Educated at Reading School (a direct grant grammar school), Mark later read Law at St Edmund Hall, Oxford. During his undergraduate days he set up his first business, specialising in publishing career handbooks.

Upon qualifying as a solicitor in 1990, Mark joined leading international law firm Freshfields as a corporate lawyer. He went on to set up his second business, Kellyfield Consulting, in 1994. A recruitment organisation serving the legal profession, it quickly acquired an enviable reputation in niche search/selection, and as one of two directors, Mark built this start-up enterprise into a company of twelve full-time staff with a turnover of £1.8 million.

Bringing business, legal and political experience to his role as a Member of Parliament, Mark has served on the frontbench under three Party leaders, including spells as Shadow Financial Secretary to the Treasury and Shadow Minister for London. In September 2010, he was appointed by the Prime Minister to the prestigious Intelligence & Security Committee, chaired by Sir Malcolm

Rifkind. He has become a prominent broadcaster and commentator, appearing frequently on BBC2 and BBC Radio 4's political programmes, Sky News and ITV's *Late Debate*, as well as writing occasional columns for the *Daily Telegraph* and *City A.M.*

He lives in Westminster with his wife and two children.

Julia Dockerill
Mark wrote *Between the Crashes* with Julia Dockerill, who has served as his Senior Parliamentary Researcher since 2006. A graduate in Social and Political Sciences from Queens' College, Cambridge, Julia is currently penning her first book on political, economic and social change in the noughties.

Also available from Biteback

MASTERS OF NOTHING

Matthew Hancock and Nadhim Zahawi

This book is about how people behave.

Not how we think we behave, or how we'd like to behave, but how
we really do.

It is a story of how a failure to understand human nature helped
cause one of the biggest crises in the history of capitalism. Of the
extraordinary extremes we witnessed from the so-called Masters of
the Universe – their greed, recklessness and irrationality. Of how
that failure led to policy mistakes that magnified the crisis. And of
how the crisis will happen again unless we get to grips with it.

288pp paperback, £12.99

**Available from all good bookshops or order from
www.bitebackpublishing.com**

Also available from Biteback

HEAVENS ON EARTH

J. P. Floru

The world's economy is in crisis. Public spending has reached
dizzying heights, national debts are crippling governments and
economic growth is lacklustre or non-existent. It has been
suggested that this is an unavoidable phase in the world's
economic development. Not so, says J. P. Floru. Rather, we
in the West have sleepwalked our way into a culture that
condemns us to economic decline while savvier nations flourish.

Heavens on Earth offers both a manifesto for creating prosperity
and a fascinating tale of global growth. It takes a sweeping view
of traditions across the world and across the centuries, introducing
us to the remarkable individuals who made it all happen.

304pp paperback, £12.99

**Available from all good bookshops or order from
www.bitebackpublishing.com**

POLITICOS.co.uk
THE ONLINE POLITICAL BOOKSTORE

WE'RE BACK

BREAKDOWNS OF THE
BEST POLITICAL
LITERATURE ON
THE HORIZON

BE REWARDED FOR YOUR LOYALTY
WITH OUR POINTS SCHEME

AN ONLINE COMMUNITY OF
POLITICAL BOOK LOVERS

THE POLITICOS.CO.UK
TEAM ON HAND TO
OFFER YOU GUIDANCE
AND BESPOKE
BOOK SUGGESTIONS

TAILORED BESTSELLERS
LISTS FROM RECESS
READING TO POLITICAL
RESEARCH MATERIALS

WEEKLY POLITICAL
BOOK PODCASTS

SPECIALIST, CONSTANTLY UPDATED,
POLITICAL CONTENT

Politicos.co.uk is owned and managed by Biteback Publishing. @Politicos_co_uk